# THE ECONOMIC HISTORY OF THE NETHERLANDS 1914–1995

What were the characteristics of economic development in Western Europe during the twentieth century? How did the structure of enterprise, the labour market and the state develop, and how did these institutional changes affect economic growth? Why was the economy of the Netherlands so successful in generating economic change? And how does this success relate to the development of a specific Dutch institutional framework?

Jan L. van Zanden in *The economic history of the Netherlands 1914–1995* answers these questions. In the first four chapters the long-term development of the economy is analysed in detail. Central to this part of the book are the rise (and decline) of managerial enterprise; the growth (and fall) of trade unions; and the expansion (and crisis) of the welfare state. The particular Dutch features of these institutional changes are highlighted. The second part of the book deals with different periods of growth (from 1914–1929, and 1950–1973), and relative stagnation (1929–1950, and 1973–1995). Moreover, Van Zanden examines the role the Netherlands played in the process of European integration, and gives an explanation of the success of the 'Dutch job machine' in the 1980s and 1990s.

*The economic history of the Netherlands* condenses all the most contemporary data and analysis into one convenient volume; it will be an invaluable resource for those studying European Economics or European History.

**Jan L. van Zanden** is Professor of Economic History at the University of Utrecht, and Director of the Netherlands Research School for Economic and Social History (N.W. Posthumus Institute). His previous publications include *The rise and decline of Holland's economy 1350–1850* (1993), and *The transformation of European agriculture in the 19th century: the case of the Netherlands* (1994).

# THE ECONOMIC HISTORY OF THE NETHERLANDS 1914–1995

A small open economy in the 'long' twentieth century

*Jan L. van Zanden*

London and New York

First published 1998
by Routledge
11 New Fetter Lane, London, EC4P 4EE

Simultaneously published in the USA and Canada
by Routledge
29 West 35th Street, New York, NY 10001

© 1998 Jan L. van Zanden

Typeset in Times by
J&L Composition Ltd, Filey, North Yorkshire
Printed and bound in Great Britain by
Mackays of Chatham PLC, Chatham, Kent

*British Library Cataloguing in Publication Data*
A catalogue record for this book is available from
the British Library

*Library of Congress Cataloging in Publication Data*
Zanden. J.L. van
[Economische geschiedenis van Nederland in de 20e eeuw.
English] The economic history of the Netherlands 1914–1995:
a small open economy in the 'long' twentieth century/
Jan L. van Zanden.
p.    cm.—(Contemporary economic history of Europe)
Rev. translation of: Economische geschiedenis van
Nederland in de 20e eeuw/J.L. van Zanden, R.T. Griffiths.
Includes bibliographical references and index.
1. Netherlands—Economic conditions—1918–1945.
2. Netherlands—Economic conditions—1945–   I. Title.
II. Series: Contemporary economic history of Europe series.
HC325.Z3613   1998
330.9492–dc21   97–6094
CIP

ISBN 0–415–15003–5

# CONTENTS

v

# LIST OF GRAPHS

# LIST OF TABLES

# EDITOR'S INTRODUCTION

By comparison with the nineteenth century, the twentieth has been very much more turbulent, both economically and politically. Two world wars and a Great Depression are sufficient to substantiate this claim without invoking the problems of more recent times. Yet despite these setbacks Europe's economic performance in the present century has been very much better than anything recorded in the historical past, thanks largely to the super-boom conditions following the post-World War II reconstruction period. Thus in the period 1946–75, or 1950–73, the annual increase in total European GNP per capita was 4.8 and 4.5 percent respectively, as against a compound rate of just under 1 percent in the nineteenth century (1800–1913) and the same during the troubled years between 1913–50. As Bairoch points out, within a generation or so European per capita income rose slightly more than in the previous 150 years (1947–75 by 250 percent, 1800–1948 by 225 percent) and, on rough estimates for the half-century before 1800, by about as much as in the preceding two centuries.[1]

The dynamic growth and relative stability of the 1950s and 1960s may however belie the natural order of things as the events of the later 1970s and early 1980s demonstrate. Certainly it would seem unlikely that the European economy, or the world economy for that matter, will see a lasting return to the relatively stable conditions of the nineteenth century. No doubt the experience of the present century can easily lead to an exaggerated idea about the stability of the previous one. Nevertheless, one may justifiably claim that for much of the nineteenth century there was a degree of harmony in the economic development of the major powers and between the metropolitan economies and the periphery which has been noticeably absent since 1914. Indeed, one of the reasons for the apparent success of the gold standard after 1870, despite the aura of stability it allegedly shed, was the absence of serious external disturbances and imbalance in development among the major participating powers. As Triffin writes, 'the residual harmonization of national monetary and credit policies depended far less on *ex post* corrective action, requiring an extreme flexibility, downward as well as upward, of national price and wage levels, than on an *ex ante* avoidance of substantial disparities in cost competitiveness and the monetary policies that would allow them to develop'.[2]

Whatever the reasons for the absence of serious economic and political conflict, the fact remains that up to 1914 international development and political relations, though subject to strains of a minor nature from time to time, were never exposed to internal and external shocks of the magnitude experienced in the twentieth century. Not surprisingly therefore, World War I rudely shattered the liberal tranquility of the later nineteenth and early twentieth centuries. At the time few people realized that it was going to be a lengthy war and, even more important, fewer still had any conception of the enormous impact it would have on economic and social relationships. Moreover, there was a general feeling, readily accepted in establishment circles, that following the period of hostilities it would be possible to resume where one had left off – in short, to recreate the conditions of the pre-war era.

For obvious reasons this was clearly an impossible task, though for nearly a decade statesmen strove to get back to what they regarded as 'normalcy', or the natural order of things. In itself this was one of the profound mistakes of the first postwar decade since it should have been clear, even at that time, that the war and postwar clearing-up operations had undermined Europe's former equipoise and sapped her strength to a point where the economic system had become very sensitive to external shocks. The map of Europe had been redrawn under the political settlements following the war and this further weakened the economic viability of the continent and left a dangerous political vacuum in its wake. Moreover, it was not only in the economic sphere that Europe's strength had been reduced; in political and social terms the European continent was seriously weakened and many countries in the early postwar years were in a state of social ferment and upheaval.[3]

Generally speaking, Europe's economic and political fragility was ignored in the 1920s, probably more out of ignorance than intent. In their efforts to resurrect the pre-war system statesmen believed they were providing a viable solution to the problems of the day, and the fact that Europe shared in the prosperity of the later 1920s seemed to vindicate their judgement. But the postwar problems – war debts, external imbalances, currency issues, structural distortions and the like – defied solutions along traditional lines. The most notable of these was the attempt to restore a semblance of the gold standard in the belief that it had been responsible for the former stability. The upshot was a set of haphazard and inconsistent currency stabilization policies which took no account of the changes in relative costs and prices among countries since 1914. Consequently, despite the apparent prosperity of the latter half of the decade, Europe remained in a state of unstable equilibrium, and therefore vulnerable to any external shocks. The collapse of American foreign lending from the middle of 1928 and the subsequent downturn of the American economy a year later exposed the weaknesses of the European economy. The structural supports were too weak to withstand violent shocks and so the edifice disintegrated.

That the years 1929–1932/33 experienced one of the worst depressions and financial crises in history is not altogether surprising given the convergence of many unfavourable forces at that point in time. Moreover, the fact that a cyclical downturn occurred against the backdrop of structural disequilibrium only served to exacerbate the problem, while the inherent weakness of certain financial institutions in Europe and the USA led to extreme instability. The intensity of the crisis varied a great deal but few countries, apart from the USSR, were unaffected. The action of governments tended to aggravate rather than ease the situation. Such policies included expenditure cuts, monetary contraction, the abandonment of the gold standard and protective measures designed to insulate domestic economies from external events. In effect these policies, while sometimes affording temporary relief to hard-pressed countries, in the end led to income destruction rather than income creation. When recovery finally began in the winter of 1932/33 it owed little to policy contributions, though subsequently some Western governments did attempt more ambitious programmes of stimulation, while many of the poorer eastern European countries adopted autarchic policies in an effort to push foward industrialization. Apart from some notable exceptions, Germany and Sweden in particular, recovery from the slump, especially in terms of employment generation, was slow and patchy and even at the peak of the upswing in 1937 many countries were still operating below their resource capacity. A combination of weak real growth forces and structural imbalances in development would no doubt have ensured a continuation of resource under-utilization had not rearmament and the outbreak of war served to close the gap.

Thus, on the eve of World War II Europe as a whole was in a much weaker state economically than it had been in 1914, with her shares of world income and trade notably reduced. Worse still, she emerged from the war in 1945 in a more prostrate condition than in 1918, with output levels well down on those of the pre-war period. In terms of the loss of life, physical destruction and decline in living standards Europe's position was much worse than after World War I. On the other hand, recovery from wartime destruction was stronger and more secure than in the previous case. In part this can be attributed to the fact that in the reconstruction phase of the later 1940s some of the mistakes and blunders of the earlier experience were avoided. Inflation, for example, was contained more readily between 1939 and 1945 and the violent inflations of the early 1920s were not for the most part perpetuated after World War II. With the exception of Berlin, the map of Europe was divided much more cleanly and neatly than after 1918. Though it resulted in two ideological power blocs, the East and the West, it did nevertheless dispose of the power vacuum in central/eastern Europe which had been a source of friction and contention in the interwar years. Moreover, the fact that each bloc was dominated or backed by a wealthy and rival super-power meant that support was forthcoming for the satellite countries. The vanquished powers were not, with the exception of East Germany, burdened by unreasonable exactions which had been the cause of so much bitterness and squabbling during the 1920s. Finally, governments no longer hankered after the 'halcyon' pre-war days, not surprisingly given the rugged conditions of the 1930s. This time it was to be planning for the future which occupied their attention, and which found expression in the commitment to maintain full employment and all that entailed in terms of growth and stability, together with a conscious desire to build upon the earlier social welfare foundations. In wider perspective, the new initiative found positive expression in terms of readiness to cooperate internationally, particularly in trade and monetary matters. The liberal American aid programme for the West in the later 1940s was a concrete manifestation of this new approach.

Thus despite the enormity of the reconstruction task facing Europe at the end of the war, the recovery effort, after some initial difficulties, was both strong and sustained, and by the early 1950s Europe had reached a point where she could look to the future with some confidence. During the next two decades or so virtually every European country, in keeping with the buoyant conditions in the world economy as a whole, expanded very much more rapidly than in the past. This was the super-growth phase during which Europe regained a large part of the relative losses incurred between 1914 and 1945. The Eastern bloc countries forged ahead the most rapidly under their planned regimes, while the Western democracies achieved their success under mixed enterprise systems with varying degrees of market freedom. In both cases the state played a far more important role than hitherto, and neither system could be said to be without its problems. The planning mechanism in eastern Europe never functioned as smoothly as originally anticipated by its proponents, and in due course most of the socialist countries were forced to make modifications to their systems of control. Similarly, the semi-market systems of the West did not always produce the right results so that governments were obliged to intervene to an increasing extent. One of the major problems encountered by the demand-managed economies of the West was that of trying to achieve a series of basically incompatible objectives simultaneously – namely full employment, price stability, growth and stability and external equilibrium. Given the limited policy weapons available to governments this proved an impossible task to accomplish in most cases, though West Germany managed to achieve the seemingly impossible for much of the period.

Although these incompatible objectives proved elusive *in toto*, there was, throughout most of the period to the early 1970s, little cause for serious alarm. It is true that there were minor lapses from full employment; fluctuations still occurred but they were very moderate and took the form of growth cycles; some countries experienced periodic balance of payments problems while prices generally rose continuously though at fairly modest annual rates. But such lapses could readily be accommodated, even with the limited policy choices, within an economic system that was growing rapidly. And there was some consolation from the fact that the planned socialist economies were not immune from some of these problems, especially later on in the period. By the later 1960s, despite some warning signs that conditions might be deteriorating, it seemed that Europe had entered a phase of perpetual prosperity not dissimilar to the one the Americans had conceived in the 1920s. Unfortunately, as in the earlier case, this illusion was to be rudely shattered in the first half of the 1970s. The super-growth phase of the postwar period culminated in the somewhat feverish and speculative boom of 1972–3. By the following year the growth trend had been reversed, the old business cycle had reappeared and most countries were experiencing inflation at higher rates than at any time in the past half-century. From that time onwards, according to Samuel Brittan, 'everything seems to have gone sour and we have had slower growth, rising unemployment, faster inflation, creeping trade restrictions and all the symptoms of stagflation'.[4] In fact, compared with the relatively placid and successful decades of the 1950s and 1960s, the later 1970s and early 1980s were extremely turbulent, reminiscent in some respects of the interwar years.

It should of course be stressed that by comparison with the interwar years or even with the nineteenth century, economic growth has been quite respectable since the sharp boom and contraction in the first half of the 1970s. It only appears poor in relation to the rapid growth between 1950 and 1973 and the question arises as to whether this period should be regarded as somewhat abnormal with the shift to a lower growth profile in the 1970s being the inevitable consequence of long-term forces invoking some reversal of the special growth promoting factors of the previous decades. In effect this would imply some weakening of real growth forces in the 1970s which was aggravated by specific factors, for example energy crises and policy variables.

The most disturbing feature of this later period was not simply that growth slowed down but that it became more erratic, with longer recessionary periods involving absolute contractions in output, and that it was accompanied by mounting unemployment and high inflation. Traditional Keynesian demand management policies were unable to cope with these problems and, in an effort to deal with them, particularly inflation, governments resorted to ultra-defensive policies and monetary control. These were not very successful either since the need for social and political compromise in policymaking meant that they were not applied rigorously enough to eradicate inflation, yet at the same time their influence was sufficiently strong to dampen the rate of growth thereby exacerbating unemployment. In other words, economic managment was faced with an awkward policy dilemma in the prevailing situation of high unemployment and rapid inflation. Policy action to deal with either one tended to make the other worse, while the constraint of the political concensus produced an uneasy compromise in an effort to 'minimise macroeconomic misery'.[5] Rostow has neatly summarized the constraints involved in this context: 'Taxes, public expenditure, interest rates, and the supply of money are not determined antiseptically by men free to move economies along a Phillips curve to an optimum trade-off between the rate of unemployment and the rate of inflation. Fiscal and monetary policy are, inevitably, living parts of the democratic political process.'[6]

Since the 1970s governments have had to wrestle with a host of problems including inflation, budgetary deficits, unemployment and renewed recession, but they have not been able to recreate the success of the immediate postwar decades. Indeed, it may be that governments are powerless, as they were in the 1930s, to solve such problems if the underlying forces of growth remain weak and at a time when the expectations of people in terms of income growth and the provision of collective goods and welfare services exceed the delivery potential of the economies in question. In a different context the former socialist economies of easter Europe had their problems and eventually these resulted in the disintegration of the regimes. In view of the current problems of Western nations the transition to market capitalism may not have come at the most propitious time.

It is not however the purpose of the volumes in this series to speculate about the future. The series is designed to provide clear and balanced surveys of the economic development and problems of individual European countries from the end of World War I through to the present, against the background of the general economic and political trends of the time. Though most of the European countries have shared a common experience for much of the period, it is nonetheless true that there has been considerable variation among countries in the rate of development and the manner in which they have sought to regulate and control their economies. The problems encountered have also varied widely, in part reflecting disparities in levels of development. While most European countries had, by the end of World War I, achieved some measure of industrialization and made the initial breakthrough into modern economic growth, there nevertheless existed a wide gulf between the richer and poorer nations. At the beginning of the period North West Europe, including Scandinavia, was by far the most advanced region and as one moved south and east so the level of development and per capita income declined. In some case, notably Bulgaria, Yugoslavia and Portugal, income levels were a third or less of those in the more advanced countries and barely one half the European average. The gap has tended to narrow over time but the general pattern remains basically the same. Between 1913 and the early 1970s most of the poorer countries in the south and east (apart form Spain) raised their real per capita income levels relative to the European average, with most of the improvement taking place after 1950. Even so, many countries still fell below the European average which in the case of Spain, Portugal, Romania and Yugoslavia was as much as 35–45 percent.[7]

Professor Van Zanden's study of the Dutch economy in the twentieth century takes up several major themes in depth from their origins in the late nineteenth century: for example the rise of managerial corporations, trade unions and the labour market, and the growth of the welfare state and government management of the economy. He shows how institutions, policies and practices have had to adapt continually to changes in the international economic environment and within the framework of a fragmented political system which has both its strengths and weaknesses. On the whole the Dutch economy has been remarkably successful for much of the period. But, as with other European economies, a question mark hangs over its future since there are signs of increasing inflexibility in economic systems leading to a loss of comparative advantage to more dynamic economies outwith Europe.

## NOTES

1 P. Bairoch, 'Europe's Gross National Product: 1800–1975', *The Journal of European Economic History* (Fall, 1976), pp. 298–9.
2 R. Triffin, *Our International Monetary System: Yesterday, Today and Tomorrow* (New York: Random House, 1968), p. 14; *see also* D.H. Aldcroft, *From Versailles to Wall Street, 1919–1929* (London: Allen Lane, 1977), pp. 162–4. Some of the costs of the gold standard system may however have been borne by the countries of the periphery, for example Latin America.
3 See P.N. Stearns, *European Society in Upheaval* (New York: Macmillan, 1967).
4 *Financial Times*, 14 February 1980.
5 J.O.N. Perkins, *The Macroeconomic Mix to Stop Stagflation* (London: Macmillan, 1980).
6 W.W. Rostow, *Getting From Here to There* (London: Macmillan, 1979).
7 See Bairoch op. cit., pp. 297, 307.

# PREFACE

I am not sure whether to introduce this book as a new experiment in twentieth-century economic history or as a thoroughly rewritten version of a previous book published by Richard Griffiths and myself in 1989. Both interpretations are somewhat beside the truth: it is not a completely new book, because I have made intensive use of certain chapters of the *Economische geschiedenis van Nederland in de 20e eeuw*. I should especially refer to the sections on the Dutch economy during the 1920s and the 1940s (in Chapters 6 and 7), which are largely based on the analysis offered in that study. However, during a stay at the University of Florida (Gainesville) in the spring of 1996, when I started working on this book, I was fortunate enough to have the time and opportunity for a complete reassessment. This resulted in a new interpretation of the long-term development of the Dutch economy in I have called the 'long' twentieth century. This has more or less forced me completely to rewrite all chapters and to add two more (the first one on the long twentieth century, and the second on managerial enterprise). Moreover, the coverage of the book was extended at the beginning (1914–1921) and the end (1985–1995) of the period. The inclusion of the 'new dynamism' of the last ten years was of fundamental importance to the understanding of the long-term processes involved. In short, the general framework of the book is new, but some of the ingredients were already present when Richard Griffiths and I tried to prepare this dish for the first time.

It goes without saying that I am particularly grateful to Richard Griffiths for the fact that back in 1985 he invited me to join his efforts to write the economic history of this century. His sharp vision of the limitations of Dutch policymaking was especially instructive. Bart van Ark and Herman de Jong generously allowed me to use all the statistical data they have gathered for a comparable project. David Colburn, who made possible my stay at the University of Florida, was an excellent and inspiring host; this created the right distance from events in the Netherlands to undertake the project of (re)writing this book. Keetie Sluyterman criticized the new chapter I added on the history of the managerial enterprise and Pierre van der Eng allowed me to use his translation of the section on 'The economic importance of Indonesia' (and added a few critical remarks). Finally, Edwin Horlings was a great help in correcting my English and helping with tables and graphs.

# 1

# THE LONG TWENTIETH CENTURY

It is not easy to write an economic history of the Netherlands in the twentieth century. First there is the problem of abundance: the number of relevant historical, economic, sociological and political studies is enormous. It is almost impossible to write anything on recent developments in the labour market or on the effects of government policies on economic growth without confining yourself in a library for many weeks. And even then you cannot be sure that you will not miss the most recent 'pioneering' dissertation on the subject. As a result, once an economic historian starts writing he is more than once seized by the fear that he failed to find the most recent papers which provide the definitive solution to his problem; there is always the temptation to continue reading.

The second problem a historian has to face is that of shortage. Historians generally prefer to do their work on somewhat more distant periods. In the Netherlands, for obvious reasons, the seventeenth century has been in strong favour, and the nineteenth century has also received more than its fair share of attention. Little basic research into archive sources has been done on the last fifty years or so, although things have recently changed for the better. What is perhaps even more important, is that the historical discussion on the nature of the twentieth century has only recently begun. Historians can give their stories a sense of unity by defining the special characteristics of economic development in, for example, the seventeenth century or the nineteenth century. But until now the twentieth century seems to be an enormous reservoir of contradictory developments without any coherence.

However, as the twentieth century draws to a close, thinking about its nature has become quite fashionable. Eric Hobsbawm has tried to bring some order into its apparent chaos by defining the 'short' twentieth century as the period between 1917 and 1991, that coincides with the life cycle of the Soviet Union (Hobsbawm 1994). This largely political definition of the century is, however, not much help to an economic history of the Netherlands. When there is a 'short' twentieth century, there should also be a 'long' one, a concept I would like to introduce here.[1] The 'long' twentieth century began in the final quarter of the nineteenth century, and its end is still unknown. The concept focuses on a number of largely institutional changes in the structure of the economy (and in society at large) that began somewhere after 1870, accelerated after the turn of the century to reach full maturity somewhere between 1960 and 1980, and now seems to be on the decline. As a result, the twentieth century has its own institutional framework that distinguishes it from the preceding century. Yet, this framework also appears to have begun to fall apart in recent years. Let me briefly review the major changes.

First, there is the growth of modern industry and, as a result of the 'second industrial revolution' of the 1880s, the rise of the managerial enterprise. In Chapter 3 I will show how almost all Dutch multinational companies were created in the relatively short period between 1880 and 1920, how they expanded enormously until about 1970, and experienced relative decline (even absolute in terms of employment) in the final quarter of this century. In other words, during the 'long' twentieth century economic growth was accompanied by an increased concentration of workers in large often multinational companies. Moreover, as a result of the separation of ownership and management the companies were controlled by managers whose principal aim was the long-term growth of the enterprise. But since the 1970s we have been witnessing the rise of a different economy in which commercial services (as opposed to industry) and small companies (as opposed to multinationals) are the most dynamic parts. And the 'revolution' of the shareholder has meant that managers have to pay much more attention to the realization of short-term profits.

The second part of the story of the long twentieth century has to do with changes in the labour market. The final years of the nineteenth century and the first decades of the twentieth century saw the rise of modern trade unions that aimed at forming a cartel of labour in order to improve their bargaining position. In the interwar period and especially during the 1940s the new structure was stabilized. Trade unions became part of the 'normal' functioning of the labour market; negotiations between employers' organizations and trade unions (and after 1945 the government) became the standard way to regulate the market. It resulted in the 'guided' wage policy of the period 1945–1963, in which a rather rigid system was applied to control the growth of nominal wages. During this period of a government-controlled labour market, the structure of wages and salaries was almost completely reorganized. The system crumbled under the pressure of market forces in the late 1950s and early 1960s, when unemployment reached an historic low. Yet, the government continued to exert a relatively strong influence on the labour market and the position of trade unions remained unaffected. The standard response to the new economic problems of the late 1970s and 1980s was therefore to strive once more for controlling wages rises, which became the official policy of the trade unions after

1982. However, the rise of new labour market institutions (such as temping agencies) and the decline in the rate of unionization after 1980 gradually eroded the influence of trade unions on the labour market and there developed a strong tendency to increase the flexibility of labour.

The rise and decline of trade unions and their influence on the labour market runs almost parallel to the growth of the welfare state, the third part of the story of the long twentieth century. In general, this century has seen an enormous increase in the role of the state in economy and society, which was probably caused by democratization, the rise of trade unions, and the emergence of mass political parties. Once again the foundations for this development were laid in the final quarter of the nineteenth century, but until the 1940s progress was rather slow. After World War II a huge expansion of social services started. Moreover, the government began to take charge of economic matters; industrialization plans and a guided wage policy are cases in point. The relatively heavy reliance on the state to solve economic problems was quite out of line with the strong 'laissez-faire' tradition of Dutch politics. During the 1980s the tide turned: a gradual dismantling of the welfare state began, budget cuts have been with us ever since (and are here to stay) and all major political parties now state that they aim at reducing the role of the government in the economy. The long-term development of the relationship between government and economy – with heavy emphasis on the rise of the welfare state – is the subject of Chapter 4.

These three long-term developments are not unique to the Netherlands. Comparable changes in the structure of the economy, the labour market and the role of the state can be found in almost all industrial nations. However, an international comparison reveals that there seems to be a clear Dutch pattern in all three. First of all, the Netherlands was a late starter in these fields: industrialization was rather slow in the nineteenth century and small-scale industry stood its ground until the 1920s. Dutch trade unions in the nineteenth century clearly lagged behind those in neighbouring countries and the Dutch state remained a model of official liberalism well into the 1930s. However, once the changes had set in, Dutch developments tended to extremes. The economic success of Dutch managerial enterprises was huge; after 1945 large multinational firms became far more important to the Netherlands than to most other Western European countries. The same applies for the development of the welfare state: after a relatively slow start, the 1960s experienced an unprecedented rise in social spending, which put the Netherlands among the (largely Scandinavian) countries at the top of the international league in terms of the share of social services in GDP. A similar story holds true for the organization of the labour market. After 1945 the labour market was under strong government control, which was rather unique to the Netherlands. Moreover, as a result of the postwar guided wage policy the influence of the unions on

3

labour relations became quite large, which has remained a feature of the Dutch labour market ever since. In short, the Dutch pattern can be described as a slow start followed by a 'big bang' in the period after World War II.

The particular Dutch version of the process of pillarization has to be introduced in the story to explain this pattern (see Chapter 2). This process ran almost completely parallel with the other major changes of the 'long' twentieth century. It had important consequences for the structure of the political system – which came to be dominated by the confessional parties – and, hence, for the development of the welfare state. Moreover, the moderate nature of Dutch trade unions, which was fundamental to their integration into a system of centralized wage bargaining after 1945, can probably also be attributed to the competition between confessional unions, moderate by nature, and the socialist unions; this competition was another result of pillarization. Finally, the pillarized society of the first two-thirds of the century was in many ways an entrepreneurial eldorado, where (multinational) companies were bound to prosper. Consequently, the 'Dutch' version of the long twentieth century is primarily connected with the process of pillarization, which will therefore receive separate attention in Chapter 2.

The Dutch pattern is one of the reasons to believe that the three long-term changes (in the structure of industry, of the labour market and of the state) are related. Of course, the close relationships between the rise of the welfare state and the growth of trade unionism are obvious and will be discussed in the chapters to come. There is however more to it. The three changes all stem from a distrust in market forces as such, and from the wish to overcome them by more efficient or just modes of organization. The debate on government intervention is a good place to start a description of the connections between the ideological frameworks of the three developments. There were basically two reasons to increase the role of government. The first one was the belief that administrative coordination – possibly with the help of some kind of plan – could be more efficient than coordination by the market. The market not only created large-scale unemployment (viz. in the 1930s) but was also unable to restructure declining industries, to operate utilities with natural monopolies, to start new basic industries, and so on. In other words, the market was (often) inefficient in the eyes of the (left-wing) reformers of the nineteenth and twentieth centuries.

A second and perhaps more fundamental reason for government intervention was that the results of the functioning of the market were often regarded as unjust, and that intervention by the government was necessary to correct (or even undo) these results. The growth of trade unions and the many changes in the labour market that came with them were another way in which to adjust the unequal results of the functioning of the labour market (and the market economy at large) that were so obvious in the nineteenth century.

The rise of managerial enterprises can at least partially be attributed to a comparable source: the efficiency of administrative coordination. For example, when during World War I Philips set out to manufacture its own glass bulbs and many other inputs instead of buying them on the market, the company internalized these markets and replaced them with its own administrative plans. In the very long run it could only do so because it was more efficient than to rely on the market for the supply of inputs. The managerial enterprise can therefore be seen as another system of administrative coordination, which is successful because it is more efficient than the markets it replaces. The rise of this type of enterprise resulted in the growth of large bureaucratic organizations – Chandler's multidivisional firm (Chandler 1990) – which operated not unlike the government bureaucracies that matured at the same time. Only the controlling influence of a (distant) market could check the growth of private bureaucracies (although after 1973 some of them have shown the same sclerosis as government administration, which has contributed to their relative decline). Both approaches – the managerial enterprise and the socialist 'planned economy' – attach great importance to economies of scale in production (and distribution), which could only be exploited optimally by a society by concentrating activities in large bureaucratic organizations.

The decades between 1914 and 1945 were characterized by the tension between the 'old' liberal economic order of the nineteenth century and the new 'anti-market' forces of a rising (welfare) state and emerging trade unions. The 1930s saw the final disintegration of the liberal, 'international' order and its replacement by all kinds of 'nationalistic' ad hoc policies aimed at softening the worst effects of the Depression. However, after World War II a new 'settlement' emerged from the apparent chaos (Eichengreen 1996). Its ideological basis was formed by the new economic ideas of J.M. Keynes that legitimized 'nationalistic' government policies towards the economy and, to a lesser extent, by the socialist tradition of economic planning. At the same time, during the occupation a new historical compromise was reached between 'labour' and 'capital' (see Chapter 5, p. 79); both parties wanted to work closely together to rebuild the economy after the liberation. The government soon became a partner in the new alliance. The second half of the 1940s witnessed the consolidation of this new institutional framework of 'organized capitalism within one country', a new synthesis of the (formerly antagonizing) forces of the 'long' twentieth century: big business, big government, and big unions. Concurrently a set of 'national' growth policies (guided wage policy, industrialization plans) was developed, which were ironically oriented more towards the supply side of the economy than towards the manipulation of demand. These policies also contributed to the success of the new 'model'.

5

Judged by its growth performance the postwar 'new settlement' was exceptionally successful. Yet, its very success created the forces that would eventually undermine the settlement. Rapid economic growth led to increased tensions on the labour market which, in the long run, undermined the profitability of industry. More importantly, the 'nationalistic' outlook of the new model was undermined by processes of economic integration which it had started. The settlement was based on a certain degree of government control over international trade and international capital movements, but at the same time governments needed larger export markets to realize their growth objectives. Out of this dilemma came a complicated process of European cooperation, which increasingly narrowed down the margins of national economic policy (Chapter 8, pp. 155–7).

The U-turn that occurred in the 1970s and 1980s is still something of a mystery, but on a few points the story can perhaps be made more clear. First of all, the model of 'organized capitalism within one country' was severely discredited by the events of the 1970s when inflation and taxes were too high and the increase in unemployment was too fast. Its ideological basis, which had not developed beyond plain Keynesianism, crumbled under the attacks of neo-liberal economists. Perhaps the changes of the 1980s should be interpreted as a 'counter-revolution' of 'capital' after it had been on the defence for a long time. The globalization of capital markets probably brought about significant changes in business strategy, which resulted in an almost continuous 'downsizing' of firms. At the same time, the margins for government intervention in the economy had become very small. Confidence in government planning and in a rational control of the economy completely disappeared and a passionate belief in the benevolent influence of the market made an exceptionally strong return. In a way, that is how and when the 'long' twentieth century came to an end. Currently we face an economy with a gradually declining share of employment in large enterprises, with a slow but persistent increase in the flexibility of labour markets (in spite of attempts by trade unions to slow down the process), and with a government that at least officially wants to reduce its role in the economy. Beneath the decay of the old structures of the 'long' twentieth century new structures are in the making, but it is much too soon to speculate about their precise nature and the reasons for their appearance. As an economic historian I aim to try and reconstruct the past, which is a sufficiently hazardous job in itself, especially for the twentieth century.

## NOTE

1 During the completion of the manuscript Erik Vanhaute drew my attention to the book by G. Arrighi (1996) who uses the term 'the long twentieth century' in a comparable way. When writing I was unaware of this important book.

# 2

# CHARACTERISTICS OF THE DUTCH ECONOMY

## A VERSATILE, SMALL AND OPEN ECONOMY: THE NETHERLANDS AT THE BEGINNING OF THE TWENTIETH CENTURY

Economic historians who study the nineteenth century have been almost obsessed with the problem of the late industrialization of the Netherlands. The fundamental issue was why 'modern industry' arose much later than in neighbouring countries such as Britain, Belgium, or even Germany (Griffiths 1996a). Sometimes it helps to approach the issue in a completely different way: why did 'modern industry' arise at all in the Netherlands in this period? During the nineteenth century most small economies seem to have moved in the direction of greater specialization and to have concentrated on activities in which they had a 'comparative advantage'. The Danish economy, for example, became increasingly dependent on the export of a small number of agricultural products, while Belgium specialized in a specific range of (semi-finished) industrial products. Why did the Dutch economy not follow a comparable path of development? The 'agro-commercial' nation of the first half of the nineteenth century was heavily dependent on its exports of agricultural products and the supply of international services to the mainly German hinterland. After 1860 the Netherlands began to develop an economic structure that was much more differentiated and balanced. In this respect the development of the Dutch economy is more comparable to that of large countries, such as Germany, France, and Italy (Griffiths 1996a).

That the Dutch economy diversified rather than specialized can to some extent be explained from developments related to the two sectors of the economy that were already strong: agriculture and international services. The modernization of agriculture resulted in the rise of agro-based industries that contributed significantly to the industrialization of a number of regions (East Groningen, West Brabant). Through various backward linkages the growth of international shipping stimulated the industrialization of the port cities of Holland. Shipbuilding is the most obvious example.

7

Yet, the gradual industrialization of the Netherlands was a far more complex process. At least two other factors played an important role: the large regional differences in economic structure and the vast colonial empire.

It is remarkable that in a small country such as the Netherlands highly different economic niches could exist simultaneously. To put it simply, the economic structure of Holland (and the other coastal provinces) was quite unlike that of the inland provinces. The history of the divergence between the economic centre of the country and its periphery goes back to (at least) the sixteenth and seventeenth centuries. The industrialization of a number of regions in the 'peripheral' inland provinces (Twente, the Achterhoek, parts of Brabant) was based on the elastic supply of proto-industrial labour. Labour intensive activities that did not demand many skills (textiles, leatherware, electric bulbs) were concentrated in regions where wages were much lower than in Holland. Improvements in infrastructure (railways) turned these regions into independent centres of economic growth – almost challenging Holland in this respect – where capital and entrepreneurship was largely supplied by the families of proto-industrial entrepreneurs (Fischer 1983).

A different structure of incentives underlay the industrialization of Holland. Since the Netherlands was poor in natural resources, all raw materials and a large part of the food supply had to be imported. Together with the rapidly growing demand for raw materials from the German hinterland, this created a great deal of employment in the two port cities, Amsterdam and Rotterdam. In the old centres of industry and trade in Holland an enormously wealthy bourgeoisie and a highly skilled labour force formed a large market for all kinds of products. In Holland the old processing industries (*trafieken*) – such as breweries, distilleries, sugar refineries, and shipyards – and a number of industries that were related to the urban supply of skilled labour (diamond cutting, printing) were the backbone of industrialization (Van Zanden 1987). Wages were relatively high in the skill and capital intensive industries.

Therefore, the industrial structure of the Netherlands that emerged during the final quarter of the nineteenth century had a dual character: labour intensive industries were located in the periphery – especially in Brabant and Twente – while skill and capital intensive industries were concentrated in Holland. This dichotomy was mitigated somewhat by the existence of agro-based industrial enclaves in Groningen and West Brabant and by the growth of the mining industry in Limburg. Nonetheless the result of the country's relatively large variation in incentives was that many different industries, ranging from highly labour intensive to highly capital intensive, were able to flourish and contribute to the industrialization of the Netherlands (Winsemius 1945).

A second factor that placed the Netherlands above 'the rank of Denmark' was its colonial empire (Baudet and Fennema 1983). In many different

8

ways Indonesia contributed to the strengthening and differentiation of the economy. The growth of international services was partially dependent on the flow of goods and services between the Netherlands and its colony. Indonesia was the main export market of cotton textile manufacturers in Twente and of various other industries (e.g. engineering), and it supplied raw materials to sugar refineries and tobacco manufacturers. The rise of the biggest (Anglo-)Dutch multinational, Royal Dutch Shell, started with the exploitation of the rich Sumatra oil fields. After 1890 *Cultuurondernemingen* – corporations specialized in the exploitation of Indonesia's vast agricultural potential – and the closely related banks (*cultuurbanken*) were probably the most profitable segments of the 'Dutch' economy (Lindblad 1996). In short, after 1830 the increasingly intensive exploitation of the colonial empire brought large profits to the Dutch economy, and contributed to the growth of a number of important industries.

As a result of these developments the Dutch economy seems to have diversified considerably during the second half of the nineteenth century. The rise of modern industries did not actually lead to a neglect of international services or agriculture. The expansion of the German hinterland stimulated the rise of Rotterdam as the main harbour for the import of raw materials and foodstuffs for the Ruhr region and for the export of many German finished products. In fact, there emerged a certain measure of specialization within Holland, with Amsterdam as the centre of trade and transport with Indonesia and Rotterdam working mainly for the German market.

Agriculture also remained a strong sector of the economy during the nineteenth century. Especially after 1890 structural changes in its organization, for example, the rise of cooperatives, specialized education, and extension services, contributed to the growth of production and exports. A favourable development of the terms of trade helped to keep the agricultural balance of trade positive in spite of a huge increase in grain imports after about 1870. This achievement was the result of the specialization in livestock farming and horticulture, both relatively labour intensive branches of the primary sector (Van Zanden 1991). It made possible (and was in turn encouraged by) a continuous expansion of agricultural employment; in the Netherlands total employment in this sector peaked quite late, in 1947.

It can be concluded that at the start of the twentieth century the Netherlands had a highly diversified economy, able to profit considerably from the economic boom that preceded World War I as a consequence of its modern infrastructure, its favourable position on the crossroads of trade in Western Europe and its strong liberal disposition. The country did of course have its shortcomings. The absence of a strong banking sector, able to finance industry, may be considered a weakness, especially when the Netherlands are compared with Germany or Belgium. After 1890 modern, large-scale industry was making rapid progress, but in many ways it was still in its infancy, lagging behind almost every other Western European country of a comparable size. But according to De Jonge (1968) and Griffiths (1996a) this was when the Netherlands underwent a modest 'big spurt', an event eagerly anticipated for so long if we are to believe the economic historians. The 'problem' of the nineteenth century was then finally resolved.

## A DECENT PILLARIZED SOCIETY

Pillarization or *verzuiling* is a special feature of Dutch society in the twentieth century. After about 1870 certain segments of the population began to organize themselves into numerous organizations on the basis of their religious or ideological convictions. Schools, trade unions, political parties, newspapers and farmers' organizations were set up for an exclusively Catholic, Protestant or socialist membership. After a while they were followed by organizations covering almost all parts of social and cultural life, from pillarized radio and television networks and nurseries to special Catholic or socialist homes for the elderly. The tightly knit Catholic pillar, which was mainly managed 'from above' by the clergy, covered almost all parts of the lives of its members. The orthodox Protestants and the socialists were almost as successful in creating their own networks of pillarized organizations, whereas the 'non-religious' or liberal community, which detested the 'voluntary' segregation of the population from the start, was not as well organized. The very existence of a fourth pillar – besides the Catholic, Protestant and socialist ones – is therefore still a matter of dispute (Lijphart 1968; Stuurman 1983; Blom 1985).

The process of pillarization was more or less complete by about 1920. This is not the place to reflect on its backgrounds, but a few remarks should be made. The rise of pillarization has been ascribed to two motives: emancipation and control. A rather popular idea is that the pillars were the result of processes of emancipation of the lower middle and working classes. For example, socialist trade unions and political parties were set up to such a purpose. They established their own newspapers, cooperative shops, leisure activities, and so on. These 'ghetto politics' were a common part of the socialist movement in the late nineteenth and early twentieth centuries throughout Europe.

The Protestant lower middle classes, who were generally more orthodox than the bourgeoisie, wanted to send their children to schools that taught their orthodoxy instead of the 'enlightened' Protestantism of nineteenth-century modern theology. The establishment of orthodox schools was therefore one way to emancipate vis-à-vis the liberal bourgeoisie. The particularly talented Protestant minister Abraham Kuyper used these feelings to create an orthodox Protestant political party, which became one of the engines behind the process of pillarization.

On the other hand, the more critical literature on pillarization stresses the motive of control. The creation of so many new organizations is considered the method by which old (and new) elites tried to bind to their own cause those groups that had newly acquired political rights. For example, when Catholic labourers were tempted to join (socialist) trade unions, the clergy began to organize their own Catholic unions, which they could control. Similarly the rise of religious parties was closely related to the ongoing enfranchisement and the 'threat' of the growth of left-wing parties (Stuurman 1983).

Whatever the theories on the origins of the pillarized society, it is agreed that pillarization resulted in a very stable political system. The electoral basis of the different parties was relatively strong: for example, orthodox Protestants voted for their own leaders, even when they strongly disagreed with their policies (as happened in the 1930s). Moreover, even though at the 'bottom' – among voters and trade unions members – the differences between the pillars were constantly underlined, at the 'top', i.e. in daily politics, they were able to work together quite well (Lijphart 1968). No pillar had an absolute majority in parliament – or could hope to attain one (probably with the exception of the socialists before 1917) – which meant that governments always consisted of more than one party. Between 1919 and 1994 the Catholic party, nestled comfortably in the middle of the political spectrum between the left (social democrats) and right (orthodox Protestants and right-wing liberals), was part of every coalition government. This fundamental continuity and the reliance of policymakers on constant negotiations between the main political parties meant that extreme changes in policy hardly occurred.

The socialist movement was perhaps the only one to challenge this very stable political system. The introduction of general (male) suffrage in 1917 made the socialists hopeful that they could win a majority, but their hopes were shattered when many of the new votes went to the Catholic (and Protestant) parties. Until 1939 they were left out of government, which many preferred to being enmeshed in the party politics of coalition governments. After World War II the newly reformed Labour Party became part of the political establishment and thereby lost its interest in opposing the pillarized political system.

As a result, in the 1950s there arose a political system with almost tedious consensus. It reflected general socio-cultural developments in Dutch society, that began in the second half of the nineteenth century. Around 1850 the values and beliefs of a large part of the population were presumably somewhat different from those of the dominant bourgeoisie. This was probably closely related to the general poverty of the working classes, which made it very difficult for them to live up to the bourgeois norms of the period. In the final quarter of the nineteenth century there began a process to civilize the working classes and make them lead a

11

'decent' life (De Regt 1984). Various groups contributed to this civilization process. In the eyes of orthodox Protestants such as Abraham Kuyper and in those of the Catholic clergy the population had to be re-Christianized. They hoped to instil (once again) the Christian norms and values on their followers by creating Protestant or Catholic organizations in all fields of life, from leisure activities to trade unions. Liberal reformers used schools, the system of poor relief, savings banks and many other institutions to educate and civilize the 'lower classes'. For its part, the socialist movement needed decent members who were completely devoted to its aims. For example, it took the lead in the battle against alcoholism because, as the socialist leader Domela Nieuwenhuys said, 'a labourer who drinks, does not think, and a labourer who thinks, does not drink'.

The development of the consumption of (pure) alcohol after 1870 is a useful indicator of the success of these movements to civilize the working classes. Alcoholism was rightly regarded as one of the worst enemies of the lower classes, and the enormous decline in alcohol consumption between 1880 and 1930 testifies to the success of the civilization process. The decline in the consumption of *jenever* (Dutch gin) was particularly dramatic; it fell continuously and by more than 80 percent between the 1870s and the 1930s. After 1900 beer also came under attack and per capita consumption declined from 42 litres in 1900 to less than 15 litres between 1935 and 1939. After 1945 alcohol consumption was slightly higher than during the 1930s (when the Depression also contributed to its decline), but until the 1960s it remained on a very low level by international standards (CBS, *Jaarcijfers*, various issues). The huge drop in alcohol consumption after 1870 is the more remarkable in that government policies played a modest role. It therefore really seems to reflect part of the process of civilizing the working classes.

Another important result of the changes after about 1870 was the changing role of married women on the labour market. Liberal reformers since the 1850s had agitated against wage labour by women (and children) because it undermined family life. The rise in real wages made it increasingly possible for married men to earn the family income and seems to have created a tendency for women to retreat to domestic activities. During the second half of the nineteenth century labour participation ratios for women declined to levels that were very low by European standards (Pott-Buter 1993). In many other countries the two world wars encouraged an increase in female labour participation, but this did not happen in the Netherlands. Married women predominantly remained at home to raise their children until the 1970s, when an upward trend suddenly began that brought female participation on the labour market to the average European level by 1990 (Chapter 6).

Until the late 1960s Dutch women appear to have specialized in reproductive activities. The strong decline in marital fertility, which occurred

12

throughout Europe after 1870, is also apparent in the Dutch figures, but it was not as steep and in some regions it was long delayed (Hofstee 1981). In the Catholic and orthodox Protestant pillars the ideal of a large family and a cosy domestic life was propagated intensely, and modern methods of birth control were strictly forbidden. This contributed to the high level of marital fertility, which was definitely highest among the orthodox Protestants and the Catholics (Van der Kaa 1980). The result was a continued rapid expansion of population. Whereas population growth in the rest of Europe slowed down markedly after about 1900, the Dutch population doubled between 1900 and 1950, and continued its growth during the following decades. After 1965 the birth rate suddenly collapsed – especially in the predominantly Catholic south of the country – which is generally attributed to the introduction of the contraception pill (notwithstanding the resistance by the Catholic clergy). The demographic regime began to converge to the European average.

The success of the civilization process that began sometime after 1870 can also be deduced from the enormous decline in infant mortality between 1870 and 1930. During the nineteenth century the Netherlands – Holland and Zeeland in particular – had a very high level of infant mortality, which was probably caused by the lack of proper fresh water and low levels of hygiene. After 1870 propaganda for breast-feeding and modern standards of hygiene, the development of better fresh water supplies and many other investments to increase public hygiene, all helped to bring infant mortality down (De Regt 1984). During the interwar period it clearly fell below the levels of neighbouring countries, even though most Dutch women still gave birth at home (and continued to do so). At the same time the number of illegitimate births seems to have fallen sharply as well, which proves once more that the Dutch population was increasingly conforming to the 'Christian' norms of a 'civilized' society (Kok 1990).

As a result of the huge success of a threefold civilization process – by the liberal bourgeoisie, by the orthodox Protestants and the Catholic clergy, and by the socialists – in the twentieth century the Netherlands had become a highly integrated society in which deviant behaviour was rare and common norms and values seem to have permeated the vast majority of the population. It is probably no coincidence that the strong decline in deviant behaviour, such as alcoholism and illegitimacy, coincided with the process of pillarization between 1880 and 1920. The depillarization, the sudden dissolution of the pillarized structure of society after about 1965, had the opposite effect and in many ways led to a convergence of Dutch society to the European pattern.

I will now try to show the relevance of these developments for the economic history of the Netherlands in the twentieth century.

13

## CHARACTERISTICS OF LONG-TERM
## ECONOMIC GROWTH

It is no surprise that the Dutch economy grew rapidly during the twentieth century which went along with an enormous increase in per capita income and the standard of living. This growth went hand in hand with a structural transformation of the economy. Industry (until 1963) and services became much more important as sources of employment and income, while agriculture relatively declined (Van Ark and De Jong 1996). Moreover, in contrast to the preceding century, in the twentieth century the price level rose almost continuously. Insofar as these developments are concerned the Dutch economy was not really unique.

A closer look at the Dutch growth record shows that the country did have a number of special features. The growth of GDP was particularly rapid and the rate of inflation was very modest throughout the century. In fact, on both counts the Dutch economy outperformed almost every other European country (Maddison 1995). Moreover, according to the much cited figures of Maddison, labour productivity was consistently higher than in most other European countries. Yet, compared to its outstanding performance in productivity per hour worked, per capita GDP was relatively low. In this section I will try to explain these special features of Dutch economic growth.

The first feature concerns inflation. Maddison's data suggest that during the twentieth century inflation in the Netherlands was much slower than in any other European country, with the exception of Switzerland (Maddison 1995). The stability of prices can first be attributed to the stable social and political system. There were no major political upheavels and, especially during the interwar period, the Netherlands was a haven of tranquility. The hyperinflation of the 1920s that wrought havoc on the economies of central and eastern Europe – with their complex social and economic background – completely passed by the Low Countries. The Depression of the 1930s led to intense socio-political conflicts in large parts of Europe, but it only increased the sense of resignation in the Netherlands. Neutrality in World War I and stern German controls during World War II ensured that inflation was quite moderate during both wars. Finally, after 1945 the close cooperation between government, trade unions and employers' organizations – with the explicit aim to control wage rises and inflation – was largely successful. The 'new settlement' between 'labour', 'capital' and the state of 1945 resulted in a country with a low level of socio-economic conflict. Among other things, this can be observed from statistics on the intensity of strikes which is shown to have been very low in the Netherlands – only Switzerland performed even better (see Chapter 5) (Flora 1981).

The effects of the stable socio-political system were strengthened by conservative financial and monetary policies. Dominant politicians such as

14

Colijn, Drees and Lubbers seem to have shared a preference for thrifty government, aimed at reducing wages and prices in order to restore and increase international competitiveness. Monetary experiments with the same purpose – such as the devaluation of the guilder – were then and are still generally detested. Colijn, the most prominent politician of the 1930s, actually denounced the idea to leave the gold standard on moral grounds, as a result of which the Netherlands would be the last European country to devalue (this time a few hours after the Swiss) (see Chapter 6). After 1945 the 'new' economic policies mainly resulted in the integration of the trade unions and the Labour Party into the effort to keep down wages and prices. And during the 1980s the standard response of the socio-political system to the growing economic problems was to form a new coalition between government, trade unions and employers' organizations with the aim of ending the rise of wages and prices. This coalition was strongly supported by the orthodox monetary policies of the Dutch Central Bank (DNB).

The Dutch tradition of financial and monetary solidity was interrupted during the 1960s and 1970s when more expansionary policies were adopted, at least by the central government (the Central Bank remained a staunch defender of the orthodox position). This probably contributed to the increase in the rate of inflation that put the Netherlands at the top of the OECD ranking in the early 1970s (see Chapter 8). After the double-digit inflation rates of the first half of the 1970s, the country slowly returned to its 'normal' path of development during the 1980s when inflation dropped to one of the lowest levels in the OECD.

As a result of the stable political system and the low rate of inflation the guilder was continually a strong currency. Once again, only the Swiss franc was able to defeat the guilder in strength. This was, however, a mixed blessing, especially in years of economic stagnation, as will be shown in the following chapters.

The growth of Dutch GDP was particularly rapid during the twentieth century – of all European countries only Norway performed better – but the increase in GDP per capita was at best equal to that in the rest of Western Europe (Maddison 1995). The paradox was simply caused by the much higher rate of population growth in the Netherlands. A second paradox is related to the first: per capita GDP may not have been particularly high but labour productivity (measured in production per hour worked) surely was. The obvious cause was the low participation rate of the Dutch population: until about 1970 female participation was far below average and during the 1970s and 1980s, when women began to reduce the gap, the participation of men began to decline (see Chapter 5). I have already suggested that there was a connection between low female participation ratios and the strong population increase between 1900 and 1970 (see Pott-Buter 1993).

The interdependence of female participation and population growth was in fact far more complicated. Labour productivity was consistently high, but rapid population growth as well as government policies aimed at improving international competitiveness kept wage costs at a relatively low average level until the mid-1960s. The expansion of the international economy and the demand for Dutch exports made for large profits and created strong incentives to increase production. Rapid economic growth went hand in hand with a large expansion of the capital stock, which was consequently of quite recent vintage. In turn this helped to increase labour productivity and keep it at a fairly high level. The infrastructure of the economy could remain relatively new as a result of the vast expansion of total output and the total capital stock.

The starting point of this line of argument is the high labour productivity of the Dutch economy. This remarkable phenomenon requires further explanation. Table 2.1 shows that during the first thirty years of the twentieth century the Dutch economy performed much better than most other European countries. This was followed by twenty years of near stagnation which caused the Netherlands to drop from first place in 1929 to third place in 1950. In 1973 the country had, however, completely recovered its leading position. Thereafter, it was more or less joined by Germany, Belgium, and France.

The high productivity of the Dutch economy at the start of the twentieth century is somewhat surprising. It developed rapidly after about 1890, but the debate on the late industrialization of the nineteenth century shows that the Netherlands was then not considered as a 'leading' economy. Yet, there is a number of reasons to take the figures seriously. First, this small and open economy was heavily involved in international trade. Low transport costs (modern infrastructure, small distances) and the proximity to two major cities ports obliged virtually every producer to compete with the most efficient competitor on the world market. Moreover, there was no protection for agriculture or industry.

*Table 2.1* Levels of labour productivity in nine European countries (US = 100)

|             | *1913* | *1929* | *1938* | *1950* | *1973* | *1992* |
|-------------|--------|--------|--------|--------|--------|--------|
| Netherlands | 78     | 84     | 72     | 51     | 81     | 99     |
| Belgium     | 70     | 64     | 61     | 48     | 70     | 98     |
| UK          | 86     | 74     | 69     | 62     | 68     | 82     |
| Germany     | 68     | 58     | 56     | 35     | 71     | 95     |
| France      | 56     | 55     | 62     | 45     | 76     | 102    |
| Italy       | 41     | 38     | 44     | 34     | 66     | 85     |
| Denmark     | 66     | 68     | 61     | 46     | 68     | 75     |
| Sweden      | 50     | 44     | 49     | 56     | 77     | 79     |
| Norway      | 43     | 45     | 50     | 43     | 60     | 88     |

*Source*: Maddison 1995: 47

A second reason may be found in the structure of the economy. The service sector was traditionally larger in the Netherlands than in neighbouring countries, and this sector generated relatively high earnings (Smits 1990, 1997). On the other hand, the agricultural sector was also rather large but very competitive and highly productive (Van Zanden 1991).

A third factor that contributed to the relatively high productivity of the Dutch economy is of a more speculative nature. The civilization process that was sketched in the previous section can also be interpreted as a movement to discipline the workers. 'Pre-industrial' customs, which harmed the efficiency of large-scale entreprise – such as Saints Monday or drinking during working hours – were effectively suppressed. Unregularized forms of shopfloor resistance were discouraged by new management techniques (Taylorism) (Bloemen 1988). This probably resulted in a disciplined labour force that was accustomed regularly to working long hours and would not resist new measures aimed at increasing labour productivity. The low level of labour conflict after 1948 further testifies to the creation of a rather docile workforce that had become accustomed to its subordinate role. In short, the decent, pillarized society had a disciplined, hardworking labour force. This is obviously a cliché, albeit an important one as it fits into the general perception of the Dutch and was often repeated in reports by foreign firms and countries on the incentives for investing in the Netherlands.

The fourth element of the explanation of the high labour productivity, the rapid growth of population and labour stock, has already been mentioned. In a way the Netherlands reaped the benefits of its slow industrialization during the nineteenth century, as there were almost no old industrial regions or declining industries to hinder the growth of the economy. However, the effects of the large demographic growth are not so easy to demonstrate. In general, in stark contrast to their early modern colleagues the economic historians of the twentieth century are not particularly interested in the demographic forces behind long-term economic development. Yet, it seems obvious that the strong growth of the market and the 'vintage' effect on the composition of the labour force – relatively young and, hence, well-educated – must have been of some importance to long-term economic development.

On the other hand, during a depression the rapid growth of population turned into a disadvantage. The fast expansion of the labour force during the 1930s and again during the 1970s and 1980s – the latter growth was a result of the echo of the postwar baby boom and the increased participation of women – made a large contribution to the sharp rise in unemployment during these decades (Drukker 1990). Insofar as unemployment is concerned the performance of the Dutch economy was consequently relatively poor.

At least until the 1960s the high level of labour productivity was combined with a relatively low level of wage costs. Table 2.2 presents some

*Table 2.2* Estimates of nominal industrial male wages in the Netherlands and in a number of major competitors, 1913–1950 (in guilders per hour, calculated using current exchange rates)

|  | *1913* | *1930* | *1950* |
|---|---|---|---|
| Netherlands | 0.22 | 0.58 | 1.12 |
| Belgium | 0.26 | 0.44 | 1.60 |
| Germany | 0.40 | 0.54 | 1.26 |
| UK | 0.70 | 1.46 | 1.76 |
| France | 0.31 | 0.52 | 0.89 |
| Denmark | — | 0.92 | 1.98 |
| USA | 0.69 | 1.47 | 5.59 |

*Sources*: ILO 1952; Van der Veen and Van Zanden 1989

evidence on wage levels in the Netherlands and its competitors, which clearly demonstrates the strong advantage of Dutch entrepreneurs. Moreover, the close proximity to the world market and the near absence of protection made raw materials and other imported inputs relatively cheap. A more favourable climate for entrepreneurial activity is therefore hard to imagine. In short, the combined influence of low (wage) costs, high productivity, a stable socio-political system and a liberal government, a disciplined workforce, a low level of inflation, and a very open economy turned the Netherlands into an 'eldorado' for entrepreneurs (Andriessen 1987). As soon as the world economy allowed for it, the economy boomed.

The special features of the Dutch economy in the twentieth century – the low rate of inflation, the strong growth of GDP, and the high level of labour productivity – are related to its unique socio-political development, which was outlined in the previous section. The decent, pillarized society had its own developmental path, which differed in certain respects from the rest of Western Europe. The resulting entrepreneurial 'eldorado' explains the strong performance of the economy in the period up to 1929 and after 1945. However, the depillarization of the 1960s deprived the Netherlands of some of its special features. The disappearance of the 'eldorado' occurred at the same time as the dismantling of the pillarized structure of society, which further strengthens the case for the intimate relationship between both developments.

## REGIONAL VARIATIONS IN ECONOMIC STRUCTURES

One of the factors behind the diversified structure of the Dutch economy at the start of the nineteenth century was the large regional variations in economic structure. These dated back (at least) as far as the seventeenth century when the economy of the western part of the country boomed spectacularly and the inland provinces saw their (relative) economic position deteriorate. Groningen and Friesland, the two northernmost coastal provinces, also appear to have profited much from the economic growth of the seventeenth century; in particular the agriculture of these provinces showed remarkable progress. During the nineteenth century the large differences in economic structure were to some extent bridged by the industrialization of parts of the 'periphery', Twente (the eastern part of Overijssel) and Brabant in particular (De Jonge 1996). Nevertheless large variations in wage levels, the cost of living, and per capita income persisted throughout the century despite the rapid increase in domestic trade and in interregional migration.

The variations in economic structure had at least two dimensions. There existed large differences in occupational structures. These remained essentially unchanged throughout the twentieth century, but the sharp contrasts were somewhat diminished. The international services – the source of the highest incomes – and capital intensive industries were concentrated in Holland. The inland provinces, on the other hand, were generally more agricultural and their industries tended to be more labour intensive as a consequence of their proto-industrial origins. Industrialization policies after 1949 and the extreme scarcity of labour in the *Randstad* (the central urban belt of Holland) during the 1950s and 1960s resulted in a more even distribution of industrial employment across the country. In the long run Brabant and Limburg became the most industrial regions of the country, whereas Twente lost most of its textiles after about 1960. Holland (and Utrecht) remained the centres of the (international) services. The growth of public administration in The Hague, of the main port, Schiphol, and of the large banks and insurance companies – all with their headquarters in the *Randstad* – further enhanced this concentration. In the remaining provinces agriculture and agro-based industries were still relatively important (for more details see: Van Zanden and Griffiths 1989: 26–9).

The regional variations in wages and prices, on the other hand, almost disappeared during the twentieth century. The rise of labour intensive industries in the periphery and the boom in its agriculture during the nineteenth century already led to a noticeable decrease in the wage gap between Holland and the rest of the country, a process that continued during the interwar period (Table 2.3). Especially in the Southern Netherlands nominal wages rose rapidly; in Limburg this was probably caused mainly by the expansion of the coal mining industry which paid high wages for dirty and dangerous work. Regional wage variations decreased rather spectacularly between 1938 and 1950: in the space of twelve years the variation coefficient declined almost as much as in the preceding one and a half century. The decrease in regional differences in income per capita was even more radical (Table 2.3, bottom line). After 1950 the new pattern of low regional disparity changed hardly if at all; the small changes that can be discerned in Table 2.3 are probably due to differences in the kinds of

*Table 2.3* Regional differences in nominal industrial wages, 1816–1983
(the Netherlands = 100)

|  | 1816 | 1906 | 1938 | 1950 | 1966 | 1983 |
|---|---|---|---|---|---|---|
| Groningen | 91 | 87 | 91 | 89 | 96 | 96 |
| Friesland | 95 | 84 | 88 | 86 | 92 | 92 |
| Drenthe | 75 | 75 | 78 | 84 | 93 | 91 |
| Overijssel | 84 | 85 | 88 | 95 | 93 | 92 |
| Gelderland | 87 | 84 | 86 | 93 | 97 | 94 |
| Utrecht | 105 | 95 | 99 | 106 | 100 | 99 |
| Noord-Holland | 145 | 123 | 110 | 102 | 104 | 108 |
| Zuid-Holland | 116 | 109 | 104 | 105 | 106 | 104 |
| Zeeland | 115 | 92 | 91 | 93 | 98 | 106 |
| Noord-Brabant | 77 | 76 | 91 | 92 | 97 | 100 |
| Limburg | 79 | 94 | 123 | 106 | 102 | 98 |
| Netherlands | 100 | 100 | 100 | 100 | 100 | 100 |
| coefficient of variation |  |  |  |  |  |  |
| wages | 0.22 | 0.15 | 0.13 | 0.08 | 0.05 | 0.06 |
| regional income |  |  |  |  |  |  |
| per capita | 0.29 | 0.25 | 0.17 | 0.06 | – | 0.05 |
| (year) | (1820) | (1910) | (1938) | (1950) |  | (1978) |

*Source*: Van Zanden and Griffiths 1989: 25

wages which are compared. In the northern parts of the country, nowadays the economically weakest region, wage levels remain somewhat below the national average. The two southern provinces have stabilized their position (after the closure of the coal mines) near the national average, and Holland continues to be the region with the highest wages and salaries.

The most remarkable development was undoubtedly the sharp levelling off of income disparities during the 1940s. This was shaped by economic and political factors. The war resulted in high profits and a high demand for labour in the agricultural sector, whereas it particularly ruined the economy of Holland. For example, the international services collapsed during the German occupation and war damage was especially severe in the region that remained occupied longest, i.e. the *Randstad*. The guided wage policy that came into existence in 1945 also played a considerable role. It led to the creation of a large formalized and institutionalized wage system in which regional differences in wage levels were largely abolished. Moreover, differences between wages for skilled and unskilled workers declined, and the increase in salaries lagged behind that in wages (see Chapter 5). The result was a sharp and general decline in wage disparities, which contributed to the reduction of regional differences.

The institutionalization of wage formation through the guided wage policy also meant that the old wage disparities would not return. The result was that the economy actually lost some of the economic 'niches' that had characterized industrialization during the nineteenth century. The Dutch economy became more homogeneous, and probably lost some of its flexibility and, in the long run, its diversity. This is especially clear from the classic example of low-wage industrialization in the Netherlands, the cotton textile industry of Twente. Its disappearance after about 1960 should probably be seen from this perspective, although it was a far more complex process.

## THE ECONOMIC IMPORTANCE OF INDONESIA

The colonial relationship with Indonesia added an extra dimension to the structure of the Dutch economy. The economic revival of the first half of the nineteenth century was achieved largely through the more intensive exploitation of the colony by means of the Cultivation System. This system not only generated a considerable surplus for the treasury, allowing the government to overcome the serious financial difficulties that had vexed the economy for more than fifty years. It also gave an important incentive for major sectors of the economy: the textile and shipbuilding industries, and international trade. The offensive against the Cultivation System by liberal politicians after 1848 was one reason for the gradual change in the relationship with the colony. Indonesia was opened up for private enterprise, which had reinforced its capacities under the Cultivation System. The trade barriers that had guided Indonesia's imports and exports to the Netherlands were broken down.

These changes led to a gradual reorientation of Indonesian international trade. In 1874 the Dutch share in exports was still as high as 60 percent, but it declined to 30 percent in 1913 and dropped below 20 percent in the interwar period (Lindblad 1988). The share of Indonesia in Dutch imports underwent a comparable decline. Dutch exports to Indonesia developed more favourably. Between 1874 and 1913 no clear trend can be discerned; it remained around 15 to 20 percent of all exports. Only after 1921, when 26 percent of Dutch exports was destined for the colony, can a decreasing tendency be discerned, with a trough of 5.4 percent in 1934 (CBS 1984).

The increasing marginalization of Dutch trade with Indonesia implied that Dutch enterprise redirected its attention to Europe while Indonesia focused increasingly on Asia and North America. This can be described as a history of missed opportunities (Lindblad 1988). It is striking that while the Netherlands maintained a considerable share in the export of 'old' plantation crops (coffee, sugar, tobacco, tea), the export of new products (petroleum, rubber, copra) that began to dominate Indonesia's foreign trade after 1900 was directed at non-Dutch markets from the start. However, it is questionable whether an analysis in terms of 'failing' Dutch entrepreneurship is entirely justified.

A comparison with the development of the economic relations between the UK and its colonies may clarify this point. These relations developed exactly in the opposite direction: the dependence of the mother country on trade with its colonies increased between 1870 and 1940. Around 1870 the UK was still strongly focused on its trade with the rest of Europe and with North America and dominated world trade in manufactures. This changed as a consequence of the rise of other industrial nations, Germany and the USA in particular. Especially after 1900 the UK lost ground to the new competitors and increasingly focused its international trade on the colonies. The apex of this process was the system of 'Imperial Preference' in the 1930s. This development has been criticized by economists and economic historians alike: the UK steered clear of international competition, allowed an insufficient renewal of its industrial base, and locked itself into colonial markets that grew slowly, showed little promise in prewar years, and evaporated after World War II with the economic emancipation of (former) colonies. The UK was therefore out of step with continental Europe after World War II and failed to benefit from the rapid expansion of the economies of Western Europe.

It was clearly favourable that the Dutch economy experienced a reverse process. Dutch manufacturing and agriculture were well prepared for competition with neighbouring countries and managed to expand their share in intra-European trade. The Dutch economy did not have to confine itself to a monopolized trade relationship with its colony in Asia – as it did during the period 1830 to 1870 – in order to recover after World War II. It managed to avoid major adjustment problems, because the economic importance of Indonesia gradually decreased over time. Only the super-competition of Japanese manufactures during the 1930s, when Dutch international competitiveness was severely handicapped by the refusal of the government to let go of the gold standard and devalue the guilder, made protective measures necessary. These were, however, largely instigated by the adverse business conditions of the 1930s.

The relative decline of trade relations between the Netherlands and Indonesia did not mean that the economic connection between the two countries diminished absolutely during the period 1870 to 1940. To the contrary, the role of Dutch companies in the trade and transport of Indonesian export commodities was increasingly overshadowed by the role of those in the production of such commodities and in the supply of investment capital and management services. Dutch direct investment in Indonesia first experienced growth during the 1870s, but did not start to expand strongly until after 1900 (Baudet and Fennema 1983: 35–6). The most spectacular growth performance was recorded in the mining sector; the exploitation of natural oil reserves was financed entirely with Dutch capital. After surviving the crisis of the 1880s plantation companies began to pump money into the sugar industry and into new activities, such as rubber and copra. The Dutch Koninklijke Paketvaart Maatschappij (KPM), established in 1891, provided a large part of the inter-island shipping services. Sizeable amounts were invested in railways. Public utilities and several companies producing for the domestic market were established with Dutch capital. Total Dutch investment in Indonesia was estimated at 4 billion guilders in 1938, which amounted to around 40 percent of the total amount of Dutch capital invested abroad and 22 percent of total Dutch capital investment. The direct contribution of Indonesia to Dutch national income in the form of dividends, interest payments and pensions has been estimated at around 8 percent for the same year. Including various indirect effects, the total contribution of Indonesia to Dutch national income could have been as high as 14 percent (Baudet and Wijers 1976).

In addition to the supply of capital – more accurately, the reinvestment of profits made in Indonesia – Dutch nationals in Indonesia increasingly moved into other employment opportunities. The public service expanded rapidly and had an increasing impact on local communities. However, the employment of Europeans outside the civil service increased much faster as a result of the rapid expansion of 'European enterprise' in Indonesia. The total number of Europeans, most of them Dutch nationals, increased from 44,000 in 1860 to 91,000 in 1900 and 240,000 in 1930 (Burger 1975, II: 4). Since many Dutch nationals remained in Indonesia only for a few years, by 1930 the number of Dutchmen in the Netherlands who had been to 'our Indies' was a multiple of this number. Hence, viewed from the perspective of the mother country, the connections with Indonesia became increasingly close.

Against this background it is understandable that after 1945 the general opinion in the Netherlands was that reviving the colonial connections with Indonesia would be of vital importance to the recovery of the Dutch economy. In addition, it was widely believed that the abundance of raw materials would enable the Netherlands to establish a positive trade balance with the USA – the way it had been before 1940 – in order to make a strategic contribution to the solution of the critical dollar shortage which impeded European recovery in the late 1940s. The Dutch put everything to work in order to restore the economic exchange with Indonesia. Dutch exports to Indonesia increased substantially, to a considerable extent in response to the demands for commodities by the Dutch armed forces in Indonesia. Dutch imports from Indonesia also increased rapidly: from 20 million guilders in 1946 to 770 million in 1951, or 8 percent of total merchandise imports in that year (CBS 1984: 134).

The formal independence of Indonesia in 1949 naturally ended all attempts to restore the economic relationship to its prewar footing. After 1951 mutual trade gradually declined, while Dutch trade with other parts of the world boomed. Mutual trade sunk to a nadir when the Dutch–Indonesian dispute on Dutch New Guinea completely disrupted relations and all Dutch enterprises in Indonesia were nationalized. The direct contribution of Indonesia to Dutch national income decreased accordingly: 2.8 percent in 1948, 4.4 percent in 1949, falling gradually to 2.1 percent in 1956 and almost nothing in the following years (Baudet and Wijers 1976). In the second half of the 1960s relations between the Netherlands and Indonesia were normalized without restoring Indonesia to even a shadow of the significance it had once had for the Dutch economy.

The opinion that the Netherlands suffered few disadvantageous consequences from the radical and sudden breach in relations with Indonesia dominates the available literature on the subject. The high rate of economic growth during the first two postwar decades indicated that the Netherlands was fully able to rely on its own economic capabilities and to redirect its economy towards Europe (or the Atlantic world in general). The process of reorientation, which had already characterized the structure of Dutch foreign trade for several decades, was rapidly completed after 1949. The vigorous Dutch economy did not need colonies to recover from World War II.

Some have suggested that the loss of Indonesia might even have contributed to the Dutch economic boom after 1945. The human capital that had previously been applied to the development of the economy of colonial Indonesia now benefited the mother country. The task of pulling two countries, the Netherlands and Indonesia, out of the economic misery of the afterwar years may well have been too big for one small country. Moreover, the loss of 'our Indies' considerably lifted the spirits of the Dutch at a time when they had to put their shoulders to the wheel. This feeling did generally prevail in Dutch society after World War II. It contributed significantly to the sacrifices (low wages) made by the Dutch population to rebuild their country after the ravages of war and to generate the economic growth that led to unprecedented prosperity.

This is not to deny that the Dutch economy suffered as a result of the loss of Indonesia (see Baudet and Fennema 1983: 136 ff). The plantation companies, the railways, the public utilities, and other companies with fixed assets in Indonesia lost most of their capital, even though the Indonesian government paid some compensation after 1965. A company such as Royal Dutch Shell could continue its activities without being disturbed owing to its dual British and Dutch ownership. Unilever also managed to avoid nationalization through a timely transfer of the headquarters of its interests in Indonesia from the Netherlands to London.

A number of industries in the Netherlands experienced structural problems aside from the loss of Dutch investments in Indonesia. The economy of the city of Amsterdam was especially affected, because of the decrease in the trade in tropical commodities and the loss of employment in the banks that financed plantation and trading companies operating in Indonesia. The production of the main textile companies in the region of Twente suffered as a consequence of the fall in the sales in Indonesia and the inability to find markets in other Third World countries. More importantly, the shipping industry lost a considerable part of its market. Until 1940 this had been an important branch of the Dutch service sector. The fall of merchant shipping also dragged down the Dutch shipbuilding industry. The loss of the colony considerably accelerated the end of the Netherlands as a mighty seafaring and shipbuilding nation. In the end, the independence of Indonesia caused the Dutch economy to lose part of its versatility.

## FROM A SMALL VERSATILE ECONOMY TO A LARGE 'SMALL ECONOMY'

This chapter opened with a description of the diversified nature of the Dutch economy at the start of the twentieth century. After 1890 its many different economic 'niches' and the strong development of the economic ties with Indonesia helped to create a highly versatile and rapidly growing economy. As a result of the combination of demographic, social, and economic forces, the economy expanded forcefully during the twentieth century. On average Dutch economic growth between 1913 and 1990 was about twice as high as in Belgium or the UK, the two pioneers of industrialization, and in the long run Dutch growth rates were only slightly lower than those of the USA (Maddison 1995). Without doubt the Netherlands became the biggest 'small economy' of Europe, a role it was to play quite often in the process of European integration.

The 'extensive' growth was, however, not matched by a comparable deepening of the structure of the economy. In fact, especially after about 1960 the economic base seems to have narrowed. Two of the causes were the loss of Indonesia and the disappearance of regional disparities. Industries that had been important to the industrialization of the first half of the century – such as textiles, shipbuilding, and metal working – declined enormously. The mines of Limburg were closed down and the shipping industry largely moved to low-cost countries. All that seems to remain of the long industrialization drive of the period 1890 to 1960 are the capital intensive and port-related industries: oil refining, bulk chemicals, basic metals, paper, and the agro-industry which thrives on the efficiency of Dutch agriculture. The importance of the Netherlands as an international centre of distribution and trade, with the two main ports of Rotterdam and Schiphol as its pivots, is continuously expanding.

It is fair to wonder if the long industrialization drive of the period 1890 to 1960 was a repetition of the magnificent flourishing of Dutch industry during the seventeenth century, albeit at different level. During its Golden Age the Netherlands in a way became the workshop of the world: fabrics from Leiden and Haarlem, Delft earthenware, ships from the Zaan, and paintings from all over Holland and Utrecht dominated international markets. Yet, after the

'Golden Age' had ended a long period of (relative) stagnation had begun, all that remained were the capital intensive processing industries (*trafieken*), a highly productive agriculture, and Amsterdam as the centre of distribution for a large hinterland. These seem to be the core activities that really persist, even in times of high wages and economic stagnation, whereas the other industries come and go with the long waves of the economy.

# 3

# THE RISE OF THE MANAGERIAL ENTERPRISE

## INTRODUCTION

The first half of the twentieth century witnessed the rise of a number of large enterprises that came to dominate the Dutch economy in the decades after World War II. Alfred Chandler, who wrote a number of books on similar developments in the USA, Great Britain and Germany, argues that this should first of all be attributed to the consequences of the 'second industrial revolution' (Chandler 1990). In the decades after about 1880 a number of fundamental technological innovations in chemicals, electricity, machine building (the internal combustion engine) and oil refining led to the growth of new industries that were to revolutionize the industrial structure of the world economy during the twentieth century. Two special features of these new technologies were their large economies of scale and their high capital intensity. The economies of scale could only be exploited optimally by producing on a very large scale, for an extensive national or preferably international market. The entrepreneurs who came to control these new industries therefore had to make huge investments in (1) production facilities; (2) a distribution apparatus; (3) the management skills needed to run the firm. As a result, there arose a new kind of firm, the managerial enterprise, which was characterized by the separation of management and ownership, and by a complex bureaucratic organization.

The establishment of large laboratories to develop new products and production techniques was another feature of this development. The merger between science and enterprise during the 'second industrial revolution' made systematic R&D one of the strong attributes of the big companies. Moreover, once the managerial enterprises had been created, they could profit from economies of scope: they were in an ideal position to diversify into new production lines and markets. The resulting drive for diversification led to the rise of the multidivisional firm, which according to Chandler signified the final stage of the rise of the managerial enterprise.

During the crucial decades after 1880 in most new industries only a few entrepreneurs were able to make the enormous investments required to

27

establish the new enterprises. Chandler refers to them as the 'first movers'. Since the first movers could profit from large economies of scale, they built up a very strong position. In other words, the barriers to entry for new entrepreneurs who wanted to set up production in the same industries – 'challengers' in Chandler's terminology – were extremely large. As a consequence the structure of the industrial 'top 100' was relatively stable: the initial first movers often remained leading companies for a very long period, often the rest of the twentieth century (Chandler 1990).

This brief sketch of Chandler's approach is relevant for the understanding of the rise of Dutch multinationals. In many ways the Dutch experience fits nicely into this theoretical framework. After a slow start of its industrialization in the period before 1870, industrial progress accelerated during the final quarter of the nineteenth century. Economic development generally profited from the new opportunities offered by the second industrial revolution. In some branches Dutch entrepreneurs were clearly 'first movers' – margarine and oil refining are cases in point – or relatively successful 'challengers', as will be shown in the next section. In retrospect it has become clear that almost all large companies which came to dominate industry after 1945 were established in the decades between 1880 and 1920 (Bloemen *et al*. 1993a). After 1920 the industrial structure expanded and diversified, and many firms were amalgamated to form even larger units. Yet, few new major industrial firms came into being. In fact, the absolute top of Dutch industry remained almost unchanged during the twentieth century. Royal Dutch Shell, Unilever, and Philips were by far the largest companies as early as the 1920s, and have remained so to this day (Bloemen *et al*. 1993a). It can therefore be argued that the basis for the successful economic development of the long twentieth century, which was in many ways caused by the expansion of industrial production and employment, was laid in the decades after about 1880.

## SIX ROADS TO THE TOP

A rough outline of the growth of Dutch multinational enterprise should start in 1871, when Henri Jurgens established a factory for the production of margarine based on the original invention by the Frenchman Mège Mouriès. The background of his move is quite obvious. Jurgens was one of the merchants who purchased large quantities of (cheap) butter in the Netherlands and Germany for sale to the ever-expanding British market. He knew that there was a huge demand for cheap butter or for a substitute that looked and tasted like butter. From the very beginning his closest competitor, Van den Bergh, was involved in the same trade. Their success was stimulated by the absence of a patent law in the Netherlands (until 1912), which made it possible to copy the original invention as well as each other's improvements without any restriction (Wilson 1954: 29 ff, 55 ff).

28

During the 1870s the industry grew in size and numbers: in 1880 there were more than 70 relatively small margarine factories in the Netherlands (Wilson 1954: 90). However, after 1880 a number of developments brought about increased concentration in the industry.

Changes in production techniques, which gradually mechanized the production process, created relatively large economies of scale. Moreover, the closing of the German market for margarine, as a part of Bismarck's protectionist policies, meant that both firms were forced to set up separate factories just inside the borders of the German empire in 1888. However, most fundamental were a number of changes introduced by the Van den Bergh family during the 1890s, which made this firm the true 'prime mover' of the margarine industry. First, systematic scientific research into the process of making margarine and its ingredients made it possible to develop a more tasteful and butterlike margarine. Furthermore, urged by the manager of the German subsidiary, Van den Bergh innovated selling methods: the firm launched its own brands with large-scale advertising campaigns. In order to bypass wholesale traders who had traditionally done much of the distribution, Van den Bergh set up its own distribution network (Wilson 1954: 72 ff). After 1900 the innovations in the German market were also introduced elsewhere, which led to an enormous increase in the production and profits of the Van den Bergh firm. The need to finance its spectacular growth resulted in the establishment in 1895 of a joint stock company that was able to attract capital on the London market.

With some delay the Jurgens company followed the example set by Van den Bergh. For example, in 1902 it too became a joint stock company. Both firms decided to work closely together and share profits in 1908 (Wilson 1954: 99). However, this agreement proved difficult to implement and, after many years of fruitless legal proceedings about its precise interpretation, they saw no other solution than to merge the two companies. It resulted in the establishment in 1927 of Margarine Unie, which merged in 1929 with the British Lever company – the leading soap manufacturer in Europe – to become Unilever. The mergers minimized the influence of the families, who still dominated the two margarine firms in 1927. Instead, there emerged a large multidivisional firm that would dominate this branch of industry until today.

In a way Royal Dutch Shell was an even more spectacular success story. It started in the 1880s in Sumatra, one of the largest islands of Indonesia, where Aeilco Janz. Zijlker began to exploit an oil field he had discovered as a planter. During the first ten years progress was slow because of a lack of capital and technical skills. In 1890 Zijlker accidentally came into contact with the distinguished banker N.P. van den Berg, who used his influence to increase the capital assets of the enterprise by creating the Royal Dutch Petroleum Company. The successful launching of the firm made it possible to extend operations and improve production facilities. It created its own brand of kerosine – the main product of the company during the first decade – which was largely sold on the Asian market. Operations expanded rapidly after Henri Deterding became manager of the firm in 1896. From the very beginning he began to build up a distribution network in order to become independent of the agents who had previously sold the kerosine. Bulk shipment and distribution, with new tankers and large tank installations ashore, replaced the costly barrels that had previously been used to pack and transport the kerosine. Moreover, the sharp rise in the demand for gasoline opened up completely new markets for the company after 1900, when it began to 'export' its products to Europe. Its first European refinery was opened in Rotterdam in 1902 and was soon followed by one in Germany. In less than ten years it had become a fully integrated company, with its own oil fields, refineries, tanker fleet, and sales organization (full details in Gerretson 1939).

Royal Dutch was still small compared to the American giant in the oil industry, Standard Oil. In its rapidly expanding markets the company increasingly met with competition from the mighty firm of Nelson Rockefeller, who aimed at creating a monopoly for Standard Oil by undercutting his competitors wherever possible. Deterding tried to meet the challenge, first by taking over the other much smaller Dutch companies in the field, and second by working closely with the largest British firm, Shell. With oil fields in Russia, Borneo, and the USA, a large tanker fleet and a well-developed sales organization in the Orient, Europe and Asia, Shell was a very attractive partner for Royal Dutch. An agreement between the two companies to coordinate sales in the Far East was signed in 1902. After a number of years that were very profitable for Royal Dutch, whose dividends soared to an average of 60 percent per year, but were rather meagre for Shell, which suffered from 'imperial overstretch' and a lack of working capital, the two companies decided to merge in 1907 on terms that were quite favourable to the Dutch (Gerretson 1939).

With the American oil industry in disarray after antitrust legislation had forced Standard Oil to break up into 33 separate organizations in 1911, the following years were exceptionally lively for the new combination. In 1912 the company extended its activities to the USA by setting up its own sales organization and by moving into oil production in California (Beaton 1957). The American branch soon became one of the most dynamic parts of the company. Royal Dutch had already set up its own laboratory in Schiedam in 1906; in 1914 a larger one was opened in Amsterdam (Gerretson 1942: 11–12). Partly on the basis of its own research, in 1927 it decided to embark upon the production of artificial fertilizer, with plants set up in IJmuiden (in a joint venture with Hoogovens, which supplied the coke gas) and in San Francisco.

After 1911 Royal Dutch Shell was increasingly recognized as one of the leading firms in the oil industry. For example, in the 1920s Deterding took a number of initiatives to form a worldwide cartel in oil, which led to the famous Achnacarry agreement of 1928 – named after Deterding's Scottish castle where the chairmen of the companies met – between Royal Dutch Shell, Anglo Persian and Standard Oil of New Jersey. By any measure the company had become a classic 'managerial enterprise' even before World War I, as it was run by managers – it had actually never been a family firm – and consisted of a number of more or less independent divisions. The British headquarters in London managed transport and marketing; The Hague was the location of the headquarters of exploration, exploitation and refining.

The start of the Dutch industry of incandescent lamps, by Gerard Philips in 1891, was also greatly facilitated by the fact that, at least on the domestic market, he did not have to worry about the Edison patents. From the beginning this 'challenger' was faced with strong competition especially from German firms, but the low costs of labour in Eindhoven (which was precisely why this place was selected as the location of the first Philips factory) gave the company an important advantage. Philips also came from a family of merchants and bankers, who could easily supply the necessary capital for the establishment of the factory. During the first decades the essence of the firm's strategy was to concentrate on the mass production of a reliable but relatively cheap lamp, which meant that much attention was paid to the improvement of production techniques (Heerding 1986: 78). This was combined with an aggressive campaign to increase market shares, as a result of which the Philips company was able to make inroads into the main European markets (Germany, England, France). From the beginning exports were a major outlet for the rapidly growing production (Heerding 1986: 63). Already at the end of the 1890s the firm dominated the (relatively small) Dutch industry of incandescent lamps. As early as 1903 the company helped to found a European cartel for incandescent lamps and was recognized by its competitors as one of the 'European players' (it negotiated a market share of 11.3 percent and was the largest non-German participant in the contract) (Heerding 1986: 109). At the same time it concentrated its efforts on the development of the metal filament lamp, again helped considerably by the absence of a patent law (Heerding 1986: 175 ff). After a series of legal proceedings, the company was however forced to pay large sums to its German competitors which controlled the (originally American) patents of this lamp. As a result, investments in R&D were raised to much higher levels and the first professional laboratory was set up (Schiff 1971: 66).

During the 1910s and 1920s the company developed into an industrial giant, certainly by Dutch standards. In 1912 it was transformed into a joint stock company, but was still controlled by the Philips family. During World War I, when German competition was largely absent, Philips was able to gain control of the American patents of the metal filament lamp, which made possible an enormous expansion of production. Moreover, in a way the company was forced by the war to integrate its production processes backwards; it set up its own production of glass bulbs, which greatly enhanced the quality of its final products (Blanken 1992: 10). The early 1920s were characterized by further forward and backward integration of activities. For example, Philips set up its own international sales agencies in order to become independent of agents abroad (Blanken 1992: 29 ff). This was followed by the establishment of foreign factories (in response to the rise of protectionism) and a complicated divisional structure for the firm. In the second half of the 1920s the company launched the manufacture of radios, which was the first important step towards a diversification of activities. The enormous success of this venture led to a renewed growth spurt, during which the number of employees tripled from about 8,000 in 1925 to almost 23,000 at the end of 1929 (Blanken 1992: 290). At the same time, the influence of managers from outside the Philips family increased markedly (Blanken 1992: 413 ff).

The Dutch were also relative late to arrive in the field of artificial fibres. The initiative was taken by J.C. Hartogs who, after having learned the trade as an employee of Courtaulds in Coventry, started the joint stock company ENKA in 1911, supported by a number of wealthy Dutch industrialists (most notably by F.H. Fentener van Vlissingen) (Dendermonde 1961: 31 ff). Once again a city at the periphery of the Netherlands (Arnhem) was selected as the location of the new industry, and the ample supply of cheap (female) labour was again one of the main considerations. And once more World War I boosted production and profits enormously, and turned a small firm into a sizeable company which could compete successfully with the big international companies. Even more than Philips, ENKA was dependent on exports as the internal market for rayon was almost nonexistent. Within ten years after its establishment it began to set up factories in other countries and to establish its own sales organization. A professional laboratory was created in 1925; a few years later the company started its own factory in the USA (Dendermonde 1961: 70). The impressive growth spurt of ENKA in 1929 resulted in a merger with the much bigger German Glanzstoff company (VGF) to form the AKU (Algemene Kunstzijde Unie) (Klaverstijn 1986: 71). Already in 1925 the main Dutch competitor was taken over by Hartogs' firm. However, the formation of AKU also meant a radical change in the organizational structure of the company, as a result of which Hartogs stepped down and a new generation of managers took over. In 1969 AKU merged with KZO (a chemical and pharmaceutical company) to form the AKZO company.

ENKA was already a joint stock company in contrast to the other companies which started as family firms. However, one entrepreneur, Hartogs, dominated its early history, just as Deterding, Philips, Jurgens and Van den Bergh dominated the rise of their respective companies. This 'personal' element is even less pronounced in the fifth company. Hoogovens, the first Dutch modern blast furnace established in 1918, was very much the product of the scarcity of raw materials and the dependence of the Dutch economy on foreign supplies during World War I. A group of wealthy industrialists and bankers, who were aware of these problems, succeeded in interesting the national government in their plan for the establishment of the Hoogovens company. The government participated in the share capital of the new firm, along with a number of big banks, shipping lines, railway companies, shipbuilders, an oil company and a few wealthy families (which once again included Fentener van Vlissingen) (De Vries 1968: 165–7).

From the beginning the company was set up as a managerial enterprise, with H.J.E. Wenkebach as its capable manager. When the first blast furnace was started in 1924 the situation had changed radically, and as a result of increased international protectionism the company encountered problems in selling its output of pig iron (a lack of capital still prevented the company from producing steel and steel products). By acquiring shares in two steel firms (one Dutch, one German) it tried to secure its sales market (Dankers and Verheul 1993: 37–8). In 1928 Hoogovens set up a joint venture, together with Royal Dutch Shell, to manufacture artificial fertilizer on the basis of the byproducts of its coke plant, which was highly successful (Dankers and Verheul 1993: 48). Only in the late 1940s, after a sharp decline in profits during the Depression, were plans realized to form an integrated steel mill. Large investments had already been made just before the outbreak of war and during the first years, but only after 1945, with the establishment of the Breedband steel mill, was the original plan completely fulfilled (again with sizeable assistance from the government) (Dankers and Verheul 1993: 113 ff).

The sixth multinational to appear on the scene was DSM, a large chemical firm that grew out of the government-owned coal mines (Staatsmijnen) which were set up in 1901 to develop the Limburg coal deposits. Within a decade it became a large organization with its own more or less independent management. The Company Act (*Bedrijvenwet*) of 1912 ruled that every (semi-)public firm had to be run along commercial lines, and that its financial administration had to be independent of government finances (De Ru 1981: 30–1).

Already in 1930 Staatsmijnen had begun to produce fertilizer as a byproduct of its coal. During the 1950s it increased its side activities by moving into (coal-based) chemicals; at the same time the production of gas became important. At the end of the 1950s it became clear that coal was becoming an increasingly expensive input for the chemical division. Management wanted to switch to cheaper oil and natural gas and concentrate more capital on the expansion of this (more profitable) part of the company (Messing 1988: 65–6). As a result, the company began to see the mines as a

33

liability, and after the coal crisis of 1958–9 it put pressure on the government to close down the first mines (Messing 1988: 281). Management tried to convince the minister of economic affairs that the long-term prospects of coal were meagre, even though the Dutch mines were among the most modern and productive of Europe. Finally, the discovery of enormous reserves of natural gas in the northern part of the Netherlands around 1960 made it clear that coal would not be able to compete much longer with this cheap source of energy. In the light of this fact Minister for Economic Affairs Den Uyl decided in 1965 to close down the Dutch coal mines over the next ten years.

After a number of requests by Staatsmijnen for subsidies for its mining activities on which it had incurred losses ever since the 'coal crisis' of 1958–9, the government decided in 1963 to give the company a share in the exploitation of the natural gas reserves (De Voogd 1993: 160). The firm that was set up to exploit these reserves, the Nederlandse Aardolie Maatschappij, was reorganized to include Shell and Esso (with a share of 30 percent each) as well as Staatsmijnen which was allotted a share of 40 percent (Messing 1988: 276). The enormous income from the exploitation of natural gas made possible heavy investments in new chemical activities and the gradual closure of the mines after 1965. As a result of the expansion of the chemical division of DSM (the new name of Staatsmijnen after it became a joint stock company in 1967) total employment fell by 'only' a third between 1958 (44,411) and 1974 (29,500) when the last mine was closed.

The following pattern can be discerned in the history of the six biggest multinationals. Two managerial enterprises grew out of the activities of 'prime movers': Unilever and Royal Dutch Shell. Philips and AKU were successful and relatively early 'challengers' in electrical equipment and synthetic fibres, and expanded rapidly during World War I, helped by the neutral status of the Netherlands. By 1929 all four companies had developed into fully-fledged 'managerial entreprises'. The merger movement in 1929, which led to the formation of Unilever and AKU, greatly contributed to the rise of managers in these firms. Finally, from the start Hoogovens and DSM were set up as large 'managerial enterprises'. Both were late arrivals to their industries and as a result they had to invest large amounts of money to overcome the barriers of entry. Hoogovens' success only began after 1945. The switch to chemicals by DSM was first financed with the profits from coal mining and later out of the large income from natural gas exploitation granted to the firm by the government. Both latecomers heavily relied on government support.

Of course, the story of these six multinationals is only part of the much broader story of the rise of managerial enterprise in the Netherlands. Many other often much smaller firms developed along similar lines. For example, the well-known Heineken brewery was set up in 1870 and already in the interwar period it had become one of the leading European companies in its field, with subsidiaries all over Europe. The 1920s witnessed the creation of two companies that would dominate the new aviation industry: Fokker, one of the most successful aircraft constructors of the interwar period (and beyond), and KLM, which became a leading airline. These examples can be multiplied at random (the best survey is Gales and Sluyterman 1993). This would generally show that below the 'top 6', which developed into managerial enterprises even before 1930, many smaller (family) firms contributed heavily to economic expansion. In an analysis of the Dutch industrial structure in 1930, Keetie Sluyterman and Len Winkelman have concluded that 'the family firm and personal relationships played an important role in Dutch industrial development' (1993: 175). They also showed that in some of the most dynamic branches of industry – chemicals and machine building – these smaller firms played a large part. It is almost impossible to disagree with them. By focusing on the small 'top' of industry, the Chandler approach is certainly biased and tends to overlook the dynamics of the smaller firms at the 'bottom'. Recent developments, which are at odds with this approach, seem to confirm this (see final section of this chapter). But the other part of the story is that even in 1930 the institutional development of Dutch industry still lagged behind that of neighbouring countries. For example, relations between industry and banking were still underdeveloped, certainly compared to Germany or Belgium. Moreover, most of the largest and most dynamic family firms of 1930 would be transformed into joint stock companies after 1945. Perhaps the late arrival of the managerial enterprise in the Netherlands in the twentieth century – although those that did break through were quite successful – does not in itself mean that the process as such was of lesser importance.

## THE ECONOMIC IMPORTANCE OF THE 'TOP 100'

There are various ways to try to get an idea of the economic importance of the growth of large managerial enterprises. The best measure would be the development of the value added or the employment of these companies, but these data are generally not (readily) available. In his large comparative study 'Scale and Scope' Chandler had to use other measures of the size of firms, i.e. the value of their assets. On the basis of this measure he reconstructed the 'top 100' of industry in the USA, Great Britain and Germany in a number of benchmark years beginning in 1913. In a separate study Erik Bloemen, Jan Kok and myself have tried to reconstruct comparable top 100s for the Netherlands using the same procedures (Bloemen et al. 1993a). This makes it possible to get an idea of the economic importance of the largest companies and of their development during the twentieth century.

A very crude indication of the economic importance of the 'top 100' is

*Table 3.1* Total value of assets of the 100 largest industrial companies as a percentage of GDP, 1913–1990 (percent)

|  | 1913 | 1930 | 1950 | 1973 | 1990 |
|---|---|---|---|---|---|
| USA | 23 | 31 | 18 | 30 | 35 |
| Great Britain[a] | 12 | 29 | 22 | 18 | 38 |
| Germany | 13 | 20 | 16 | – | 31 |
| Netherlands | 20 | 38 | 62 | 88 | 77 |
| Without Royal Dutch |  |  |  |  |  |
| Shell | 14 | 27 | 34 | 52 | 42 |

*Source*: Bloemen *et al.* 1993a, b
[a] Market value of shares.

the relationship between the total value of its assets and the size of the national economy, measured by its GDP, both at current prices (see Table 3.1). The first point that should be made about this comparison is that in twentieth-century industrial countries the ratio between GDP and the total capital stock is usually between 2.2 and 2.7; this relationship seems to remain fairly stable (Maddison 1993). Keeping this in mind, Table 3.1 demonstrates the large importance of the top 100 to the Dutch economy compared with the three major industrial countries. It is really surprising that as early as 1913 the ratio between the total value of assets and GDP was higher in the Netherlands than elsewhere. Until 1950 its growth was indeed spectacular, the more so because in the other countries the trend was only slightly upward. The bottom line of the table presents the same statistic, but without the huge assets of Royal Dutch Shell. When this company is left out of the comparison, the Dutch figures become less abnormal, which testifies to the enormous size of the absolute number one. What is perhaps equally striking is the relatively strong decline of the Dutch top 100 compared with GDP after 1973, a decline that was not found in the other countries.

The data on the capital value of the top 100 give an impression of a strong rise until the 1970s, after which stagnation or even decline set in. A more detailed study of total employment in the same group of companies can corroborate this finding. Of course, employment is a much better index of the impact of the large enterprises on the economy, but unfortunately for the years before 1970 systematic data are not available. For only a dozen 'top 100' firms it was possible to reconstruct the growth of employment starting in about 1929. Moreover, almost from the start a large part of the employment in these firms was located outside the country. The two largest firms were Anglo-Dutch (Unilever and Royal Dutch Shell), and most other companies had an important part of their factories, mines, plantations or distribution networks abroad. The comparison in Table 3.2 between 'total industrial employment' in the Netherlands and total employment with the

*Table 3.2* Total labour force of largest Dutch industrial companies compared with total industrial employment, 1929–1993

|  | *1929* | *1950* | *1960* | *1973* | *1993* |
|---|---|---|---|---|---|
| Royal Dutch Shell | (50) | 256 | 214 | 168 | 117 |
| Philips | 40 | 90 | 211 | 402 | 252 |
| Unilever | 7 | 81 | 293 | 353 | 294 |
| DSM | 21 | 35 | 40 | 30 | 22 |
| AKZO | 8 | 8 | 14 | 106 | 61 |
| Hoogovens | 1 | 7 | 13 | 76 | 24 |
| *Total top 6* | *(127)* | *467* | *785* | *1135* | *770* |
| Of which in the Netherlands | (70) | (150) | 170 | 200[a] | 120 |
| Dutch share in employment (%) | (55) | (32) | 22 | 18 | 16 |
| Rest of top 100[b] | ? | (200) | (300) | 512 | 634 |
| *Total top 100* | ? | *(667)* | *(1,185)* | *1,647* | *1,404* |
| *Total industrial employment in Netherlands* | 822 | 1,100 | 1,279 | 1,116 | 960 |
| Share in total industrial employment (%) | | | | | |
| Total top 6 | (15.4) | 42.5 | 61.4 | 101.7 | 80.2 |
| Total top 6 in the Netherlands | (8.6) | 13.6 | 13.3 | 17.9 | 12.5 |
| Total top 100 | ? | 60.6 | 92.7 | 147.6 | 146.3 |

*Sources*: Klarenbeek 1995. Employment in Royal Dutch Shell in 1929 on basis of Deterding 1934: 15; Beaton 1957: 352
*Notes*: Figures in brackets are rough estimates.
[a] 1971. [b] 1950 and 1960: rough estimates based on employment in only six companies (Ahold, Fokker, Gist Brocades, Thomassen & Drijver, ENCI and Zinkwit Mij)

top 6 or top 100 is therefore certainly flawed, but it can give an impression of the relative strength and importance of these companies vis-à-vis the Dutch economy.

This comparison shows that the 'top 6' underwent a fivefold increase in employment between 1929 and 1950, when total employment in industry grew at only a slow rate. Employment with Royal Dutch Shell expanded enormously and the growth of Unilever was almost as impressive. As a result the 'share' of the 'top 6' in total industrial employment almost tripled. During the 1950s and 1960s the very rapid expansion continued; only Royal Dutch Shell showed a completely different pattern with a slow but incessant decline in total employment (since the business history of Shell in this period has unfortunately not been written the causes can only be the subject of speculation). Total employment in the big six peaked in the early 1970s – probably exactly in 1973 – followed by a strong decline during the late 1970s and 1980s, a decline which still seems to continue (for example, between 1990 and 1993 all members of the big six reduced employment by an average of 9 percent). Philips, the biggest employer in 1973, has had to lay off more than a third of its employees since then; AKZO fared even worse and closed down its former core activities in synthetic fibres. The huge decline of Hoogovens, however, is partially explained by the dissolution of ESTEL, the merger with the German steel company Hoesch, in 1982. In the final section of this chapter we will take a closer look at these developments.

After 1973 the companies below the top 6 performed relatively much better. During the 1980s a number of companies such as Ahold (mainly retail distribution, but with a large industrial division) and KNP (paper) made their way into the very top of Dutch industry; in 1993 both firms employed more people than DSM or Hoogovens. By focusing on the 'traditional' top 6 of Dutch industry the decline after 1973 is somewhat overstated (the top 6 employers in 1993 enlisted 831,000 people, 8 percent more than the 'traditional' top 6 of Table 3.2).

In the previous section it was shown that already before World War I large companies such as Jurgens, Van den Bergh and Royal Dutch were truly international. During the 1920s and 1930s AKU and Philips developed the same feature and acquired large production facilities outside the Netherlands. The actual share of the 'top 6' in Dutch industrial employment was therefore much smaller than the figures in Table 3.2 suggest, because an important part of the labour force of these firms was employed outside the Netherlands. Already in 1929 the Dutch share in total employment of the top 6 was perhaps as low as 55 percent. In 1950 this had declined to probably about a third, and it was to fall to less than 16 percent in 1993. As a result the 'real' share of the top 6 in total industrial employment did not change much after 1950. There was probably an increase during the 1960s and certainly a fall after 1973, but these developments were less remarkable than the large changes in the total employment of these industrial companies.

To test Chandler's hypothesis that the managerial enterprise is concentrated in the new industries of the second industrial revolution, the top 100 companies were classified according to their main activity. As it turns out in the Netherlands these large companies were also mostly found in oil refining, foodstuffs, and, increasingly, in electronics, but also in basic metals and chemicals (Table 3.3). Foodstuffs is very much the exception, but the other industries fit well into the definition of the 'new industries' given by Chandler.

An international comparison with the three countries analysed by Chandler shows that – on the basis of their share in top 100 activities – the Dutch had a particularly strong position in food processing and oil refining, and were underrepresented in basic metals and engineering. In fact it turns out that the Dutch profile of top 100 industries was almost exactly the opposite of the German profile. Where the Germans had a

*Table 3.3* Industrial structure of the top 100 companies in 1913, 1950 and 1990
(percentage shares in the total value of assets)

|  | *1913* | *1950* | *1990* |
|---|---|---|---|
| **Process industries** | | | |
| Oil refining | 31.0 | 45.1 | 36.4 |
| Foodstuffs | 27.5 | 24.0 | 16.2 |
| Chemicals | 5.0 | 3.9 | 10.5 |
| Basic metals | 2.7 | 3.1 | 3.3 |
| Paper | 2.6 | 1.0 | 2.6 |
| *Total* | 68.8 | 77.1 | 69.0 |
| **Other industries** | | | |
| Textiles | 7.3 | 4.3 | 0.4 |
| Woodworking | 4.7 | 0.3 | – |
| Machine building | 4.6 | 2.7 | 2.1 |
| Building materials | 3.6 | 0.8 | 1.4 |
| Transport equipment | 5.9 | 3.9 | 2.7 |
| Metal products | 1.6 | 0.8 | 1.5 |
| Electronics | 1.5 | 9.2 | 18.0 |
| Printing/publishing | 0.6 | 0.1 | 3.3 |
| Other | 1.4 | 0.8 | 1.7 |
| *Total* | 31.2 | 22.9 | 31.1 |

*Source*: Bloemen *et al.* 1993a

strong position (basic metals and engineering), Dutch industry was relatively underrepresented, and conversely the Germans were weak in oil refining and food processing. Generally, Dutch strength seems to have been concentrated in processing industries, such as the manufacture of basic metals, refined oil, paper, beer, and bulk chemicals, made out of imported crude oil. The strong position of agriculture, which underpins the important role of food processing, also seems to play a role in determining the relative strength of Dutch industry (Bloemen *et al.* 1993a: 12–14).

The rise of the managerial enterprise during the first half of the twentieth century had consequences for technological change as well. In the nineteenth century the Netherlands was a country of technological diffusion, which did not contribute much to worldwide research and development (Davids 1995). This changed markedly after about 1900, partly as a result of the establishment of laboratories by the new multinationals. The number of scientists working in the laboratories of industrial firms grew from 350 in 1915 to about 1,800 in 1939; during the 1930s the five multinationals financed about half of total industrial R&D (Bloemen 1981: 156). In the afterwar period, R&D was largely concentrated in the same five largest Dutch multinationals (Philips, Unilever, AKZO, DSM, Shell); their share in total industrial R&D rose from 60 to 70 percent. Only in Switzerland was R&D more dominated by the big five; Sweden came in as a good third (OECD 1972: 132; OECD 1978: 172).

The sharp increase in R&D in the first half of the twentieth century can probably best be read from statistics on the number of patents issued abroad to inhabitants of the Netherlands. In Eric Schiff's (1971) study of *Industrialization without National Patents*, he has drawn attention to the fact that the Dutch share in the patents issued by other countries (Germany, Great Britain, France, USA) was relatively small at the turn of the twentieth century. Most other small European countries had a higher (per capita) output of patents, which points to a lack of R&D, and perhaps of technological creativity in general, in the Netherlands in that period. To find out what happened thereafter, the Dutch share in international patents of Germany and the USA has been analysed. To put these figures into perspective, Dutch patenting activity has been compared with that of five other small economies, namely Belgium, Switzerland, Denmark, Sweden, and Norway.

Let us first concentrate on the comparison with Belgium which compares best with the Netherlands in terms of population and GDP. The results of this comparison, presented in Table 3.4, show that the Netherlands did indeed lag behind its southern neighbour until World War I, when Dutch patenting activity was at best half the Belgian level. But whereas Belgian patenting went into a long-term relative decline, the output of Dutch R&D increased rapidly during the 1920s, 1930s and 1940s to reach a peak in the (early) 1950s. When the issuing of patents resumed in Germany in 1951, after a break during World War II and the Allied occupation, the Dutch share began at almost 17 percent; only in this year was the Netherlands able to beat the Swiss. Belgium, the pioneer of industrialization on the continent, was the only small economy whose share in international patenting was greatly reduced in the course of the century. The Netherlands, on the other hand, was the only country significantly to improve its relative position (Table 3.4). The decline that began in the 1960s has much to do with the increase in patenting from outside Europe, especially from Japan (and, more recently, from other Asian countries). Within Europe the Dutch share has more or less stabilized since the 1950s.

It is tempting to explain the huge increase in international patenting by Dutch inhabitants as due to the rise of the managerial enterprise. In this view the Belgian decline resulted from the fact that in the same period there did not emerge comparable managerial enterprises, and that its economic history was dominated by the relative decline of the 'old' industrial structure. The comparison with Switzerland and the three Scandinavian countries is also quite illuminating. The three countries that nursed a relatively large number of multinational enterprises – the Netherlands, Switzerland, Sweden – generally had much higher levels of patenting than the three other countries. In the long run the first group improved

Table 3.4 Share of six small economies in the total number of foreign patents issued by the USA and Germany, 1880–1990 to 1990–1993 (percent)

| | Netherlands | | Belgium | | Switzerland | |
|---|---|---|---|---|---|---|
| | Germany | USA | Germany | USA | Germany | USA |
| 1880–89 | – | 0.3 | – | 1.4 | – | 2.7 |
| 1890–99[a] | 1.6 | 0.5 | 3.9 | 1.3 | 5.1 | 2.3 |
| 1900–09 | 2.0 | 0.6 | 3.6 | 1.5 | 6.8 | 2.5 |
| 1910–19 | 3.0 | 0.8 | 3.3 | 1.0 | 10.8 | 3.2 |
| 1920–29 | 3.0 | 1.4 | 2.6 | 1.2 | 13.5 | 4.3 |
| 1930–39 | 4.4 | 2.7 | 2.2 | 1.0 | 14.6 | 4.7 |
| 1940–49 | – | 3.7 | – | 0.8 | – | 7.2 |
| 1950–59 | 9.6 | 6.1 | 1.7 | 1.3 | 14.9 | 8.5 |
| 1960–69 | 6.8 | 3.9 | 1.4 | 1.3 | 10.0 | 6.9 |
| 1970–79 | 4.0 | 2.8 | 0.9 | 1.2 | 8.5 | 5.7 |
| 1980–89 | 4.4 | 2.4 | 0.6 | 0.8 | 7.9 | 3.9 |
| 1990–93 | – | 2.1 | – | 0.8 | – | 2.8 |

| | Denmark | | Sweden | | Norway | |
|---|---|---|---|---|---|---|
| | Germany | USA | Germany | USA | Germany | USA |
| 1880–89 | – | 0.7 | – | 1.0 | – | 0.3 |
| 1890–99[a] | 1.4 | 0.5 | 2.9 | 1.6 | 0.7 | 0.4 |
| 1900–09 | 2.4 | 0.9 | 2.9 | 2.0 | 0.7 | 0.5 |
| 1910–19 | 2.5 | 0.9 | 3.5 | 2.7 | 0.9 | 1.1 |
| 1920–29 | 1.9 | 1.0 | 3.8 | 3.3 | 1.3 | 1.0 |
| 1930–39[b] | 1.3 | 0.6 | 4.2 | 3.4 | 1.1 | 0.6 |
| 1940–49 | – | 0.6 | – | 4.5 | – | 0.4 |
| 1950–59 | 1.3 | 0.9 | 5.8 | 5.8 | 0.9 | 0.8 |
| 1960–69 | 1.1 | 0.7 | 4.0 | 4.2 | 0.4 | 0.4 |
| 1970–79 | 0.9 | 0.7 | 3.4 | 3.6 | 0.3 | 0.4 |
| 1980–89 | 0.9 | 0.6 | 2.7 | 2.7 | 0.3 | 0.3 |
| 1990–93 | – | 0.5 | – | 1.7 | – | 0.2 |

[a] Germany: 1893–99. [b] Germany: 1930–36.
Sources: Annual Report of the Commissioner of Patents, 1880–1993; Blatt für Patent-, Muster-, und Zeicherwesen, 1894–1990

its relative position in international patenting, whereas Belgium and to a lesser extent Norway and Denmark fell behind. When comparisons are made on a per capita basis it turns out that Dutch patenting levels improved very much during the first half of the century and more or less stabilized after the 1950s (in comparison to the other small European countries). Dutch patenting productivity was more or less on a par with the Swedish level, but was still way behind the Swiss. Levels of patenting 'productivity' in the other three countries were generally much lower after World War II. This again leads to the conclusion that big multinational enterprises were a decisive force behind the development of R&D during the twentieth century.

Patent statistics reveal that the contribution of Dutch multinational firms to international patenting was indeed huge. In the period 1969 to 1973 two firms, Philips and Shell, registered as many patents in the USA as the total number of patents issued to Dutch inhabitants (3,240 against 3,237) (US Dept of Commerce 1975). Part of the explanation is that many patents were applied for by foreign subsidiaries of these firms (for example, the huge British or American branches of Shell, or Philips' subsidiaries in the USA), and were therefore registered as British or American patents. The same source shows that the share of private inventors in total patents declined from about 80 percent in 1900 to only 16 percent in the 1960s and 1970s (US Dept of Commerce 1979). This was matched by a comparable increase in the share of companies.

## MANAGERS AND SHAREHOLDERS

The rise of the large corporations led to the separation of ownership and management. In the long run this had important consequences for the way in which companies responded to economic changes. In the nineteenth century a joint stock company was considered to be a contract between a number of owners or shareholders with the aim of making profit. It had no 'independent' legal basis of its own. As a result almost all profits were distributed to the shareholders. The legal basis for economic life, the *Wetboek van Koophandel* of 1836, also mentioned the possibility of creating reserves from extraordinary profits, but the main purpose of this was to stabilize dividends. The formation of a separate reserve made it possible to continue paying dividends in years with losses (Immink 1892: 5). This began to change with the rise of a 'class' of managers. Whereas shareholders were first of all interested in high dividends, managers preferred to concentrate on the long-term growth of the firm, and the retention of part of the profits was a relatively cheap way to finance growth. In 1919 J.G. de Jongh analysed these changes in some detail: he noticed that the creation of reserves had become normal and that managers were the driving force behind this change. He sketched the manager as a person who is 'rich in phantasies for discovering new necessities for the formation of new reserves'. This development could not be explained by a decline in the appetite of shareholders for large dividends, but was mainly due to the ambition of managers to expand the operations of the firm (De Jongh 1919: 12–13). In the same vein Dr A. Sternheim, one the leading financial analysts of the interwar period, commented on the increased importance of these reserves; he mentioned that the old rule that 10 percent of extra profits should be reserved had been abandoned and that the desire of the companies to expand was the main force behind the increased importance of retained profits (De Kroniek, 1928–29: 202).

Estimates of the pay-out ratio in this period show that in normal years about 70 to 80 percent of net profits was distributed to shareholders. During the Depression of the 1930s relatively high dividends continued to be paid; in four years more than 100 percent of net profits was paid out. The desire to please the shareholders was an important reason for this measure. As a result the value of reserves decreased rather sharply during the 1930s (De Kroniek 1938–39: 121).

Table 3.5 presents estimates of the change in the pay-out ratio since the 1920s. Although these data are fraught with difficulties and margins of error are consequently relatively large, some conclusions can clearly be derived from them. After 1945 the relatively high pay-out ratios of the prewar period gave way to a much lower share of dividends in total net profits. During the 1950s retained profits were by far the most important source of growth; almost all investments were financed out of this source (Rietkerk 1991: 34). This was stimulated by government policies, such as tax deductions for investing firms. During the 1960s and 1970s the profit-ability of the largest firms declined, which led to a further reduction of the share of dividends in net profits. It reached its lowest level in the early 1980s. The decline in the pay-out ratio is in stark contrast to the response of these firms to the low profits of the 1930s.

To summarize, the contrasting reactions to declining profits show the change in business strategy as a result of the rise of managers. In the nineteenth century it was normal to pay out almost all profits and to attempt to stabilize dividends. According to De Jongh (1919) after 1900 managers

*Table 3.5* Development of the pay-out ratio (share of dividends and bonuses in net profits), 1923–1929 to 1990–1994 (percent)

| | |
|---|---|
| 1911–13 | c.80 |
| 1923–29 | 72.1 |
| 1930–35 | 139.6 |
| 1936–39 | 73.8 |
| 1947–49 | 62.3 |
| 1950–59 | 64.4 |
| 1960–69 | 51.3 |
| 1970–79 | 45.3 |
| 1980–84 | 38.4 |
| 1985–89 | 46.0 |
| 1990–94 | 57.8 |

*Sources*: 1911–13: Van Oss 1915–16. 1923–39: Post 1972: 41. 1947–64: CBS, *Statistiek der (grotere) naamloze vennootschappen* 1949–1966. 1965–94: CBS 1984, 1989, 1994–6
*Notes*: 1911–13: sample of the largest joint stock companies. 1923–39: all joint stock companies (NVs). 1947–64: only the largest joint stock companies. 1965–94: all companies listed on the Amsterdam Stock Exchange.

had to develop a reserve policy and use their imagination to increase the share of reserves in total profit. The situation after 1945 was exactly the opposite: the interests of the firm dictated that a large part of profits was used to finance growth, and (high) dividends were only paid when profits were high enough.

Behind this change from reserve policy to dividend policy were fundamental alterations in the 'balance of power' within the firm. The position of the managerial class became ever stronger at the 'expense' of the influence of shareholders. The firm, which in the nineteenth century was the absolute property of the shareholders, developed into an 'independent' body with its own rights and duties. The revision of the *Wetboek van Koophandel* of 1928 still confirmed the idea that a joint stock company was a contract of shareholders and did not take into account the changes that were taking place (Bloembergen 1943). However, a famous judgment by the Dutch Supreme Court of 1949 maintained that companies (i.e. the board of supervisors) had to give prevalence to the interests of the company, even if these conflicted with those of the shareholders (Blanco Fernandez 1993: 51). The government also recognized this change when it introduced corporate taxation (in the nineteenth century taxes were only levied on the dividends).

The manager was the dominating figure in the new corporation and saw himself as the mediator between the different interests of labour, government, capital (i.e. shareholders) and customers. Yet, managers also had their own objectives. Empirical and theoretical research has shown that they were primarily interested in expansion, in the long term growth of activities (Marris 1967). Therefore they advocated investments in R&D, the capture of new markets, and the development of new products, even at the expense of a short-term loss.

The position of the managers was strengthened by a number of institutional developments. In 1898, when the emerging Dutch oil industry was in danger of being taken over by Standard Oil, the first protective device in Dutch modern history was introduced. The Minister for Colonial Affairs, J.Th. Cremer, proposed a reorganization of the ownership structure of Royal Dutch in such a way that a hostile takeover would be almost impossible. He was also able to overcome the strong resistance of the Ministry of Justice against such an innovation (Gerretson 1939, II: 71ff). After 1914 many companies followed the example set by Royal Dutch. Moreover, during the transition from family firm to joint stock company the original family often tried to maintain its influence on the management of the firm by introducing comparable legal constructions to safeguard their position. For example, Philips created a separate institution (*stichting*) which controlled the company's priority shares to which the right to appoint the directors of the firm was attached. The 'shares' that were traded on the stock exchange were issued by a different body which had no influence on management (Lakeman 1991: 77). Comparable constructions were introduced in almost all major companies; a recent survey showed that more than half of the 193 firms listed on the Amsterdam Stock Exchange had issued 'priority shares' (Voogd 1989: 43). This was, however, just one of the many oligarchic devices used to strengthen the position of the managers.

Of comparable importance was the change in the position of the board of supervisors. Since the early 1800s the board of directors of most joint stock companies had been controlled by a board of supervisors (*raad van commissarissen*), which appointed the members of the board of directors and took major decisions on strategic issues. Normally this board of supervisors was appointed in turn by the general meeting of shareholders, which gave shareholders an indirect say in the management of the firm. Yet, as the locus of power in the big firms shifted towards management during the twentieth century, the board of supervisors also became increasingly independent of the shareholders. Companies introduced the rule that new members of the board of supervisors should be appointed by the general meeting of shareholders according to a binding recommendation of the board itself, and the same happened with the appointment of members of the board of directors. The new company law of 1971 introduced a model for the joint stock company in which this became the rule; the board of supervisors became an oligarchic institution, which selected its own members (Voogd 1989). Personal relationships between management and the board of supervisors were generally strong; for example, after retiring from the board of directors, managers often became a member of the board of supervisors.

Shareholders not only lost influence in the management of the firm, they also lost real income. A reconstruction of the development of the real value of shares quoted on the Amsterdam Stock Exchange shows that throughout the century the prices barely kept pace with the general increase in price level (Graph 3.1). The pre-World War I level of real share prices was never again surpassed. What is perhaps most remarkable is that the economic growth of the 'golden years' (1950 to 1973) led to a strong decline in real share prices after 1960–61, a decline that continued into the 1980s. Only after 1983 did real share prices recover and rise to a level almost comparable with that of 1913.

In the 1960s and 1970s the position of managers reached its apex; the new company law of 1971 which formalized their strong hold over the company is probably the best evidence. This is particularly important to understand the economic development of the 1960s. The growth-oriented business strategy of the managers lay behind the combination of declining profitability and increased investments that occurred during the 1960s (see Chapter 8). Again the development of Philips is an excellent case in point: the company saw its profits decline rapidly during this decade, in spite of

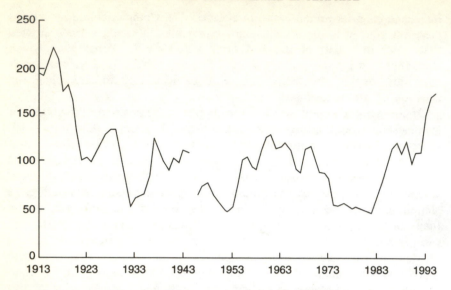

*Graph 3.1* Index of real share prices on the Amsterdam Stock Exchange, 1913–1995 (1970 = 100)
*Sources*: Share prices: 1913–1921: Brandes de Roos 1927 (only share prices of industrial companies); 1921–1970: De Vries 1976; 1970–1995: CBS 1994, 1996. Index of the cost of living: Maddison 1991; CBS 1996
*Note*: Real share prices are calculated by dividing indices of nominal share prices by an index of the cost of living

an almost megalomaniac growth strategy that resulted in a doubling of its size (in terms of employment) (Lakeman 1991: 153 ff).

A number of processes caused a rather sudden change of course during the 1980s. Some 'famous' bankruptcies focused attention on the failures of management and on failed supervision by the board of supervisors (Lakeman 1984). The bankruptcy of the construction company OGEM led to legal proceedings by shareholders in order to recover some of their losses from the members of the board of supervisors who had neglected their job and had continued protecting management. In 1986 the Vereniging voor de Effectenhandel (Society for the Trade in Shares), the body that manages the Amsterdam Stock Exchange, began an offensive against legal constructions that restricted the influence of shareholders. In their view, Dutch shares were undervalued as a result of oligarchic devices. This offensive resulted in the introduction (in 1989) of rules against the accumulation of such devices (Rietkerk 1991: 169). The globalization of capital markets was a strong force behind this 'revolution' of the shareholder, because it made capital highly mobile and firms much more dependent on the whims of the stock exchange. A final proof of the increased importance of 'capital' can be found in the data on the pay-out ratio, which started to increase again during the 1980s (and continues to do so during the 1990s) (Table 3.5).

## THE DECLINE OF DUTCH MULTINATIONALS

During the 1960s and early 1970s the trend towards larger companies accelerated as a result of a number of developments. The process of European economic integration, which gained momentum after the Treaty of Rome of 1957, not only involved the rapid expansion of export markets, but also meant that firm size was increasingly compared on an international basis. With its relatively small internal market, most Dutch industrial firms, insurance companies and banks found themselves relatively insignificant compared to their competitors from Germany, France or Britain. In the same period the introduction of large computer systems (mainframes) to automatize operations in some branches of industry, banking and insurance led to the creation of important economies of scale, which further accelerated the tendency towards larger units of operation. The merger movement that swept through the Dutch economy in the late 1960s was largely motivated on these grounds. Moreover, a strong belief in the (economic) blessings of scale and scope was imported through American business ideologies, that came to dominate thinking about the future of enterprise in this period. It was therefore quite logical that concentration in larger units was thought to be the panacea for the decline of certain industries (textiles, shipbuilding), which meant that mergers were forced upon them by the goverment whenever demands for support were discussed. For example, in 1971 under strong pressure from successive ministers for economic affairs large parts of the shipbuilding and metal products industries were amalgamated into RSV, which received handsome subsidies to develop new lines of production (and slowly close down the old ones) (Wassenberg 1983).

Moreover, the persistent decline in profit in large parts of Dutch industry stimulated a drive towards diversification. The 'ideal' of the multidivisional company, which uses the cash flow it generates in markets it had already captured to invest in new products and activities, lent a rationale to this drive. Hoogovens, for example, found itself locked into a steel industry with at best meagre long-term economic prospects. With ample government support it set up new activities in aluminium in the early 1960s (Dankers and Verheul 1993: 278 ff). AKU diversified into a wide range of chemical products as the markets for artificial fibres became increasingly saturated. The formation of AKZO in 1969, when pharmaceutical activities and electrochemicals were integrated in the new company, was another step in the move away from its former core business (Klaverstijn 1986). The development of DSM is a classic example of a switch out of a declining coal industry. Even Royal Dutch Shell, which since its formation

47

in 1907 had mainly grown through the broadening of its own activities, took over the mining company Billiton. In the early 1970s there followed a few large international mergers (Hoogovens formed ESTEL with the German steel company Hoesch and the aeroplane manufacturer Fokker merged with VFW) whose aim was to rationalize operations and to share markets and distribution networks (De Smidt and Wever, 1990, 176 ff).

This spectacular drive towards large-scale production ended in the 1970s. The first signs of change were perhaps the dissolution of the two German–Dutch mergers, both of which were failures. In 1978 Fokker regained its independence, followed in 1983 by Hoogovens. Both mergers had created more problems than they solved, to put it mildly, and the harsh economic climate of the late 1970s had not given the new companies the time to ripen slowly. The bankruptcy of RSV in 1983 meant that industrial policies towards this important sector of the economy had failed (see also Chapter 9), and it discredited the 'strategic thinking' that had lain at their foundation.

In general, the 1980s saw a decisive return to 'core activities' in response to the urgent economic problems of the day. Diversification as a strategy was discredited and many firms began to sell the acquisitions of the 1960s. On the ideological level the belief in the superiority of the 'corporate strategy' of the 'multidivisional corporation' was followed by the rediscovery of the efficiency of small and medium-sized enterprise. Relatively small enterprises turned out to be not only more efficient, but also more innovative and flexible. Various studies showed that in many branches of industry economies of scale were becoming less important; for example, the mainframes of the 1960s were replaced by relatively cheap networks of personal computers. Moreover, large corporations also discovered the efficiency of their suppliers and began to contract out an increasingly large part of their activities – from catering to the making of sizeable parts of the end product. Decentralized and flat Japanese models of business organization, which made better use of the human resources of highly skilled employees, replaced the American-style 'top heavy' structures. All these changes, which were often introduced as cost-cutting measures to keep ahead of international competition, led to the gradual slimming down of the large companies.

Moreover, the large companies became increasingly footloose. The reduction in the number of production plants in high-cost regions such as the Netherlands continued, followed more recently by administrative and R&D departments. This has added to the decline in the share of Dutch employment in the workforce of these firms (Table 3.3). Of course, this does not imply that the large firms are going to disappear. In certain sectors the development of new products (chips, aircraft) requires such enormous investments that only very large companies are able to finance it. The consumer market is largely dominated by special brands – from

Coca-Cola to Sony – which require huge investments in marketing and advertising. In these sectors large firms will certainly persist, but their organization has changed markedly since the 1970s and their relative importance in the economy seems to be on the decline.

Another influence behind the decline of the large-scale enterprise was the 'revolution' of the shareholder, that was sketched in the preceding section. This 'revolution' and the globalization of capital markets have added to the pressure on management to increase profitability in the short run in order to pay out higher dividends and push up share prices. As a result, the downsizing of the multinationals was not only a reaction to the economic distress of the 1970s and early 1980s, but continued during the years of big profits after 1985. At the same time share prices soared on the Amsterdam Stock Exchange, like they did elsewhere (see Graph 3.1).

There is, however, another side to this story: the revival of entrepreneurship during the 1980s. Management buy-outs and other ways to sell subsidiaries led to the creation of new firms. Small and medium-sized firms profited from increased subcontracting. Highly schooled men and women, who were unable to find a job as a result of the high unemployment of the 1980s and 1990s, decided to set up their own companies. The rapid expansion of demand for all kinds of service activities – from baby-sitting to consultancy – highly stimulated this development (see also Chapter 5). During the 'long' twentieth century the number of entrepreneurs in the Dutch economy has probably declined as the average size of firms had gone up markedly. For example, the average number of workers per establishment in industry increased from 6.9 in 1930 to 10.5 in 1950 and 17.7 in 1978 (CBS 1984: 88). A huge rise can be registered after 1984, when reliable figures on the total number of enterprises first became available, which was especially pronounced in the business services (Table 3.6). There was also a noticeable increase in industry, whereas until about 1983 the number of industrial firms had been declining.

Although often arising out of the economic difficulties of the 1980s, the

*Table 3.6* Number of enterprises in industry and services, 1984 and 1994 (in thousands)

|  | 1984 | 1994 | Increase (%) |
| --- | --- | --- | --- |
| Industry and mining | 44 | 57 | 30 |
| Construction | 39 | 46 | 18 |
| Trade/hotel/catering | 205 | 254 | 24 |
| Transport/communications | 20 | 27 | 35 |
| Business services | 85 | 177 | 108 |
| Other services | 53 | 89 | 68 |
| *Total* | 447 | 650 | 45 |

*Source*: CBS, *Statistical Yearbook*, 1985, 1995

rapid growth of the number of companies and the renewed flourishing of entrepreneurship to which it testifies are important signs. In the long twentieth century the typical Dutchman became an employee of a large enterprise or of government. This choice of a secure job was no longer available for most people who entered the job market in the 1980s. Entrepreneurship, almost despised in the 1960s and early 1970s, has been rehabilitated during the 1980s and attracts more and more people. It is perhaps possible to draw a parallel with the final quarter of the nineteenth century, with which this chapter opened, when another burst of entrepreneurship woke up the Dutch economy. Yet the consequences of this new wave of entrepreneurial spirit will almost certainly be vastly different from the preceding one.

# 4

# THE POLITICS OF A PILLARIZED SOCIETY AND THE DEVELOPMENT OF THE WELFARE STATE

## THE ANALYTICAL FRAMEWORK

In the preceding chapter Chandler's framework was used to analyse the rise of the managerial entreprise. Unfortunately, a comparable 'classic' study covering the growth of the state, in particular the rise of the welfare state, is not at hand. The relevant literature offers an enormous array of explanations, which means that almost every attempt at interpretation has to be eclectic (see, for example, Wilensky 1975; Flora 1981; Kaelble 1990; a recent review in Lindert 1994). In this brief sketch of the increasing role of the state in social and economic development during the twentieth century, the focus is on factors that seem to be particularly relevant for understanding the Dutch case.

There is some agreement that the rise of democracy and of political mass movements was of fundamental importance to the rise of the welfare state. The enfranchisement of the (lower) middle and working classes led to the rise of political parties that represented their interests – the social democrats are the most obvious case in point. This could result in countermeasures by the elite to stem their growth (Bismarck's *Sozialistengesetze* are often interpreted as such) or to 'genuine' social reforms once these parties gained access to government. Aristotle already noticed that in democracy 'the poor have more sovereign power than the men of property; for they are more numerous and the decisions of the majority prevail' (cited in Lindert 1994). Economists such as Downs (1972) have elaborated these ideas into models which predict that the extension of the franchise will eventually lead to domination by political 'entrepreneurs' who aim at redistributing the income of the (few) rich to the (many) poor.

The extension of the franchise was a general process in Europe in the second half of the nineteenth century and the first decades of the twentieth, but there were many differences in pace and timing. More important perhaps was the question who succeeded in capturing the support of the new voters, how they perceived their own interests, and how actively they

51

participated in the political process. Were they primarily interested in increasing expenditure on better education, which would facilitate upward social mobility for their children, or in old age pensions for themselves? Peter Lindert (1994), for example, suggests that a rapidly growing young population would be more interested in the former, whereas a stagnant, relatively old population will favour the latter.

The degree and nature of political participation was another important factor: did the poor actually begin to vote? Did a socialist party capture their allegiance or did they participate in political 'machines' that were demarcated along religious lines, such as the Dutch Catholic and orthodox Protestant *zuilen* (pillars). According to the Scandinavian 'model' the rise of welfare spending was connected to the growth of trade unions and social democratic parties. Once these parties started to dominate government their 'classic' welfare state could take shape and income disparities began to level off, thus confirming the predictions of Aristotle and Downs (Esping-Andersen 1985). But this was only one of many possible outcomes of the rise of democracy. Ideology and religion could create political affiliations beyond sharply defined class lines. These class lines were perhaps not as sharp in a relatively homogeneous country such as the Netherlands (with a rather large group of farmers until the 1950s).

Another factor, often stressed in the literature, was the growth of per capita income. 'Social transfers' are a relative 'luxury' to which only rich countries can afford to allocate a sizeable part of their income. In the daily practice of welfare politics, economic growth means higher tax revenues which make it possible to finance welfare transfers without cutting into the budgets of others. Moreover, sustained economic growth makes it relatively easy to raise tax levels as long as the real incomes of all parties involved are still growing. On the other hand, economic stagnation and the resulting increase in unemployment generate a rise in the 'demand' for social transfers, which may also give an impulse to the (re)organization of the welfare services. The ageing of the population may have comparable effects and will probably broaden the electoral basis for (higher) old age pensions.

Finally, some consideration should be given to a factor that is often overlooked in the literature, namely the persistence and viability of private (pre-industrial) welfare provisions. The literature seems to agree that under the onslaught of industrialization and urbanization older welfare arrangements must have disappeared or at least fallen short of the task of guaranteeing basic levels of welfare. However, this does not seem to hold true, especially in a country which was already highly urbanized in the seventeenth century (and before). The nineteenth century saw the growth of all kinds of private welfare arrangements – ranging from mutual funeral funds to savings banks for the lower classes – which all contributed to the stabilization of income during the life cycle (Van Gerwen 1993). More-

52

over, the trade unions quickly discovered that by offering insurances against unemployment, sickness and other hardships, they could bind their members closer to their cause. Of course, the main disadvantage of these private welfare provisions was that they only included the better-off labourers; broadly speaking the people most in need were not union members and had no money to save. The rise of the welfare state meant that at least part of these private arrangements was replaced by collective welfare provisions, a process that accelerated whenever the 'old' systems were no longer able to cope. Two inflationary shocks – during the 1910s and the 1940s – undermined the traditional welfare arrangements as the value of private savings dwindled during both periods; the Great Depression of the 1930s also put a lot of pressure on these private arrangements.

In this chapter some of these insights will be applied to the Dutch case. In fact, I have broadened the subject by trying to account for the general growth of government activities during the twentieth century. The rise of social transfers was only one part of a much larger movement towards increased intervention by the government in economy and society, which can at least partly be explained by these theories. For example, government intervention in agricultural production and pricing, which started in the 1930s, was not only a response to the increased 'demand' for intervention from this sector, but was also motivated by competition between the dominant political parties for rural voters (this factor was completely absent in the preceding agricultural depression of the 1880s, which therefore did not elicit a comparable response from the government). As a result, a 'welfare state' for farmers was set up, which developed into the Common Agricultural Policy of the EEC during the 1960s. I will use this example to go into the dynamics of intervention and to illustrate the segmented structure of policymaking in the Netherlands in the post-World War II period. But first I will turn to the early history of the Dutch welfare state.

## THE SLOW RISE OF THE WELFARE STATE

From its inception in the final decades of the sixteenth century the Dutch state had been dominated by the 'liberal' bourgeoisie of the cities of Holland. In the final quarter of the nineteenth century this dominance was challenged by the process of pillarization and by the emancipation of the lower and middle classes. Abraham Kuyper, the founder of the orthodox Protestant pillar, was also the first to set up a mass political party. The conflict which started his involvement in politics was primary education, i.e. the officially 'neutral', non-religious character of subsidized public schools. Kuyper and his followers wanted either a 're-Christianization' of these schools or equally large subsidies for their own orthodox Protestant schools. The decision of the liberal government to increase subsidies to public schools in 1878, which would improve their competitive position vis-à-vis the Protestant and Catholic (or confessional) schools, led to the formation of the first modern political party (in 1879), the ARP, which successfully opposed the measures. The costs of schooling and the ways in which public and confessional schools should be organized would dominate Dutch politics until 1918 (Woltjer 1994: 37 ff).

The process of enfranchisement that began in 1887 worked clearly to the advantage of the Protestant and Catholic groups in parliament. Aided by the parallel movement of pillarization and by the development of their own programme of social reforms, they were able to mobilize a large part of the working and lower middle classes, especially in the countryside. In fact, during the final decades of the nineteenth century the basis was laid for a political structure in which the Catholic party (the RKSP) was to dominate political life. By their very nature confessional parties tend towards the middle of the political spectrum, because they represented labourers, farmers, and employers alike. Leaders of confessional trade unions, confessional agricultural organizations, and confessional employers' organizations participated in the governing bodies of the parties and were elected to parliament as their representatives. The political agenda of the confessional parties was an intensely debated compromise of the desires of their various wings. The crucial middle position of the Catholic party (in particular) meant that between 1887 and 1994 it was present in almost every Dutch government, always in combination with one of the Protestant parties (Kuyper's ARP and the more moderate CHU). Because no party or pillar could hope to achieve an absolute majority, governments were usually made up of three or more parties, but the Catholic party could more or less decide who would participate in the coalition governments and who would not, which gave it a crucial edge over its competitors (for more details: Lijphart 1968; Woltjer 1994).

The growth of the electorate also led to the rise of a socialist party, but it remained modest in size as a result of the strong competition of the confessional parties. In 1913, when about 68 percent of adult males were allowed to vote, it won about 18 percent of the votes, a share which increased to about a quarter after the introduction of universal male (1917) and female (1919) suffrage. But the ideological differences between the socialists and the Christian parties foreclosed almost any form of cooperation until 1939. The liberal groups were the big losers in the democratization process, but they remained influential as allies of the confessional parties.

The early development of the welfare state must be viewed against this background. After 1848 the laissez-faire orientation of the political establishment meant that the level of government intervention was reduced to a minimum. In 1869, for example, even the outmoded patent law was abolished and it was not until 1912 that a new one was introduced. As a result, the Netherlands was arguably the most liberal economy in Europe, even outperforming Great Britain. In a flurry of left-liberal activism a measure to outlaw child labour was adopted in 1874, but because nothing was done against its widespread violation the law remained more or less a dead letter. During the 1890s left-wing liberalism regained its momentum, which led to the adoption of an industrial accidents insurance law in 1901, after many bitter controversies about how to organize its implementation. Two views on the future of welfare legislation were in conflict. The confessional parties, especially Kuyper's ARP, wanted a decentralized system of administration in which every entrepreneur was allowed to manage the insurance scheme. The centralizing force of the state was deeply distrusted by the orthodox Protestants; in their view the establishment of welfare schemes was the responsibility of employers and employees, and state interference should be kept at an absolute minimum. The left-wing liberals (radicals) and the socialists (although they did not play a large part in the debate) clearly preferred a strong degree of guidance by the state, as it was clear that most employers would not voluntarily set up welfare schemes (De Vries 1970).

The compromise that emerged in 1901, in which a large degree of autonomy for branches and individual entreprises was integrated into the system, became characteristic of Dutch welfare legislation. Until 1913, however, stalemate between the right (the confessional parties) and the left (the liberals and socialists) persisted. Kuyper, who became prime minister in 1901, was unable to implement the social reforms that were part of his programme; but the same was true for the liberals. Consequently, welfare legislation stagnated (Woltjer 1994: 62).

World War I led to a breakthrough. Against the background of a strong increase in the membership and strength of unions, a historical compromise between the various political groups was reached: the left would get universal suffrage and the right full subsidization of confessional schools. Almost at the same time a number of important social reforms was introduced, such as government subsidies for the unemployment insurance schemes administered by the unions (1915), old-age and disability pensions for limited groups of labourers (1919), and the official eight-hour working day (1919). Moreover, the *raden van de arbeid*, institutions in which labour and capital could cooperate (for example, concerning wage negotiations) were set up and subsidies for the improvement of housing conditions were greatly expanded in these years.

These (and other changes) had a considerable effect on the general level of government expenditure. Graph 4.1, which shows the relationship between government expenditure and national income, demonstrates the discontinuity: before 1913 government expenditure was almost perfectly stable at about 8 percent of national income. After 1914 the sharp rise in expenditure on war-related issues resulted in a strong rise of this ratio. The 1920s did not witness a return to normalcy: the share of expenditure on

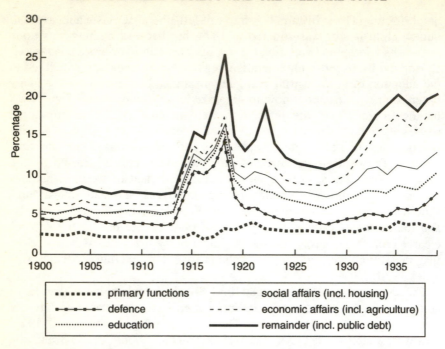

*Graph 4.1* Share of government expenditure in net domestic product
(market prices), 1900–1939
*Sources*: Database of government expenditure made available by Prof. Merkies,
Free University, Amsterdam; net domestic product: Van Bochove and Huitker 1987;
CBS 1994

'social categories' remained at a much higher level than before the war,
although strong cuts by successive ministers of finance during the first half
of the 1920s did result in a slight decline. Not only social transfers profited
from the 'democratic revolution' of these years, expenditure on education,
as part of the historical compromise of 1917, also expanded rapidly.
Compared with the period before 1913, the share of government expenditure in total income rose by about 50 percent (see also Stevers 1967). As a
result social transfers as a share of GDP went up during the war, and in this
respect the Netherlands converged to the European level (Table 4.1).

After the sharp rise of welfare spending during the period 1917 to 1921
not much happened during the rest of the interwar period (Table 4.1). This
stagnation of the welfare state seems to be at variance with the standard
theory, which predicts a strong increase in social transfers after the introduction of universal suffrage. The viability of private welfare arrangements
may help to explain the stagnation: unions were increasingly active in the
field of unemployment insurance (subsidized by the state), and resisted
more intervention from government because it would rob them of impor-

*Table 4.1* Social transfers as a percentage of GDP, 1910–1990 (percent)

| | 1910 | 1920 | 1930 | 1950[a] | 1960 | 1970 | 1980 | 1990 |
|---|---|---|---|---|---|---|---|---|
| Belgium | 0.4 | 0.5 | 0.6 | 9.6[b] | 13.1 | 19.3 | 30.4 | 19.2[c] |
| Germany | – | – | 5.0 | 12.4 | 18.1 | 19.5 | 25.7 | 25.3[d] |
| UK | 1.4 | 1.4 | 2.6 | 5.7 | 10.2 | 13.2 | 16.4 | 16.2 |
| France | 0.8 | 0.6 | 1.1 | 11.3 | 13.4 | 16.7 | 22.6 | 27.4 |
| Italy | 0.0 | 0.0 | 0.1 | 9.3[e] | 13.1 | 16.9 | 21.2 | 22.8[f] |
| Denmark | 1.8 | 2.7 | 3.4 | 5.8 | 12.3 | 19.1 | 27.4 | 29.0 |
| (1) Unweighed average | 0.9 | 1.1 | 2.1 | 9.0 | 13.4 | 17.5 | 24.0 | 23.3 |
| (2) Netherlands | 0.4 | 1.1 | 1.2 | 6.6 | 11.7 | 22.5 | 28.3 | 25.6[c] |
| (2) (1) | 0.44 | 1.00 | 0.57 | 0.73 | 0.87 | 1.29 | 1.18 | 1.10 |

*Sources*: 1910–1930: Lindert 1994: 1960–1990: Lindert 1996: 1950: Kohl 1981: 339
*Notes*: Figures for 1950 and 1990 are not strictly comparable with the other data.
[a] As a share of GNP. [b] 1953. [c] Only central government. [d] 1989. [e] 1955. [f] 1988, only central government.

tant services they supplied to their members. Moreover, World War I and the boom in social expenditure that followed resulted in large government deficits. After 1921 the reorganization of finances was given priority, and during the 1930s economic decline caused a renewed drive to cut social transfers (see Chapter 6).

Yet the financial and economic problems of the interwar period cannot completely explain the lack of progress in the field of welfare spending. The huge increase in expenditure on agriculture during the Great Depression is sufficient proof of this (see pp. 58–60). In addition, during the economic boom of the second half of the 1920s social transfers were not a priority of the cabinet. The impotency of the social democrats, who remained isolated in Dutch politics until 1939, and the lack of interest among the confessional and liberal parties in social spending, are the main explanations for the tardy development of the welfare state until World War II. Confessional parties and the social democrats hardly competed for the votes of labourers; the ideological (and geographical) barriers between the different pillars were solid and, within those pillars, the ideological commitment to the leadership was very strong. One of the reasons the Catholic parties did not want to form a coalition with the social democrats was that it would give them an air of respectability, and could thus lower the barriers for voter mobility between the two (Woltjer 1994: 96).

In the long run the stabilization of politics in 1917 resulted in a return to conservative policies. Before 1913 there was broad consensus that social reforms were necessary, but because of a lack of agreement on the exact contents and organization of these reforms, little progress was made. In a way the war and its many side effects, such as the enormous growth of the trade unions, made it possible to implement at least part of the programme that was discussed before 1914. After 1921, however, this consensus disappeared and the policies of the confessional parties became more conservative. Apart from the social democrats no major party sought the favours of the working classes by supporting new welfare schemes, as the confessional parties and the radicals had done before the introduction of universal suffrage. The explanation for this unexpected outcome is that after 1917 the major parties did not compete for working-class votes as a consequence of the high degree of pillarization in society. A further test of this analysis can be offered by looking at the one field in which much progress was made during the 1930s, namely agricultural policy.

## AGRICULTURAL POLICIES AND THE 'GREEN FRONT'

During the interwar period floating voters were probably concentrated in the middle and upper classes – among the liberal Protestants – and there was a much greater electoral overlap between the confessional parties and the liberal parties than between them and the social democrats. In general, the degree of pillarization became stronger towards the bottom of the social pyramid, while it was weakest or non-existent among the nobility, employers, professionals and other parts of the elite. The old Protestant elite actually disliked the whole process of splitting up Dutch society into segments. The result of the correlation between social position and the degree of pillarization was that political parties only competed for the votes of the well-off. For example, during the 1930s the orthodox Protestant leader Colijn was able to attract a large part of the upper-class liberal electorate by acting as the 'strong man' of Dutch politics who would restore law and order, and by sticking rigidly to the gold standard, a policy strongly favoured by right-wing liberals (Blom 1989: 28 ff). In doing so he met with hardly any opposition from within his own party, nor did he lose part of his electorate; orthodox Protestants were bound to vote for the ARP anyway. As a result, his relatively small orthodox Protestant party was able to dominate policy formation during the greater part of the 1930s (Woltjer 1994: 129 ff).

Another part of the electorate for which competition was relatively strong wase the farmers. The pillarization of the farming community had begun in the 1890s and had been particularly strong in the Catholic south of the country. The Protestants had not been so successful and in the north of the country the traditionally liberal farmers were not really part of a clearly demarcated pillar. Moreover, the organizations that represented farmers' interests in The Hague were dominated by the liberal farmers from the north. However, the countryside was generally regarded as the natural habitat of the confessional parties – whereas the socialists and the liberals had their strongholds in the cities – which meant that for them the agrarian vote was of crucial importance.

This political structure helps to explain why in the early years of the 1930s – between 1931 and 1933 – government intervention in the agricultural sector experienced an unprecedented increase. Of course, other factors also played a role. World War I had demonstrated the importance of agriculture for the supply of basic foodstuffs; the enormous decline in agricultural prices after 1929 actually threatened to destroy the sector. Moreover, already during the second half of the 1920s, when the rest of the economy profited from the international boom, prices had been on the decline, which led to many complaints about the distress in the agricultural sector (Knibbe 1993: 179–80). This prelude surely helped to convince politicians that something had to be done, but the amazing speed and scale of the policies after 1931 were surprising indeed.

In 1930 the first proposals for far-reaching protectionist measures were put forward by representatives of the Groningen farmers, who worked closely with national farmers' organizations (Krips-van der Laan 1985: 39 ff). This resulted in protection for wheat-growing farmers in 1931. But as the depression in agriculture spread from arable farming to livestock and horticulture, it became necessary to extend these measures to other products. Within a few years a virtually comprehensive system of agricultural protection was set up, which regulated almost every part of the sector. Halfway through the 1930s the contribution of government subsidies to total value added in agriculture peaked at over 40 percent, which gives an idea of the enormous amounts of money that were involved (see also Graph 4.1) (calculated from CBS, *Jaarcijfers*, 1934–40 and Van den Noort 1965).

It is relatively easy to protect a sector that has a net trade deficit, i.e. of which domestic consumption is higher than domestic production: import duties can do the job and government finances can actually profit from their proceeds (although the consumer will pay the price). Attempts to protect a sector with a large export surplus will, however, produce major financial problems because the government has to find funds to pay for the export subsidies. By definition protection keeps internal prices above world market prices, and in the case of an export surplus this has to be dumped on the world market. In the 1930s the main Dutch political parties were willing to pay this price at the expense of continuous budget deficits and high internal food prices. Moreover, as Klemann (1990) has shown, the need to sell the surplus of horticultural and dairy products was also constantly felt in international economic policies. This often meant that other interests, e.g. those of the colonies or manufacturers, were sacrificed in international trade negotiations (see Chapter 7). The Dutch economy therefore paid a relatively high price for the protection of this politically 'sensitive' sector.

Moreover, the close cooperation between agrarian interest groups and the government in the 1930s led to the creation of what has been called the

59

'green front'. In all major political parties representatives of the agrarian interest were able to lobby successfully for their cause. Since then agricultural specialists – recruited from the various farmers' organizations – have come to dominate parliamentary decision-making on agricultural matters. Moreover, a separate Ministry of Agriculture and Fisheries was set up in 1935 and until 1994 would invariably be headed by a specialist with the same training and background. As a result, a separate political subsystem came into existence in which all major decisions on agrarian matters were taken by specialists who had received training in one of the agrarian organizations and pressure groups (Louwes 1980).

This political subsystem has proven to be enormously resilient. When the Depression of the 1930s came to an end, the organization set up to manage the agricultural policies was transformed into an administrative body for food production and distribution in anticipation of World War II. In this respect the Dutch were well prepared in 1940; until the autumn of 1944 the system performed very efficiently. After 1945 it continued to operate as a system to guarantee low food prices and became an important element of the policy to keep down prices (and wages) in order to restore international competitiveness (see Chapter 7). The political subsystem was further elaborated by the creation of a separate Advisory Council, the Stichting voor de Landbouw. On all matters the minister had to consult this body, in which the agrarian interest groups were assembled, and he could often use their advice to strengthen his stance for agricultural protection (Louwes 1980).

The basic guideline of the postwar system was that farmers should receive a just reward for their efforts, i.e. that agricultural prices should reflect production costs plus a certain margin for the farmer. Detailed estimates were made of the production costs of an average farm, which formed the basis for negotiations between the Stichting voor de Landbouw and the minister on the yearly changes in the price level. This guideline made it possible to keep prices below world market prices until the mid-1950s. Freezing rents at their 1941 level also contributed to this effort (rent was obviously a part of production costs) (Weststrate 1959: 183 ff).

After 1951, when agricultural prices on the world market began a steep decline and increasingly large surpluses of agricultural products became available for export, this policy ran into difficulties. As in the 1930s one of the basic aims of Dutch international policy was to find export outlets for these surpluses, knowing that other producers (Denmark, for example) were able to produce at lower costs. Benelux, the economic union between Belgium, the Netherlands and Luxemburg that began in 1948, created the first preferential export market for agricultural products, but this solved only a small fraction of the problem (traditionally Germany and Britain had been far more important as export markets) (Meade *et al.* 1964: 114–28). As a result, after 1951 – the creation of the European Community for Steel and Coal – the Dutch Minister for Agriculture Sicco Mansholt tried to set up a more or less comparable preferential trading system for agricultural products. He was convinced that only such an organization could rescue Dutch agricultural protection in the long run. His persistence led to a separate paragraph on agriculture in the Treaty of Rome (1957), which formed the basis of the EEC (Milward 1992: 300 ff). This paragraph announced the creation of a Common Agricultural Policy (CAP), but left unspecified what this would actually imply. In 1958 Mansholt became the first European Commissioner for Agriculture and could start negotiations about its organization. The results of these negotiations, which are too complicated to deal with here, was that on a European scale a system was introduced which looked very much like the Dutch one: guaranteed prices for the most important products (cereals, milk), subject to annual negotiations by the ministers for agriculture of the member states (Burger 1993).

Seen from the Dutch perspective this system worked rather well until the late 1970s. The share of direct government subsidies in the value added of Dutch agriculture rose to 17.5 percent in 1958, which testifies to the magnitude of the problem in the late 1950s (calculated from Dercksen *et al.* 1982: 206–9). This measure of the degree of protection declined to only 2.3 percent in 1970–2 (in the EEC as a whole) as a result of the creation of a preferential export market and the fact that the EEC as a whole was not yet self-sufficient in agricultural products (Meester and Strijker 1985: 40). Foreign, mainly German, consumers instead of Dutch taxpayers were now paying the price for agricultural protection. Moreover, within the EEC trade area the Dutch were arguably the most efficient producers in livestock farming and horticulture, and both industries were able to capture large European markets (and, in the process, became even more efficient). The growth of agricultural production – sustained by the CAP – inevitably led to a crisis, because it rapidly outgrew the sluggish increase in consumption. In the late 1970s the EEC became a net exporter of agricultural products and had to dump increasingly large surpluses on the world market. In 1973–74 about 6 percent of total consumption of agricultural products of the EEC was imported; in 1980–1 this had changed into an export surplus of about 7 percent of total consumption (Thiede 1984).

Consequently, the costs of the CAP exploded. Already in 1984 direct subsidies amounted to more than 15 percent of value added in agriculture, and the CAP came disproportionately to dominate the EC budget (Meester and Strijker 1985: 40). Moreover, the many changes in exchange rates during the 1970s made it impossible to maintain one price level throughout Europe. This would have meant, for example, that every devaluation of the lira was followed by a concomitant increase in Italian farm prices, and a revaluation of the Deutsche Mark by a similar reduction. Instead, a complicated system of national prices levels came into existence, which made a mockery of the original aims of the CAP, i.e. to create one unified market.

The gradual reform of the CAP that began in the 1980s is of no concern to this analysis. In this section I have focused on agricultural policies because it is the first example of far-reaching government intervention, beginning in a period when conservative politicians were reluctant to do so, a phenomenon that should be explained. Moreover, this case study shows the persistence of agricultural policies and of the political subsystem that produced them. The 'green front' was able to adapt rather smoothly to the changes brought about by World War II, the reconstruction policies and the process of European integration. The political subsystem that was formed in the 1930s – based on the close links between political parties, interest groups, and government officials (especially of the Ministry for Agriculture) – still dominates policymaking on agriculture in the 1990s. When the first Dutch cabinet without the confessional parties was formed in 1994, the (right-wing) liberal who was appointed as Minister for Agriculture was not a 'specialist' in the field and had never been a member of one of the agricultural interest groups. Certainly, after almost 60 years of rule by 'one of their own' this proved hard to swallow; resistance against his 'liberal' proposals to reform agricultural policy has been strong. More fundamentally, particular sections of the 'green front' have come to question the continuation of protection on basis of the conviction that some parts of Dutch agriculture are now efficient enough to meet any competition. So very slowly the 'green front' has been crumbling, perhaps one of the most significant signs that the long twentieth century is coming to an end.

## THE BIG BOOM IN GOVERNMENT SPENDING 1945–1980

By any standard government spending, especially on social transfers, exploded in the decades after World War II. Of course, the war had led to a huge increase in government measures to regulate the economy and exploit it to the advantage of the German occupier. Policies to control inflation and to distribute the limited supplies of foodstuffs and raw materials led to the growth of huge costly bureaucracies. After 1946 these measures were gradually relaxed and the bureaucracies dissolved, which brought about a decrease in the share of government in national income until the second half of the 1950s (Graph 4.2). Nevertheless, just as after World War I, this level remained much higher than before 1939. Compared to the 1920s the share doubled (from about 12 percent of net domestic product income to about 25 percent) (see also Stevers 1967).

Until the 1950s the development of government spending was in line with the 'platform' theory of Peacock and Wiseman (1967). This theory postulates a strong 'ratchet effect': after a sudden rise in government spending during a war, it will decline after the end of hostilities, but by much less than the original increase during the first years of the war. Other

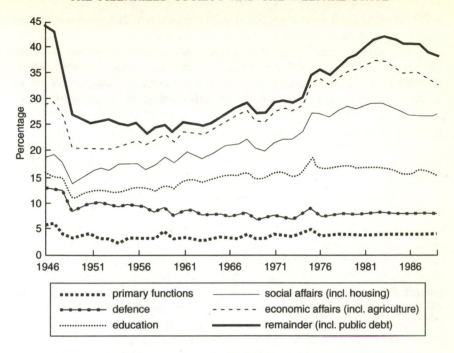

*Graph 4.2* Share of government expenditure in net domestic product
(market prices), 1946–1989
*Sources*: Database of government expenditure made available by Prof. Merkies,
Free University, Amsterdam; net domestic product: Van Bochove and Huitker 1987;
CBS 1994

shocks to the economy – such as the Great Depression of the 1930s – can
have a comparable effect on the relationship between government expenditure and GDP. However, according to Peacock and Wiseman (1967), the
ratio between government spending and GDP will be more or less stable
between such 'crises'. Such 'platforms' existed in the Netherlands before
1914, in the 1920s and in the 1950s (Graphs 4.1 and 4.2). Yet, this really
changed in the 1960s when there began a strong rise in government
spending relative to national income, which continued until the early
1980s (Graph 4.2).

To explain these developments – the afterwar 'ratchet effect' and the
continuous rise between 1960 and 1980 – we have to dig once more into the
development of the socio-political structure. During the 1930s the socialist
party, aware of its isolation and impotence, moved towards the political
centre, which is the way 'rational' politicians are expected to act in such
situations. A group of moderate politicians – inspired by the reformist ideas
of the economist Jan Tinbergen – gained the upper hand (Knotter 1980;
Woltjer 1994: 168–71). In 1939 this was rewarded: the socialists were

63

asked to participate in the coalition government, which they accepted (in anticipation of the harsh times that were to come).

During the German occupation, ideas about a radical 'break' with the pillarized structure of society and politics circulated widely, stimulated by the experience of the resistance against the Germans, which seemed to unify all parts of the population. In 1945 this led to the creation of a new, supposedly 'post-pillarization' Labour Party (PvdA), in which the socialists and relatively small groups of left-wing liberals and Christian democrats merged. This new party broke with the socialist orthodoxy of the past, and, as it was the clearest expression of political renewal caused by the occupation, it laid strong claims to government. In fact, the first postwar government (1945–6) was dominated by its members (Woltjer 1994: 208 ff).

And yet, the first afterwar elections of 1946 would show that pillarization had not disappeared. The confessional parties (and a right-wing liberal party) returned to the scene without having lost their electorate. The communists were stronger than ever, but were quickly isolated by all other parties. Whereas in quantitative terms little seemed to have changed (the electorate of the new Labour Party was even somewhat smaller than the combined electorates of the parties that had merged into it), the fact that from 1945 onwards the social democrats became a 'natural' part of government coalitions made a real difference. Until 1958 politics would be dominated by coalitions of the Labour Party and the Catholic party (renamed KVP), supplemented with one or two of the other (Protestant or liberal) parties. From 1948 to 1958 these coalitions were led by the social democrat Willem Drees, whose main aim was to consolidate and extend the system of social spending. His most famous law – the 'noodwet Drees' of 1947 – was an 'emergency measure' to introduce a modest state pension for the elderly (Woltjer 1994: 347).

This was not the only significant change in social spending during the immediate afterwar period. The 'noodwet Drees' was motivated by the fact that private savings, an important source of income for the aged, had lost a large part of their value as a result of inflation during and directly after the war. The same reason, the collapse of private arrangements, was behind the changes in unemployment insurance. Already in the 1930s the trade unions were no longer able to finance their unemployment funds despite heavy government subsidies. In 1949 government took over completely and extended coverage to all employees. A few other measures were taken as well; together these help to explain the sharp upturn in social transfers between the 1930s and 1950 (see Table 4.1). However, in view of the large structural problems of the Dutch economy in these years, benefit levels were kept at a bare minimum. In general, welfare legislation was quite parsimonious, which accounts for the relatively low level of spending in comparison with the rest of Western Europe in the 1950s (Table 4.1).

However, this changed radically during the 1960s and early 1970s. Only in the Netherlands did the share of social transfers in GDP double between 1960 and 1970 (Table 4.1). In 1970 the Netherlands was already topping the league, dropping to a second place after Belgium in 1980. This 'big bang' in welfare legislation and social spending of the 1960s is one of the major problems to be solved in Dutch economic and social history of the period.

There is no simple political explanation for the boom in social spending during the 1960s. In fact, although this became a cliché in the 1980s, it is very difficult to blame this boom on the social democrats, because they had hardly participated in government coalitions between 1958 and 1973 (apart from a short-lived cabinet headed by Cals in 1965–6). The problem to explain is why (before 1958) social-democratic and Catholic coalition governments managed to keep social spending at an internationally low level, whereas coalitions of Catholics and right-wing liberals between 1958 and 1973 were more generous than ever before (and since). To do this we have to return to the socio-political structure sketched in preceding sections.

World War II did not end the pillarized structure of Dutch politics, and the lack of voter mobility between the social democrats and the confessional parties probably persisted. Of course, the former socialists became far more respectable and there was increasing fear that Catholic workers would defect to the Labour Party. In 1954 the Dutch bishops reacted with a renewal of their decision of 1918 that Catholics were not allowed to join the Labour Party or the socialist trade union; the latter would even result in excommunication (Windmuller and De Galan 1970, I: 108). This ultimate attempt to restore pillarization was probably successful in the short term – the position of Catholic trade unions and parties became stronger during the 1950s – but it failed in the long term. The centralized wage policy of the 1950s led to intensive contacts between trade unions of different denominations, since they were obliged to work closely together in wage bargaining as well as advisory work for the government. Until 1958 the two big unions – the NVV (socialist) and the NKV (Catholic) – worked together to support the policies of 'their' social-democrat and Catholic coalition government.

After the dissolution of this coalition in 1958 the NKV was faced with a conflict of interest; either it had to cooperate with the Catholic party, which shifted to the right between 1958 and 1963 (see Chapter 8), or it could oppose this shift together with the NVV. In 1963, shortly before the general elections, the two unions presented an ambitious programme for large-scale increases in social spending that was to have major influence (Woltjer 1994: 423). During the next years almost all their proposals were implemented; it also spelled the end of the move to the right in the Catholic party. In 1976 the close cooperation between the two unions culminated in their fusion, one of the most significant moments in the de-pillarization of the Netherlands.

What actually happened during the 1960s was that the ideological barriers which had prevented Catholic and Protestant workers from voting for the social democratic party (or other non-confessional parties) were gradually disappearing, a process that accelerated after 1965. Political scientists such as Arend Lijphart (1968) have analysed the instability that came along with de-pillarization. As might be expected, there began a renewed competition for the votes of the lower (middle) classes. The left wings of the confessional parties became much more influential; even the orthodox Protestant party (ARP) developed a powerful left wing, which came to dominate the party during the mid-1970s. New left-wing parties arose – sometimes led by former members of the confessional parties – and this increased competition for the leftist vote also prompted the Labour Party to move in that direction.

The spectacular economic success of this period gave a strong impetus to these developments. After more than a decade of rapid expansion, a growth of GDP of 4 or 5 percent was believed to be natural. The progressive tax system did the rest: taxes grew at a higher rate than incomes, which gave politicians ample opportunity to fulfil their wishes. In the early 1960s a new budgetary system was introduced by the Minister of Finance, Jelle Zijlstra, which was based on the proposition that the long-run growth of tax income determined the yearly increase in spending, so that politicians only had to decide how to distribute the proceeds (Sterks 1982: 140 ff). This new system and the beginning of a flow of funds from the exploitation of natural gas all helped in taking off the pressure.

De-pillarization, a renewed competition for lower-class votes, and a continuous increase in tax revenues at an unparalleled level created the strong desire to shape a complete system of social transfers, which would provide social security from the cradle to the grave. What finally contributed heavily to the expansion of social transfers during the 1960s (and 1970s) was that the new welfare legislation was quite generous. Like other parts of the legal system, welfare legislation is generally rather lethargic: old laws almost never die and they are at best adapted to new circumstances. The welfare measures taken during and before the first half of the century had generally been rather parsimonious. In most countries these laws were extended and updated after 1945, without seriously changing their character. In a study of unemployment insurance schemes in Western Europe, Jens Alber found that there existed a strong negative relationship between the age of a scheme and the duration and level of its benefits; the Dutch scheme, one of the youngest, was by far the most generous (Alber 1981: 169). Since the Netherlands was a relative latecomer in the field it created a very 'modern' system which was, however, relatively generous and expensive.

During the mid-1960s the most important laws (on family allowances (1963), general assistance (1965), disability insurance (1966) and sickness benefits (1967)) were mainly the work of Catholic ministers (G.M.J. Veld-kamp, M. Klompé), who were strongly supported by 'their' unions. At the same time expenditure on education, health care and subsidized housing increased rapidly, spurred on by the same forces (see Graph 4.2). Although many politicians were aware of the dangers of an excessive increase in government spending, and although between 1967 and 1973 the cabinets urged for the need to control expenditure, they failed in the face of these strong forces.

The coalition government that took over in 1973 – headed for the first time since 1958 by a social democratic, J.M. den Uyl – was in many ways the climax of this development. Its programme was aimed at spreading income, knowledge and power more evenly among the population, and to this end a number of welfare measures was introduced during its first years. Moreover, it strongly increased minimum wages, especially those of the young. Yet, it was soon confronted with the economic downturn of 1973 which, politically and ideologically, ended the leftist euphoria that began in the 1960s. Certainly, the share of government in national income continued to rise between 1975 and 1982, but this was largely caused by the increased claims on the various social arrangements, rather than by their extension.

## THE CRISIS OF THE WELFARE STATE

The ambitious project of the 1960s, to build an all-encompassing and relatively generous welfare state, already ran aground in the late 1970s. Since the mechanisms behind the 'crisis of the welfare state' have been the subject of intensive study, I cannot do much more than give a rough sketch of the different causes.

First of all, the 'free' supply of collective goods – of education, social security, health care, subsidized housing – led to an enormous expansion of their demand. Expenditure on medical consumption, (higher) education and low-cost housing grew much more rapidly than GDP (Van Zanden and Griffiths 1989: 69–71). The 'Baumol effect', the fact that the price of these labour intensive activities rose much more than the general price level, also contributed to the increase in the claims on funds.

During the 1970s the sharp rise in spending on social security was connected with the downturn of the economy. Naturally, expenditure on unemployment benefits rose. A much more expensive problem was the huge increase in the number of people who received benefits under the 'Disability Act' of 1966. These benefits were generally higher and lasted longer than the unemployment benefits, so that during lay-offs employers and employees combined to classify as many people as possible as 'disabled'. Older employees whose chances of finding a new job were relatively small especially 'profited' from this system. The generous allowances of the collective insurance against illness also helped to increase sick leave. All this led to a huge rise in collective spending (government spending and collective insurances) because at the micro level – where these collective goods were considered free – there was no trade-off between costs and benefits.

In financing the huge increase in expenditure, the 'welfare state' i.e. the attempt to redistribute income through the state in favour of the poor, more or less ran into its 'natural' limits. The possibilities for taxing the rich were already exhausted in the early 1960s, when a marginal tariff of 72 percent was introduced for the highest income levels. The continued growth of welfare spending therefore had to lead to an increase in the tax burden for the middle and lower classes. Moreover, collective insurance premiums were increasingly considered to be just another kind of tax. These problems were not really acute during the 1960s, when the prosperous state of the economy made it easy to pay for the growth of government expenditure. The economic downturn after 1973 made a big difference. Resistance against the heavy burden of taxes and social security premiums gradually built up. Grey and black economic circuits expanded; tax evasion became a (profitable) national sport, especially for the wealthy; and the poor went their own way by cheating with welfare benefits.

Resistance against heavy taxation certainly played a role in the move to the right that occurred in Dutch politics after 1973. The huge government deficits that arose after 1977 – in spite of a big increase in government income from the exploitation of natural gas resources – created a sense of urgency that something had to be done to control government spending (Knoester 1989: 153 ff). This, however, proved to be very difficult.

One of the reasons why the fiscal crisis of the state of the late 1970s and early 1980s was so persistent was that a lot of 'automatic' links were built into government expenditure. For example, social security benefits, pensions and salaries of government employees were tied to the general increase in wages in the private sector. In turn, these were almost automatically linked to the increase in the cost of living and some estimate of the increase in labour productivity (see Chapter 5). This meant that in periods of sharp inflation the growth of government expenditure would rapidly get out of control.

Yet, behind this system of automatic links was a much more formidable problem. The Dutch political system had become heavily segmented, dominated by relatively strong coalitions of politicians, pressure groups, and bureaucrats. The 'green front', that was sketched in the previous section, is just one example of such a powerful political subsystem. Health care, 'social affairs' (dominated by the trade unions), or 'housing' are other examples of segments of the political system that had become increasingly independent. A fully developed political subsystem consisted of the following elements: strong pressure groups, able to mobilize the media; an official advisory board in which the minister consulted or even negotiated with the pressure groups on the desired policies; a department with its own budget, headed by a strong minister of their own bred; and, within each large party, a number of specialists who would dominate the relevant debates in parliament (every party in parliament would delegate debates on certain issues to its own 'specialists', who were often recruited from the relevant pressure groups). Backed by 'his' pressure groups, government officials, press, and parliamentary specialists, a minister tried to build up a strong position for the decisive negotiations in the cabinet, where the decisions on the yearly budgets were made. He had to convince his colleagues, but especially the Minister of Finance, that his department needed more money. A successful minister was defined as one who could get a larger share of the pie; 'weak' ministers were the ones who failed in this respect (Van Zanden and Griffiths 1989: 71).

The Minister of Finance is the only hero of the tale. He is confronted with the demands for larger budgets by his fellow specialist ministers. Moreover, it is an unwritten rule that during the crucial negotiations in the cabinet the specialists do not oppose each other's proposals for more money (Toirkens 1988). This is the task of the Minister of Finance, who is however easily outvoted by a majority of specialists. As a result, the expansion of expenditure is built into the system.

Various attempts have been made to contain these forces. The best known is the structural budget system introduced in the early 1960s, which linked the growth of government expenditure to the predicted long-term increase in tax income and thus tried to impose a ceiling. But after 1973, when there began an unanticipated decline in the long-term growth rate of the economy, this system allowed for a much too rapid expansion of expenditure because growth was still based on the expected long-term growth rate of the period until 1973.

The need to cut budgets and reduce the deficit on the one hand and the resistance of the powerful forces that opposed such measures on the other increasingly conflicted during the late 1970s and 1980s. José Toirkens (1988) has shown that it led to a long series of budget cuts that were very 'soft' or were evaded by the department that had to implement them. Window-dressing and rhetoric, the manipulation of funds and official statistics, every trick was played to delay real cuts. It was soon found out that, once a minister had assumed office, he or she was very skilful in evading any attack on the budget. The only way to reorganize finances was by making very detailed agreements with coalition parties and cabinet members during the negotiations leading up to the formation of a cabinet (Toirkens 1988).

However, in the end this slow and painful process has been rather successful. After 1982 collective expenditure, that is government spending and social security transfers, as a percentage of GDP slowly started to decline, from a peak level of over 66 percent (in 1982 and 1983) to 53.8 percent in 1995 (CPB 1995: 162–3). Spending by the government did not decline as much, but also showed a remarkable turn in the 1980s (Graph 4.2). This decline was largely the result of three major changes. Government salaries, particularly in education, were lowered (in 1982–3) and continued to lag behind wages in the private sector. Moreover, after 1988 employment in the government sector started to decline (its share in total employment was reduced from 15 percent in 1982 to 12.5 percent in 1995). As a result, the share of salaries paid by the government in GDP fell from 12.6 percent in 1982 to 9.6 percent in 1995.

The second part of the reforms consisted of a large number of measures to lower the level of social security benefits, decrease their duration, and increase entrance barriers. Especially during the first half of the 1980s old age pensions and other benefits declined in real terms; thereafter at best they kept pace with inflation. However, the number of people receiving benefits continued to rise as a consequence of the gradual ageing of the population, the extension of early retirement schemes and the increase in the number of people receiving disability benefits (WAO). The net effect of growing numbers and decreasing real benefits was a decline of social transfers as a share of GDP by 4.4 percent (from 29.4 percent in 1982 to 25.0 percent in 1995) (CPB 1995: 162–3).

Third, transfers to industry were another source of major budget cuts. The generous system of investment subsidies, introduced in 1975 (WIR), was abolished and direct capital transfers were reduced after the discrediting of industrial policies in 1984–5 (see Chapter 9). The privatization of the postal services (PTT) and of the supply of loans to housing corporations also pushed down direct transfers (Van Popta 1995: 223). Other less important sources of savings were the reduction of defence expenditure after the end of the Cold War in 1989, and continuous cuts in the budget for (higher) education.

In general the groups that had benefited most from the reforms of the 1960s and early 1970s, the poor and the young, fared worst by these measures. A slow upturn in income inequality, after its gradual fall during the 1960s and 1970s, was one of the results of the process (Arts and Van Wijck 1994).

Other factors have contributed to the swing to the right in Dutch politics in the decade after 1973. Political participation has been on the decline since about 1970, when the duty to vote (*opkomstplicht*) was abolished. Before 1970 more than 92 percent of voters went to the ballot, but this declined drastically to 80.6 percent in 1982 and 78.3 percent in 1994 (CBS 1994; CBS, *Statistical Yearbook*, 1995). Like elsewhere, non-voters are overrepresented among the lower classes. Moreover, the traditional basis of the social democrats, the industrial labourers, was rapidly eroded during the 1970s and 1980s: industrial employment fell, as did the rate of union-ization after 1977 (see Chapter 5). The merger of the three confessional parties into the CDA strengthened the traditional centre of Dutch politics; the left wings of the confessional parties almost disappeared in the process.

With the ongoing de-pillarization the old ties that bound parties and voters together have largely disappeared. Ideological differences have almost vanished and the largest parties have tried to broaden their electorate by moving to the centre of the political spectrum (see Chapter 9). The ideological gap which made cooperation between the Labour Party and the right-wing liberals (VVD) impossible, was greatly reduced in the process. As a result, in 1994, for the first time since 1917, a government without the Christian democrats took office. In a way, this ended a 'long' century of pillarized politics.

# 5

# THE LABOUR MARKET

## THE LATE RISE OF TRADE UNIONISM

An economy consists of a coherent system of markets on which products and production factors are traded at certain prices. The labour market is special for a number of reasons. This is where humans and their work capacity are traded, which means that human welfare is highly dependent on its efficiency. The labour market has therefore been subject to more institutional changes than other markets. Trade unions emerged in response to the superior bargaining power of employers, and they won the right to bargain collectively. Trade unions established collective insurance schemes against unemployment, sickness and disability, with an eye to decreasing the degree of direct dependence on employers. Special institutions were set up to bring together supply and demand. Finally, for a number of reasons, government began to regulate the market. As a result the labour market has been radically transformed: whereas it was almost completely 'free' for the greater part of the nineteenth century – until 1869 unions were officially forbidden in the Netherlands – after 1945 it probably became the most regulated market of the economy. In this chapter some of the factors behind the transformation and some of its consequences will be studied.

The rise of the trade unions was probably the most fundamental change in the labour market, and it triggered a large part of the other institutional developments. The late rise of Dutch unionism has been the subject of some debate, which in fact started already in 1902 when the first 'modern' economic and social history of the Netherlands was published by the socialist writer Henriette Roland Holst (1902). The first attempts to set up something approaching the model of a 'modern' trade union were made around 1870 and were largely restricted to Amsterdam, but until about 1900 progress was slow. The start of the modern trade union movement during the first decade of the century was initiated by socialists who had studied the unions in Germany and Great Britain and who introduced the model of 'new unionism' in the Netherlands. The ANDB – the union of diamond workers in Amsterdam established in 1896 – became the first successful example of a centralized union, which built up large reserves and supplied all kinds of services to its members (Windmuller and De Galan 1970: I, 24). Insurances, in particular against unemployment, were part of the package. After the national strike of 1903, which showed the limitations of the anarcho-syndicalistic movement, this model quickly came to dominate the socialist trade union movement. In 1906 fifteen national unions established a federation, the NVV, which was to dominate the socialist trade union movement during the next 70 years. The founders made it clear from the start that their aim was to improve the position of the workers by wage bargaining – especially through the conclusion of collective bargaining agreements (in Dutch CAO) – and by political actions aimed at protective labour legislation (Windmuller 1969: 31). To summarize, in practice the organization was highly reformist.

Around the same time the development of Protestant and Catholic trade unions gained momentum. The 'threat' of the socialist unions was often behind attempts to set up confessional unions, which were much more conservative and inclined to cooperate with employers. Moreover, the Catholic unions were usually controlled by members of the clergy, who acted as 'spiritual advisers'. In 1908 and 1909, shortly after the foundation of the NVV, there followed the creation of national organizations of the Catholic and Protestant unions. Compared with the socialist unions that could count on 80,000 members in 1914, the two confessional federations were relatively small; in 1914 their combined membership was about 40,000 or half the size of the NVV (Windmuller and De Galan 1970: I, 25 ff).

To sum up, the two decades before World War I saw the rise of the trade unions and their national federations which were to dominate wage bargaining during the rest of the century. In response to the failure of the anarcho-syndicalist movement, the socialist federation NVV was strongly centralized and reformist. It was able to grow rapidly due to its successes in wage bargaining, and as a result of the services it supplied to its members, of which unemployment insurance was probably the most important. It thus solved the classical free-rider problem (Van Leeuwen 1996). As part of the general process of pillarization and in reaction to the rise of socialist unions the orthodox Protestants and Catholics set up their own unions and national federations.

The late industrialization and the parallel movement of pillarization produced a rather complex structure of the trade unions, characterized by strong national federations and, at times, fierce competition between the socialist and confessional trade unions. This probably induced the socialist unions, who needed to be recognized by employers as at least one of the official partners in wage bargaining, to become even more moderate. One of the most important goals of the socialist unions until 1940 was to become recognized as the partner, or one of the partners, for the conclusion of a collective wage agreement (CAO) (Schrover *et al.* 1992). It is obvious that employers preferred to bargain with the most moderate unions and attempted to exclude the socialists. In their study of the history of the trade union movement, Ger Harmsen and Bob Reinalda (1975), who made no secret of their commitment to the cause of the socialist unions, show that the confessional unions often undermined strikes that were called for by the socialist unions. Although their story may be biased, this was probably the logic of the situation that had come into existence. It forced the socialist unions to become very moderate; the strong centralized structure of the NVV contributed to keeping the more radical elements in the socialist trade union movement in check.

## EXPANSION AND CONSOLIDATION 1914–1940

Until 1914 trade unions had been rather peripheral to the labour market. No more than about 16 percent of the dependent labour force was organized (in 1914), and the number of industries in which collective wage bargaining took place was even smaller (see Table 5.1). But in the decade before World War I the movement had definitively gained momentum and during the war membership and collective wage negotiations grew explosively. The share of the dependent population that was organized went up to 30 percent in 1920, after which came a period of some decline (see Graph 5.1). In a few years the trade unions made up the backlog they had had during the nineteenth century (Table 5.2).

*Table 5.1* Number of collective bargaining agreements and their coverage, 1911–1989

| | Industrywide | | Companywide | Total | Employees covered (1000) | As a share of dependent labour force |
|---|---|---|---|---|---|---|
| | Nation | Region | | | | |
| 1911 | – | – | – | 87 | 23 | 1.3 |
| 1920 | – | – | – | 984 | 274 | 12.6 |
| 1930 | – | – | – | 1,554 | 386 | 15.5 |
| 1940 | 31 | 354 | 1,159 | 1,544 | 352 | 12.6 |
| 1947 | 7 | 91 | 54 | 152 | ? | – |
| 1951 | 48 | 77 | 239 | 364 | 900 | 29.7 |
| 1956 | 149 | 118 | 322 | 589 | 1,749 | 51.9 |
| 1960 | 170 | 118 | 398 | 686 | 2,073 | 57.9 |
| 1970 | 196 | 66 | 484 | 746 | 2,310 | 50.1 |
| 1980 | 162 | 23 | 543 | 728 | 2,762 | 51.8 |
| 1989 | 198 | | 694 | 892 | 3,253 | 54.7 |

*Sources*: Korver 1993: 393. Dependent labour force: Van der Bie 1995; Den Bakker and Van Sorge 1996; CBS 1994

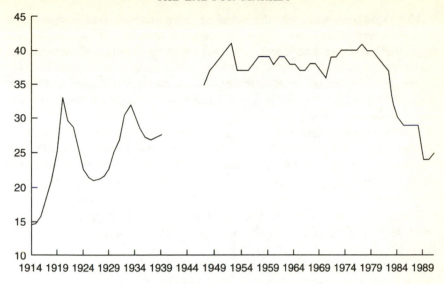

*Graph 5.1* Union density in the Netherlands, 1914–1991
*Sources*: 1914–1940: Harmsen and Reinalda; dependent labour force: Den Bakker and Van
Sorge 1996; 1947–1991 Van Cleef and Kuijpers 1991
*Note*: Due to differences in definition and in the underlying series of the dependent labour
force this series does not correspond completely with the estimates made by Crouch 1993.

*Table 5.2* Union density in the Netherlands and seven other West European
countries, 1900–1990 (union membership as a percentage of the total number of
employees, percent)

|             | 1870  | 1900  | 1914 | 1925 | 1938 | 1950 | 1963 | 1975 | 1990 |
|-------------|-------|-------|------|------|------|------|------|------|------|
| Netherlands | < 1   | < 5   | 16.2 | 23.0 | 31.1 | 42.3 | 42.1 | 38.0 | 24.0 |
| Belgium     | 3.6   | 4.8   | 11.2 | 30.8 | 37.0 | 59.0 | 64.8 | 75.2 | 62.0 |
| Germany     | 0.6   | 3.8   | 17.2 | 28.4 | –    | 34.6 | 37.2 | 34.9 | 32.0 |
| UK          | 11.3  | 16.5  | 26.9 | 31.8 | 36.9 | 45.4 | 48.5 | 56.4 | 43.0 |
| France      | 0.3   | 5.0   | 3.5  | 7.6  | 33.7 | 23.9 | 20.7 | 22.8 | 8.0  |
| Denmark     | 1.8   | 12.3  | 19.7 | 36.0 | 38.1 | 53.5 | 64.7 | 75.5 | 82.0 |
| Sweden      | –     | 3.6   | 12.5 | 31.0 | 55.1 | 65.5 | 74.3 | 84.8 | 83.0 |
| Norway      | –     | 3.9   | 13.8 | 20.1 | 57.3 | 56.7 | 56.7 | 72.0 | 61.0 |

*Source*: Crouch (1993)

These were years of relatively easy progress: prices were rising rapidly
as were profits, and with some show of force the trade unions could realize
major wage rises. This enhanced their status and led to an increase in
membership (Kuijpers and Schrage 1992). Moreover, in 1915 the government came to the rescue of the unemployment insurance schemes that had
been set up by the unions; the resulting government subsidies made it quite
attractive to become a member.

The rapid expansion of the number of collective wage agreements (CAO) during these years was sometimes also favoured by the employers' organizations (that had come into existence in 1901). When such an agreement was implemented in all companies in a certain branch it led to the uniformization of labour conditions and put an end to 'unfair' competition in this respect. In some industries, i.e. printing, brick production, employers' organizations were not sufficiently strong to force their members to implement the CAO and to reduce cut-throat competition. Trade unions had to do the job, assisted by the larger more efficient companies and in effect they thereby 'regulated' competition within the industry. The very first successful modern union, the ANDB of 1896, owed its existence to a comparable situation (Van Tijn 1974, 1976).

The gradual acceptance of the CAO as a means to regulate and make uniform labour conditions in industry was also encouraged by Catholic ideas about a corporatist restructuring of society. In 1919 a High Council of Labour was established to serve as a permanent point of contact between the government, organized labour, and employers' organizations (Windmuller 1969: 63). One of its principal aims was to clarify the legal status of collective wage agreements. In 1927, after long negotiations, the resulting law was approved by parliament. A crucial extension followed in 1937 when the government (i.e. the Minister for Social Affairs) obtained the right to approve the agreements and extend them to all firms in a given industry, or to nullify them when it would be contradictory to 'the public interest' (Windmuller 1969: 74–8). The detailed government intervention in certain industries during the Great Depression had made this extension necessary. Thus, although the trade unions were generally on the defensive during the two decades of deflation after 1920, the number of collective wage agreements gradually increased, and their role in wage bargaining became more and more accepted.

One of the big questions about the role of the trade unions is whether their rise led to a decline in wage flexibility, which could result in unemployment. Following the classic study of H.G. Lewis (1963) many authors have tried to estimate the effects of unions on wage formation by comparing the development and level of wages of unionized and non-unionized industries. Lewis, for example, showed that in periods of deflation, i.e. during the 1930s, wages in unionized industries declined far less than in the rest of the economy. By comparing wage formation before and after World War I we can get an idea of the impact of the unions on wage bargaining in the Netherlands. The first thing to note, however, is that wages have always been rather sticky. One of the most famous examples is probably that nominal wages in the western part of the Netherlands remained the same between about 1640 and 1850 despite large fluctuations in the cost of living and the level of employment (De Vries and Van der Woude 1995: 706).

Ship carpenters who went on strike for the first time in 1869 complained that their wages had not been altered since 1664.

This extreme inflexibility disappeared in the second half of the nineteenth century, but the relationship between prices (i.e. the cost of living) and wages remained loose. For example, the (agricultural) depression of the 1880s saw a strong increase in real wages, the effect of falling food prices. On the other hand, during the big growth spurt in the two decades before 1914, nominal wages hardly kept pace with prices (Van der Veen and Van Zanden 1989). Money illusion seems to offer the best explanation for these 'perverse' trends in real wages. In other words, employers and employees believed that in the long run prices were stable, a proposition that was not completely out of line with the long-term development of the price level in the nineteenth century.

The inflationary boom of World War I made an end to this 'money illusion'. Changes in the price level began to play a large role in wage bargaining (Kuijpers and Schrage 1992). The introduction by the Amsterdam Bureau of Statistics in 1917 of an index number of the cost of living, which gave an exact measure of the change in the price level, certainly helped the unions in this respect. As a result, after World War I changes in the price level became a major determinant of wage formation. The inflationary boom and the much increased role of the unions in a way led to more (upward) flexibility and a greater conformity to market forces.

The Depression of the 1930s makes it possible to have a closer look at the effects of unionism on wage formation. Economic policies after 1931 focused to an important degree on the lowering of prices and wages in order to restore international competitiveness (see Chapter 7). Naturally, trade unions tried to resist those pressures. In 1930 and 1931 they were rather successful and real wages went up rapidly (Table 5.3). After 1931, however, nominal wages began to decline fairly quickly, even more than the ongoing decline in the cost of living. The sharp rise in unemployment during these years helps to explain the fall in nominal wages.

The fact that the 'real product wage' sharply increased during the early 1930s and remained on a high level until the end of 1936 should largely be explained out of rigidities in the structure of prices. Between 1929 and 1935 nominal wages and the cost of living fell by almost the same percentage (Table 5.3), but the 'real product wage' increased sharply because industrial output prices fell much more than the cost of living. Sticky rents, increased margins in retail trade, and agricultural prices that were kept at an artificially high level largely explain the discrepancy (Keesing 1947: 111–12, 171–2). The fall in the 'real product wage' (and the return of profitability in industry) only occurred after devaluation of the guilder in 1936.

The 'real' test of the bargaining power of the unions is probably what happened to wages in unionized industries compared with those in non-unionized sectors. However, such a clear dichotomy did not exist in the

*Table 5.3* Wages and prices in the 1930s (indices, 1926–1930 = 100)

|  | Nominal wages | Cost of living | Real wages | Output prices | Real 'product' wages |
|---|---|---|---|---|---|
| 1929 | 102 | 101 | 101 | 99 | 103 |
| 1930 | 104 | 97 | 107 | 93 | 111 |
| 1931 | 102 | 91 | 112 | 84 | 122 |
| 1932 | 95 | 85 | 112 | 73 | 130 |
| 1933 | 91 | 84 | 109 | 70 | 129 |
| 1934 | 88 | 84 | 105 | 68 | 129 |
| 1935 | 85 | 81 | 105 | 67 | 128 |
| 1936 | 83[a] | 77 | 107 | 66[a] | 125[a] |
| 1937 | 84 | 82 | 103 | 79 | 107 |
| 1938 | 88 | 83 | 106 | 76 | 116 |

*Source*: Keesing 1947: 111, 116, 171, 249, 254
[a] Until the devaluation of September that year.

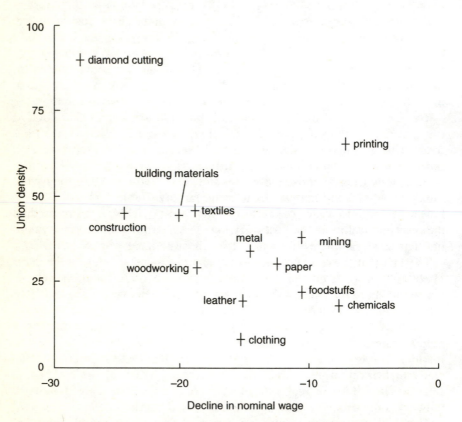

*Graph 5.2* Decline in nominal wages between 1930 and 1935 and union density in 1930 in thirteen industries
*Sources*: Rijksverzekeringsbank 1935; CBS 1935

78

Netherlands. Rates of unionization in 1930 varied from 100 percent (in diamond cutting) to about 10 percent (in the clothing industry), but in most industries it hovered somewhere between 20 and 40 percent. As an alternative to measuring the 'union/non-union wage differential' I have tried to find a relationship between the level of unionization and the development of nominal wages during the first half of the 1930s. The result (Graph 5.2) presents us with a paradox: in the highly unionized diamond cutting industry wages declined much more than in clothing or chemicals. In general, there seems to be a negative correlation between unionization and wage rises, which is certainly unexpected. A few extreme values lend themselves to interpretation. The Depression was particularly intense in diamond cutting, an export industry largely working for the American market. The printing industry may be the one example of strong positive effects of unionization, as it had a closed shop system (and as a sheltered industry it was better insulated from the vagaries of the world market). But in general this comparison suggests that the existence of unions and collective bargaining, which was closely connected with the degree of unionization, probably made it easier for employers to enforce wage reductions. This striking result helps to explain why the system of collective wage bargaining could count on growing support by the government during the 1930s.

## GUIDED WAGE POLICY AND THE CENTRALIZATION OF WAGE BARGAINING

In many ways the famous guided wage policy that was introduced in 1945 was an extension of the system of collective wage bargaining of the interwar period. An equally important 'input' into the new system was the experience of the German occupation, which 'created the psychological basis for agreement on the forms and spirit of institutionalized cooperation in the postwar period' (Windmuller 1969: 90). The most concrete example of this was the establishment of the Stichting van de Arbeid (Labour Foundation) as a result of secret negotiations between representatives of the three federations of trade unions and employers' organizations during the war. The aim of this new institution was to lay a solid basis for cooperation between unions and employers after the war (Van Bottenburg 1995).

The legal basis of the guided wage policy that was introduced after the war was the Extraordinary Decree on Labour Relations of October 1945. It reinstated a special *College van Rijksbemiddelaren* (Board of Mediators) which had the right to intervene in almost every aspect of wage bargaining and had to approve all collective bargaining agreements. Moreover, it increased workers' rights; for example, it improved legal protection against dismissal (Windmuller and De Galan 1970, II: 9 ff).

Between 1945 and 1963 wage bargaining was a highly centralized process. The first step was a directive issued by the Minister for Social Affairs on the permitted wage increase during a particular year. Naturally, before he could do so he had to consult unions and employers' organizations, united in the Stichting van de Arbeid. On this basis wage bargaining in industries and big companies was started; the resulting CAOs had to be approved by the College van Rijksbemiddelaars, which could then extend them to all companies in the industry. In theory the Board could also reject a CAO in which case negotiations had to start all over again. However, this did not happen often.

Three phases can be discerned between 1945 and 1963 (Windmuller and De Galan 1979, II: 58 ff). After some initial problems, between 1946 and 1953 wages were generally linked to the increase in the cost of living. At the same time, a minimum wage was introduced and wages of unskilled labourers were increased far more than those of white-collar workers. After 1953 the rise in labour productivity (and in GDP per capita) also began to determine the permitted wage increases. The aim of wage policy became to keep the share of wages in national income at a constant level. In 1959 there began experiments to decentralize wage bargaining by linking wages to the rise in labour productivity in the various sectors of the economy. These experiments more or less prepared the way for the official dissolution of the guided wage policy in 1963 (see next section).

The introduction of the guided wage policy led to a strong centralization in wage bargaining and to the official recognition of the trade unions as the representatives of the workers. In some industries, for example, cotton, resistance against the (socialist) trade unions had remained strong, even in the 1930s. This resistance disappeared because it was now included in the formalized structure of wage bargaining. In this way the guided wage policy strengthened the position of the trade unions; especially the role of the national federations, which were already relatively strong, was greatly enhanced by the establishment of a national framework for wage bargaining. The share of the dependent labour force for which a CAO was concluded by the unions rose from 12.6 percent just before the war to more than 50 percent in the 1950s (Table 5.1).

At the same time union membership rose (Graph 5.1) and the unions became generally accepted as 'social partners' which were (held) responsible for economic development and the growth of employment together with the employers' organizations and the government. Until 1958 the Department of Social Affairs was invariably headed by a member of the Labour Party, who worked closely with the unions to improve labour conditions and extend welfare schemes.

The centralist tendency in the new system is clear from data on the number of collective bargaining agreements, which declined enormously during the 1940s, whereas the numbers of workers involved expanded rapidly (Table 5.1). Before 1940 an average CAO would regulate labour conditions for about 220 to 280 workers (and this average was slowly falling); most of the CAOs were concluded with individual companies and only a few related to national industries. Between 1940 and 1947 company-wide agreements almost disappeared and were replaced by regional and, during the 1950s, national CAOs. The average number of employees covered jumped to almost 2,500 in 1947 and continued to grow thereafter.

As a result of this development, the wage structure became much more transparent, which must have lowered transaction costs. However, in the process it also lost much of its previous flexibility. The strong levelling tendencies of these measures on regional wage variations have already been sketched in Chapter 2. In the same period wage differences between industries also became much smaller, as did wage disparities between blue-collar and white-collar workers (Weststrate 1959).

The control of the implementation of the directives of the Minister for Social Affairs by the College van Rijksbemiddelaars made it necessary for wage agreements to become very detailed, specifying and regulating all aspects of labour conditions. Of course, much was done to circumvent the detailed guidelines of the Minister. New wage systems (i.e. piece rates instead of hourly rates) and new systems of work classification were introduced with the hidden aim of raising pay beyond the limits set by the government. Especially during the 1950s, when the economy boomed and the demand for labour exploded, wage drift became a nearly universal phenomenon, which was particularly strong in the most rapidly growing industries and regions (Windmuller and De Galan 1979: II, 104–6). Yet these 'destabilizing' forces started from a wage structure which was changed radically during the 1940s and operated within a system largely governed by the collective wage bargaining between unions and employers' organizations.

The preceding makes it clear why the trade unions were cooperating with a system aimed at controlling the increase in wages. It was already noticed that this greatly strengthened the position of the unions and especially of the national federations. This also helps to explain the structural changes that occurred in labour relations in general. During the first quarter of the century strikes had been a rather common element of labour relations, although strike intensity was never as high as in neighbouring countries (Germany, Britain or Belgium) (see Flora 1981: 354–6; Albeda and Dercksen 1985: 155 ff). During the 1920s and 1930s the number and magnitude of strikes had already decreased markedly. The longest and most bitter conflicts were concentrated in a few industries in which employers did not want to recognize the unions as the representatives of labour (Alberts *et al*. 1982).

However, this source of conflict disappeared after 1945. Especially after

1948, when the 'threat' of the communist trade union was contained, strikes became very rare indeed. The communist-led EVC (Eenheidsvak-centrale), which had been set up during the war, was not allowed to participate in the new framework of centralized wage negotiations. It resisted the new policies, but after having lost a number of strikes it quickly lost membership. Moreover, for the other unions to go on strike after 1945 they had to disagree with the directives of 'their own' Minister for Social Affairs, who had set the limits to wage bargaining. Any strike therefore became political and would undermine cooperation with the government and the employers' organizations.

Of course, labour conflicts did not disappear, but often had to take the form of wildcat strikes. Whereas before 1940 only about 20 percent of the strikes were not organized by the unions, this share rose from 50 percent to 80 percent after World War II (Albeda and Dercksen 1985: 168). Lacking support by the unions, which worked closely together, these strikes soon ended and were mostly unsuccessful. As a result after 1948 the Netherlands became a showcase of almost completely appeased labour relations.

The big question is of course how successful these policies were in keeping down the wage level. This issue will be returned to in Chapter 8 in an attempt to show that between 1945 and 1953 wage policy and the closely related price policy succeeded in improving the competitiveness of Dutch industry. After 1953 the labour market became so tight that things were increasingly running out of hand, and after 1959 the guided wage policy had become largely ineffective. But the initial success has been instrumental in creating a very favourable environment for economic growth during the 1950s.

In another way the new system would affect wage bargaining in the long run. The inflationary boom of World War I had led to the inclusion of changes in the cost of living in wage determination; changes in labour productivity, however, did not yet enter into the wage formation process. This changed after 1953, when economic growth became one of the bases for the permitted wage increase. Labour productivity became one of the determinants of wage formation (see Van Hulst 1984: 231 ff). The effects that this had on wages during the 1960s and 1970s will be the subject of the next section.

## FROM THE GUIDED WAGE POLICY TO 'WAGE LEADERSHIP'

During the 1950s pressure built up on the guided wage policy. Employers in a number of branches – especially in construction and the metal industry – complained that they were not allowed to raise wages to attract the workers they needed. This put the unions in an awkward position, because they were confronted by employers who were prepared to pay (much) more. It resulted in wage drift, an increase in wages larger than the raise laid down in the CAO, which undermined collective wage bargaining. Already in 1955 a number of socialist unions were dissatisfied with the meagre results of centralized bargaining. They demanded more freedom to get better deals for their members. But the national federation (NVV), whose role was greatly enhanced by the new system, was able to suppress these demands (Windmuller and De Galan 1979: II, 70). In politics, the Labour Party remained faithful to the guided wage policy, but the other parties gradually began to move away from it.

In 1959, when the Labour Party did not participate in the coalition government for the first time since the war, attempts were made to reform the policy. The new directive of the Minister for Social Affairs stated that the increase in labour productivity in the relevant sector should be the basis for wage rises (Windmuller and De Galan 1979: II, 72 ff). In practice it was, however, difficult to measure productivity, which made it almost impossible for the College van Rijksbemiddelaars to monitor the implementation of the new directive. It was almost forced to become very compliant because there were often sound reasons to agree on a substantial wage rise.

In the same year the new system was put to a test. In the first CAO concluded under the new directive a large increase of 5 percent was agreed upon in the metal industry, which was more or less in line with the estimated increase in labour productivity. In construction, where labour productivity grew much more slowly, the same increase was proposed. The College van Rijksbemiddelaars decided to approve this second CAO as well, on condition that the price of buildings would not be increased. This was unacceptable for the employers, who decided to withdraw from collective bargaining, a step unheard of in the afterwar period. In their turn, the unions called for a strike, which became one of the biggest of the afterwar period (it lasted for two weeks). The government found a way out of the conflict by announcing an official price stop for construction (that was, however, almost impossible to control), which forced the employers to accept the CAO (Windmuller and De Galan 1979: II, 74–6).

The events of 1959–60 are characteristic for the new system of wage formation that came into existence in the 1960s. In theory attempts to decentralize wage bargaining by allowing for inter-industry differences in the growth of productivity could solve some of the problems of the strongly centralized system of the 1950s. But this solution did not take into account the high degree of centralization and coordination of the trade unions. The new system that arose has been called one of 'wage leadership' (Driehuis 1975) and was based on the strong position of the unions. Wage bargaining usually began in a sector in which growth was strong and labour productivity rose rapidly; in this respect the metal industry was the unions' favourite. The nice result of bargaining in this 'wage leader' was then used as a starting point of negotiations in the rest of the economy. Once the trend was set by the new CAO in the metal industry, the unions usually succeeded in achieving an (almost) comparable wage rise in the other sectors. In order to compensate for the rise in wage costs, employers in other industries and services therefore had to increase their prices, just as employers in construction had wanted to do in 1960. As a result, the new system was highly inflationary. Branches of industry which had to compete internationally and were unable to pass their rising wage costs on to their costumers, such as textiles, clothing or leatherware, were the primary victims of the new system (see Chapter 8).

In practice the new system of wage negotiations did not result in larger wage disparities between industries. They even declined slightly during the 1960s and 1970s. The wage explosion that followed in the first years of the new decade brought about the official abolishment of the moribund guided wage policy in 1963. But the strong centralized forces in wage bargaining remained a feature of wage formation. During the 1950s and 1960s collective bargaining agreements were also extended to the service sector where they had not traditionally been found. As a result the labour conditions of almost the entire dependent labour force became regulated by a CAO (Korver 1993). A number of times the government tried to stem the inflationary tide by issuing new directives on the permitted increase in wages, but these attempts to return to the guided wage policy of the 1950s were largely unsuccessful (Van Hulst 1984). Regular meetings between the government, the unions, and the employers' organizations in the framework of the Stichting van de Arbeid, where wage bargaining and its results were discussed, became part of the yearly political ritual. Yet not until the 1980s would these meetings meet again with success.

## THE RISE IN UNEMPLOYMENT 1973–1983

The story of the changes on the labour market during the twenty years after 1973 is quite complex. The decline in employment in industry is perhaps the most fundamental process. It generated unemployment and a fall in union membership, which in the long run undermined the position of the unions. There is, however, a more positive side to this story: the de-pillarization of the 1960s and 1970s brought along a revolution in female work participation. The strong increase in the supply of (part-time) labour was matched by growing employment in a number of branches of services. Moreover, attempts to restrain the increase in wage levels became highly successful after 1982, and this combination of forces – an increasingly flexible supply of low-wage (female) labour and wage restraints – created the Dutch version of the American 'job machine' (Kloosterman and Elfring 1991).

We should first turn to the rise of unemployment. Official unemployment statistics for the 1970s and 1980s are a mess. At present three different statistics are available and only one, with the most unreliable and highest estimates, goes back to the period before 1988 (Hartog and Theeuwes 1993: 5–8). However, even these high estimates tend to underestimate the 'true' rate of unemployment, because a sizeable part of the people who benefit from early retirement schemes or disability pensions are probably 'hidden' unemployed. There is, however, some consensus that already in the years after 1967 unemployment slowly began to rise, in spite of the substantial growth of GDP. Like elsewhere, the growth of unemployment accelerated after 1973, stabilized during the second half of the 1970s, and showed an enormous increase during the 'second oil crisis' of 1979 to 1983. In fact, the Dutch 'peak' of unemployment was much steeper than in the EEC as a whole, but after 1984 decline set in rather early compared with the other EEC countries (Hartog and Theeuwes 1993: 2–3).

In order to explain the huge increase in unemployment – from about 1 percent in the early 1960s to almost 12 percent in 1983–4 according to the OECD statistics – some attention has to be paid to its different causes. The theoretical literature, which proliferated in the 1980s, distinguished between three kinds of unemployment: frictional, structural, and cyclical.

Frictional unemployment is related to the efficiency of the labour market: how well do supply and demand match? A number of studies has shown a strong growth of frictional unemployment after 1967, which has raised a variety of issues related to the efficiency of the Dutch labour market (Driehuis and Zwan 1978; Hartog and Theeuwes 1993: 57 ff). According to one estimate it increased from 1.3 percent in 1960 to 3.3 percent in 1983 (CPB 1986: 113), which indicates that employees need much more time to find a new job independent of the level of unemployment. Two forces are probably behind the decreased efficiency of the labour market. The first one is that the relatively generous allowances of the welfare state made it possible to take more time to select a job. Although attempts to quantify the effect of the welfare state on the duration of unemployment have not always shown clear results, it probably was of some importance (Hartog and Theeuwes 1993: 70–1).

The second force behind the rise in unemployment concerns more fundamental changes in the labour market, which deserve some attention. Historically, until the early 1960s the most important change in the structure of the labour force has been the decline of agriculture and the rise of industry as the main sources of employment. This meant that largely unskilled labourers from agriculture had to find employment in industry, which did not create huge matching problems. However, after 1967 employment in industry began to decline, whereas employment tended to increase in the service sector. The structure of this growing demand, however, was very different from the 'new' supply of former industrial workers. The labour market of the new service industries was basically bimodal: demand grew relatively rapidly for highly educated personnel (in government, business services and health care) and for largely unskilled work in all kinds of personal service (leisure, catering, etc.) (see next section). Both segments were captured by different groups of new entrants to the labour market. Highly skilled professionals with a university degree or higher secondary education dominated the first segment; female part-time labourers and new entrants with only basic eduation filled the ranks of the second segment. There were however few new jobs for skilled industrial workers. Moreover, everyone knew or sensed this problem and these particular workers were often retired (very) early or became beneficiaries of the disability scheme.

Finally, the educational profile of the labour force changed dramatically between 1960 and 1987 (see Table 5.4), which probably contributed to the matching problems on the labour market. This rise in the level of education can be interpreted as an increase in specialization: the unskilled worker with only basic education can perform much more varied jobs in agriculture, industry, or services than the physician or lawyer who leaves university. Unemployment among academics became a normal feature of the labour market in the 1980s and the highly specialized unemployed were allowed to seek 'suitable labour' (*passende arbeid*), labour that fitted their level of education and employment record. Note that in the 1930s labour force agencies were much harsher: it was almost proverbial for the intensity of the 'Great Depression' that university engineers had to work as tram conductors.

These developments were fundamental to the significant changes in the functioning of the labour market. A large part of the debate on the causes of unemployment in the 1970s and 1980s was, however, about the relative importance of structural versus cyclical unemployment. The basic idea behind this distinction was that a number of supply-side forces − basically the strong rise in real wages and the concomitant decrease in profitability − reduced productive capacity during the 1970s and early 1980s, which resulted in a slack demand for labour (Den Hartog and Tjan 1974, 1976). This reduction in capacity caused 'structural' unemployment. Investments were needed to increase capacity; the related employment and these investments were in turn dependent on the profitability of industry. On the other

*Table 5.4* Educational distribution of the Dutch labour force, 1960, 1971, 1987 (percent)

| Workers with: | 1960 | 1971 | 1987 |
| --- | --- | --- | --- |
| Only basic education | 56 | 40 | 17 |
| Lower intermediate education | 33 | 40 | 23 |
| Upper intermediate education | 7 | 12 | 40 |
| Higher education | 3 | 9 | 21 |
| Total | 99 | 101 | 101 |

*Source*: Van Ark and De Jong 1996: 224

86

hand, fluctuations in demand – the downturn after 1973 and again after 1979 – were the cause of 'cyclical' unemployment, a Keynesian phenomenon. In theory cyclical unemployment can be solved by expanding demand, for example, by increasing the budget deficit (which was the policy of the Den Uyl government during the downturn of 1974–5). However, such a policy did not solve structural unemployment. It would probably increase the supply-side problems, since an increase in government spending tends to lower profitability in the private sector.

The bottom line of this interpretation of the source of unemployment in the 1970s and 1980s, which was put forward by the Central Planning Bureau, was that it was caused largely by the excessive increase in wage levels during the 1960s and 1970s. Wages had to go down in order to solve unemployment. One of the problems was that wages in the Netherlands did not seem to react strongly to the increase in unemployment (Grubb *et al.* 1983). This wage rigidity was a rather recent phenomenon. Between 1953 and 1973 an increase in unemployment of 1 percent led to a reduction in the growth of wages by about 0.9 percent, but this measure of wage rigidity declined to about 0.3 percent in the period 1973 to 1985. One explanation is afforded by the concept of hysteresis: as a result of the duration of unemployment a large part of the unemployed does not really compete on the labour market. They do not apply for jobs or are not considered viable candidates when they do (Hartog and Theeuwes 1993: 65–6). Again the allowances of the welfare system make it possible for this situation to persist. The share of people who have been unemployed for more than one year increased from less than 10 percent in 1970 to more than 50 percent in 1985. What contributes to the problem is that this 'hard core' of unemployed is concentrated in the big cities and among the allochthonous population (Kloosterman 1994).

In short, the causes of unemployment in the years after 1973 were highly different from those in the 1930s, when it was largely the result of a huge decline in demand. Structural unemployment, according to the tale told by the CPB, caused by the high level of real wages and increased friction on the labour market, probably related to the growth of the welfare state and to structural changes in the labour market; this was much more important than cyclical employment, caused by demand related forces. This diagnosis, which was more or less accepted by all parties involved – the major political parties, the unions, and the employers' organizations – prepared the way for concerted action aimed at reducing unemployment.

## WAGE RESTRAINT AND THE DUTCH 'JOB MACHINE'

In the early 1980s the trade unions became increasingly sensitive to the appeal for wage restraint by the CPB and successive governments. One of the reasons was that they were quickly losing members as a result of the decline in industrial employment. The most 'radical' federation, the FNV (formed in 1976 as a result of a merger of the socialist and Catholic federations), lost almost 200,000 members between 1980 and 1985 due to the closure of industries in which the socialist and Catholic unions had traditionally been strong, such as shipbuilding and textiles. Moreover, the position of the unions had been weakened by the extension of the welfare state in the preceding decades. Before 1940 unions had been very active in the field of social security, but this had been completely replaced by the state. As a result of deindustrialization and the loss of these functions union density fell by about 10 percent in the 1980s (see Graph 5.1). Moreover, the enormous increase in unemployment put a lot of pressure on the unions to moderate their demands.

The General Agreement of 1982 between the government, the unions and the employers' organizations is often cited as the beginning of a new phase of wage restraint (Hartog and Theeuwes 1993: 38). Its essence was that employers would reduce working hours from 40 to 38 hours per week and that in return unions would moderate their claims for wage rises for a number of years. Finally, the government promised not to intervene any longer in wage bargaining as it had done unsuccessfully in the late 1970s. The unions hoped to reduce unemployment by sharing the existing jobs through the reduction in working hours, but after a couple of years it became increasingly clear that the effects of this policy were quite small. Wage restraint was, however, very effective, and during the 1980s and early 1990s real wages in the Netherlands grew much less than in most other EEC countries (see Chapter 9).

Government policies to increase flexibility in the labour market and lower wage costs added to the success of wage restraint. After the forced increase in minimum wages in the 1970s the minimum wage was lowered in 1984 and held constant for another four years (a typically Dutch compromise slowly to lower its real value) (CBS 1994). The benefits of the various social insurance schemes were decreased step by step, and tax incentives were introduced to stimulate employment among unskilled workers at the minimum wage level.

Wage restraint has once again become one of the ingredients of Dutch economic 'success' during the 1980s and early 1990s. Changes in the supply of labour were another ingredient. De-pillarization and women's emancipation caused an upsurge in the supply of female labour in the 1970s and 1980s. The female participation ratio (the part of the female population in the age group of 15 to 64 years that was employed) had been as low as 20 to 26 percent in the 1950s and 1960s but increased spectacularly to about 51 percent in 1989 (Hartog and Theeuwes 1993: 12). The custom that after marriage women withdrew to household activities rapidly disappeared and many married women re-entered the labour market (Kloosterman and Elfring 1991: 154–5). However, the institutional setting

*Table 5.5* Structure of employment in the 1980s (thousands of employees)

|  | 1979 | 1990 | Diff. |
|---|---|---|---|
| Agriculture | 250 | 258 | 8 |
| Industry | 1,612 | 1,441 | −171 |
| Business services | 454 | 663 | 209 |
| Distributive services | 1,055 | 1,232 | 177 |
| Personal services | 329 | 391 | 62 |
| Collective services | 1,274 | 1,564 | 290 |
| Total services | 3,112 | 3,850 | 738 |
| Other* | · 48 | 120 | 72 |
| Total | 5,022 | 5,669 | 647 |

*Source*: Kloosterman and Elfring 1991: 81, 101
* Personnel working through temping agencies which cannot be allocated to one of the sectors.

was not conducive to this change; nursuries were either non-existent or very expensive, schools supposed that a parent would be permanently at home, etc. This implied that many women tended to work part-time and even among men part-time work made some progress.

The total labour force grew much less as a result of a decline in male labour participation (from 98 percent in 1960 to 80 percent in 1989). However, compared to other European countries, the Dutch labour force grew rapidly as a result of the rise in female participation.

Fortunately, after the big decline in employment in the early 1980s, the demand for labour began to grow quite rapidly. Kloosterman and Elfring (1991) have analysed the Dutch job machine in more detail (see Table 5.5). They show that employment in industry and agriculture stopped falling, which was already a major achievement, and that the big growth of employment was in services. Notably, business services expanded rapidly; hotel and catering (which was mainly responsible for the growth of employment in personal services) and the retail trade were other growth industries. In collective services the share of government employment fell – the result of strong pressures to reduce the budget deficit – but education and health care continued to expand. By far the biggest increase occurred in labour employed by temping agencies, which have contributed much to the increase in flexibility on the labour market.

According to Kloosterman and Elfring (1991) the Dutch job machine was rather similar to the American one, where almost the same 'growth industries' have been identified. However, the structure of new employment was quite different from the 'traditional' one of industrial employment, as Table 5.6 shows. Most of the employment growth was in low-wage jobs; the 'McDonald's (or hamburger) economy' (i.e. all kinds of low-wage catering and leisure activities) expanded rapidly. Another source of employment growth was highly skilled jobs in business services (lawyers, accountants,

*Table 5.6* Structure of employment in the 1980s according to wage classes (percent)

|  | Industry | | Services | |
| --- | --- | --- | --- | --- |
|  | *1979* | *1988* | *1979* | *1988* |
| Low wages | 21 | 22 | 27 | 35 |
| Medium wages | 60 | 54 | 44 | 44 |
| High wages | 19 | 24 | 29 | 21 |

*Source*: Kloosterman and Elfring, 1991: 149

software designers, etc.) and health care. But the broad 'middle class' of skilled labourers, which had dominated employment in industry, underwent a relative decline and until the middle of the 1980s it even fell in absolute terms. These workers had great difficulty in finding new employment opportunities.

These changes have a major impact on Dutch society and politics in the 1990s. In general the degree of polarization within Dutch society is gradually increasing, moving slowly in the direction of the American 'model'. Moreover, these processes have undermined the position of the trade unions, which are weak in the lower segments of the labour market (of the 'hamburger economy' and the temping agencies, where a large part of the young and the part-time (female) labour force is employed), but are also underrepresented in the highest segments (for example, business services). However, institutional rigidities have so far prevented radical changes in the position of the unions in wage bargaining; almost 100 percent of the wage-dependent labour force is still covered by a CAO (Korver 1993). The major outcome of these changes in the position of the union is a tendency to decentralize wage bargaining; for example, the number of companywide agreements has increased (Table 5.2). In wage bargaining the unions have to pay much more attention to the specific problems of the relevant industry, but this has not led to large increases in wage disparities between industries. The legacy of the centralized system of wage bargaining of the past still seems to be quite strong.

# 6

# THE BEST OF BOTH WORLDS: CATCHING UP 1914–1929

## MACROECONOMIC PERFORMANCE

The decision of the German army to respect the neutrality of the Netherlands – because it might need the country for the supply of goods – in a way determined Dutch (economic) development in the fifteen years before the Great Depression. During the war large parts of the Dutch economy benefited from the neutral status. Agriculture and international trade (which supplied the Germans with many goods in spite of the Allied blockade) and large parts of industry were able to reap substantial war profits. Once peace was established in 1918 the bonus was probably even larger, because industry was eager to supply war damaged Europe with all the goods it needed. As a result the Dutch economy made great progress during the period 1914 to 1921, certainly in comparison with its neighbours (Van der Bie 1995: 85). Moreover, the return to a 'peacetime economy' was relatively successful. Whereas most neutral countries found it difficult to adapt to the postwar economy and were confronted in the 1920s with the backlash effects of overexpansion during the 1910s, the Netherlands fared relatively well. For a number of reasons the international downturn of 1921–3 did not do much damage to the Dutch economy; only banking went through a major crisis. The boom that followed after 1923 was in many ways a continuation of the industrialization process that had started in the second half of the nineteenth century.

Recent work on the national accounts for World War I and the interwar period make it possible to analyse the economic growth in more detail (see Table 6.1). During World War I growth was more rapid than in Western Europe, and especially GDP per hour worked increased markedly (as a result of the official reduction of working hours to 8 hours per day in 1919). As Ronald van der Bie (1995) has shown, Dutch economic growth was even faster than in other neutral countries, such as the Scandinavian nations and Switzerland. In fact, the Netherlands was probably the only European country in which per capita income and production per hour worked increased between 1913 and 1921 (Van der Bie 1995: 85 ff).

*Table 6.1* Growth of GDP in the Netherlands and North West Europe, 1913–1929
(growth rates)

|  | GDP | | GDP per head | | GDP per hour | |
|---|---|---|---|---|---|---|
|  | *Neth.* | *NW Eur.* | *Neth.* | *NW Eur.* | *Neth.* | *NW Eur.* |
| 1913–21 | 2.10 | −0.43 | 0.64 | −1.04 | 2.78 | – |
| 1921–29 | 4.69 | 4.83 | 3.17 | 3.95 | 3.14 | – |
| 1913–29 | 3.39 | 2.16 | 1.92 | 1.42 | 3.79 | 2.14 |

*Source*: Van Ark and De Jong 1996: 201

During the 1920s growth rates were quite spectacular and higher than ever before. In the second half of the nineteenth century growth rates of GDP were about 2 percent on average and seldom surpassed the 4 percent mark for more than two or three years in a row (Maddison 1995). The growth spurt of the 1920s was an international phenomenon. The smaller European countries did especially well in these years. For most belligerents (Germany, Belgium, France) rapid growth was the result of recovery from the low levels of 1918–19, but most neutral countries had a comparably strong performance. Because the international literature is heavily dominated by the countries that fared worst – Britain in particular – the 'growth spurt' of the 1920s has not received the attention it deserves. It can be shown that the economic growth of these years links the industrialization process of the nineteenth century with the 'golden years' between 1950 and 1973.

One way to try and explain economic growth is by means of 'growth accounting'; that is, by analysing to what extent the change in GDP can be attributed to the increase in the various inputs (labour, capital) and to the 'residual' or 'unexplained' part of growth which remains after the contributions of the inputs have been subtracted. Such an exercise is put forward in Table 6.2. For comparative purposes, the growth accounting estimates for the final years of the nineteenth century and for the 'golden years' after World War II are also included. It turns out that growth during World War I can easily be explained from the growth of inputs (and the decrease in working hours). Total factor productivity even declined a little. However, the 1920s saw a strong growth in total factor productivity, which compares well with the increase in the residual during the golden years after 1947. The difference with growth before World War I is also quite clear: growth rates were much lower before 1913 and the increase in total factor productivity was relatively small. Viewed from this perspective the performance of the Dutch economy during the 1920s was similar to that of the 'golden years' after 1947.

Other indicators of macroeconomic performance also show a rather favourable picture. Notwithstanding peaks in 1915 and again in the early 1920s, unemployment was relatively low (Van der Bie 1995). Maddison

*Table 6.2* Growth accounting for the interwar period compared with the preceding and following periods (growth rates of GDP, inputs, and the residual), 1850–1973

|  | GDP | Persons employed | Hours per person | School. per person | Capital stock | R&D stock | Total factor productivity (residual) |
|---|---|---|---|---|---|---|---|
| 1850–1913 | 2.05 | 1.03 | −0.20 | 0.65 | 2.37 | – | 0.26 |
| 1913–1921 | 2.10 | 1.12 | −1.76 | 0.64 | 4.58 | 7.29 | −0.16 |
| 1921–1929 | 4.69 | 1.51 | 0.00 | 0.64 | 2.48 | 6.38 | 2.23 |
| 1929–1938 | 0.33 | 0.14 | −0.08 | 0.64 | 2.72 | 8.56 | −1.50 |
| 1938–1947 | 0.72 | 2.07 | −0.18 | 0.64 | −0.67 | 3.10 | −0.86 |
| 1947–1973 | 5.07 | 1.51 | −0.89 | 0.98 | 4.52 | 4.74 | 2.50 |

*Sources*: 1913–1973: Van Ark and De Jong 1996, except for the data R&D stock: the output of R&D is measured as the number of US patents granted to inhabitants of the Netherlands; the service life of R&D is estimated to be 30 years (source: *Annual Report Patents*, 1880–1993). 1850–1913: the same method was applied, using yet unpublished results of the Dutch national accounts project; capital stock and schooling from Clemens *et al.* 1996

estimated an average unemployment rate for the 1920s of about 2.4 percent, compared with 4.4 percent in North West Europe (Maddison 1991). Recent estimates of Den Bakker and Van Sorge (1996) are higher, but still show that the Netherlands did better than the other neutral countries (as well as Britain), which all had rather high levels of unemployment in these years (a problem which is returned to).

## DEPRESSION AND BOOM DURING WORLD WAR I
## 1914–1921

In many ways World War I struck a hard blow at the Dutch economy. Export markets for Dutch products were disrupted, financial markets were paralyzed and trade flows were blocked. The initial reaction of the economy to the outbreak of the war was therefore one of contraction from which only agriculture seems to have escaped (Table 6.3). In spite of the increased demand for labour as a result of mobilization, unemployment went up rapidly (from a low of about 1 per cent in 1913).

However, conditions changed already in the course of 1915. Financial markets recovered quite quickly; the run on the banks that followed the closure of the Amsterdam Stock Exchange on 28 July 1914 could be stopped by a number of emergency measures of the Central Bank that restored confidence in the guilder and the banking system (De Vries 1989: 61 ff). The suspension of the gold standard was one of these measures. The internal market recovered equally quickly. A large part of foreign competition was suddenly eliminated, which allowed industrialists to (re)capture markets that had been dominated by foreign enterprise before the war. As the war progressed the problem was no longer to find markets outlets, but

93

Table 6.3 Development of GDP of different sectors of the economy and of
unemployment, 1913–1921 (growth rates)

|  | GDP | Agriculture | Industry | Services | Unemployment* |
|---|---|---|---|---|---|
| 1914 | −1.5 | 12.2 | −5.3 | −2.4 | 5.4 |
| 1915 | −4.5 | −3.2 | −11.3 | −2.5 | 6.2 |
| 1916 | −1.3 | 1.4 | −6.3 | 2.4 | 3.0 |
| 1917 | −9.1 | 7.0 | −20.6 | −8.7 | 4.6 |
| 1918 | −4.0 | −14.8 | −16.4 | 2.6 | 5.2 |
| 1919 | 9.1 | −11.4 | 31.4 | 11.8 | 5.8 |
| 1920 | 13.4 | 19.4 | 19.0 | 10.4 | 4.4 |
| 1921 | 18.0 | 1.5 | 26.5 | 18.1 | 7.2 |
| 1913–21 | 2.1 | 0.9 | 0.4 | 3.6 | 4.8 |

Sources: Van der Bie 1995; Knibbe 1993: 292; and unpublished results of the National
Accounts project
* as a percentage of the labour force.

to acquire the inputs (raw materials and coal) needed to keep production
going. This bottleneck created enormous problems after the beginning of
the unrestricted submarine war in 1917, when it became almost impossible
to ship goods into the country. The branches of industry that were most
dependent on imported raw materials – textiles, diamond cutting, paper,
and a large part of the food industry – fared worst, whereas construction,
mining, printing and utilities were still able to expand production (Van der
Bie 1995: 107). On average, output in industry declined sharply during the
war years, and especially in 1917 and 1918, whereas the decline in agriculture and services was much more moderate (Table 6.3). Fluctuations in
agricultural output were also influenced by weather conditions, but also in
this sector the shortages of fertilizers and imported fodder (essential in
livestock farming) caused a moderate downward trend in production.

The sharp contraction in economic activity during the final years of the
war did not result in a huge increase in unemployment. A comparison with
the Depression of the 1930s is illuminating. Between 1913 and 1918 GDP
fell by almost 20 percent, which was twice as severe as the decline of the
1930s (between 1929 and 1934 GDP fell by almost 10 percent) (Den
Bakker et al. 1987). The peak in unemployment in the 1930s was about
19 percent (in 1935–6), whereas it never exceeded 6 percent during World
War I (Van der Bie 1995; Den Bakker and Van Sorge 1996). Labour
hoarding is the best explanation for the low level of unemployment. As a
result of the generally strong increase in demand, the price of products
went up rapidly and profits increased enormously in these years despite a
decline in output (see below). Entrepreneurs therefore had no incentive to
lay off workers, and in a way they invested in their labour force in the
expectation that at the end of the war they would need them to step up
production. Rising prices and stagnating nominal wages caused a decline in

real 'product' wages of about 17 percent between 1913 and 1917 (whereas these increased during the early 1930s), which helps explain the hoarding of labour (Van der Bie 1995: 93). Of course, it brought about a decline in labour productivity, but labour hoarding probably also made possible the unprecedented increase in production in the boom of 1918 to 1921.

The social consequences of the contraction in GDP were therefore much less serious than in the 1930s (but see Kuijpers 1996). Real wages declined as policies to suppress the inflationary tide were not completely successful, but the demand for labour actually increased during the war years (employment in 1918 was 6.4 percent higher than in 1913).

The boom that was unleashed in the final months of 1918 after the German surrender in November was perhaps the most spectacular one in Dutch economic history. Postwar demand for products and capital goods (such as ships) was indeed enormous and Dutch industry was ready to fulfil it. The restoration of the sea routes with Indonesia, among others, led to an enormous growth spurt in international trade, since Europe was craving for coffee, tea, rubber and oil to replenish stocks. Reconstruction demand from Belgium and France was high because both countries supposed that German war reparations could be used to finance it. The shipbuilding industry expanded as it never had done before to rebuild the merchant fleet which had partly been destroyed by the war. The boom was fuelled by monetary financing (see below) and created large external imbalances as the huge increase in investments was not met by an equally strong increase in domestic savings. As a result, there appeared large deficits on the balance of payments and confidence in the guilder declined; its value against the dollar fell by about 30 percent in 1919–20 (Keesing 1947: 20).

In short, the postwar upturn resulted in double-digit growth figures for industry and services, a growth spurt unparalleled in Dutch economic history. The economy gained so much momentum that the downturn of the international economy, which began in the closing months of 1920, almost passed by the Netherlands. The year 1921 was still one of considerable growth, despite an ever sharper fall in prices (Table 6.3). However, one sign of the coming economic problems was the (modest) increase in unemployment (Table 6.3).

The war forced the government to intervene in almost every part of economic and social life, but it was ill-prepared to do so. Two fields were given priority, namely securing the food supply (at reasonable prices) and managing international trade. The first priority made it necessary partially to restructure agriculture. The sector had specialized in livestock farming and horticulture; it produced largely for export markets and was highly dependent on imported foodstuffs and fertilizers. As the war went on, demand from the German market became almost insatiable and prices on the other side of the eastern border were enormously attractive. If trade had been left to itself the strong pull of the German market would have led to an enormous increase in prices and a strong fall in domestic consumption. Moreover, the mounting problems with imports of bread grains and fodder made it necessary to step up production and expand arable agriculture. As a result, the distribution of bread grains and other foodstuffs was introduced, the expansion of grain growing was stimulated and exports were limited. These policies were only partly successful, because they had to be introduced in a rush and without proper consideration of their effects on the economy. Moreover, it took a long time to establish a competent bureaucracy able to implement and monitor the policies. Especially in 1914 and 1915 their implementation relied heavily on the voluntary cooperation of communities, merchants and producers, who more often than not could profit from evasion of the rules (Kuijpers 1996). Ill-conceived measures also contributed to the problems. For example, the price of the main foodstuffs was kept at a relatively low level, which induced farmers to concentrate more on unregulated industrial crops (which were exported to Germany). As a result, the acreage devoted to bread grains actually declined between 1914 and 1917 – in spite of attempts to increase domestic food production – which obliged policymakers to introduce compulsory schemes for the breaking up of pasture (Broekema 1920: 300 ff). Through this ad hoc approach and by learning from the many mistakes that were made government intervention into agriculture increased step by step.

Although these measures were not without success, the general impression is that the food and distribution policies were inefficient and at times chaotic, and that small groups of merchants and entrepreneurs (war profiteers) did very well by (evading) them. The solution for the regulation of international trade was probably somewhat more effective. This was a delicate issue for a neutral country such as the Netherlands. The Allies tried to cut off the German supply of foodstuffs and raw materials, but they could not block imports destined for the Dutch economy. Yet, what to do with imports that were processed by Dutch industry into exports for the Germans? If the Netherlands would cooperate with the Allies and cut off German food supply, it would risk its neutral status. Moreover, the high prices on the German market made it very attractive to continue some of the traditional exports. The compromise that was found was to establish a private company, the NOT (Netherlands Overseas Trust Company) which was given the monopoly on the international trade of the country. Since the company was managed by private enterprise – a number of large bankers and merchants – the Dutch government could not be held responsible for any mistakes made in the process (i.e. the export of sensitive goods to Germany or an overly vigorous ban on exports to the eastern neighbour). The allocation of shipping space and import and export licences among private enterprises became the responsibility of the NOT, which (secretly) negotiated with the British and Germans on the ways to conduct its business. That a crucial part of foreign policy was handed down to a group of entrepreneurs did not really bother the government (Dc Vries 1989: 73 ff).

In general, this solution seems to have been quite efficient because it made possible the continuation of a relatively large international trade, especially with the Germans. Sizeable quantities of 'non-sensitive' products, such as coffee and tobacco, were re-exported, often after having changed hands and brands in one of the port cities. Exports of agricultural products were also kept at a rather high level, notwithstanding the increased scarcity at home. In this way the Netherlands lived up to the expectations of the German army commanders, who had decided not to invade the country in order to have a 'breathing lung' for the German war economy.

On the positive side the war created new opportunities to experiment with all kinds of government policy. Already in the 1870s left-wing liberals (radicals) had developed ideas about a more active government which would take responsibility for the general welfare of the population. When the radicals gained momentum in the 1890s they had been advocates for social reform, the 'nationalization' of public utilities and other monopolies and the stimulation of economic development through large public works, of which the plan to enclose the Zuiderzee and create a number of large polders was the most important part. Some of these plans had been implemented before 1913 (for example, the industrial accidents law and the Mining Act in 1901), but the list of plans was still long. Stalemate between the left and the right had blocked progress since 1901, but this changed during the war when a (historical) compromise was reached between liberals and the confessional parties (see Chapter 4). The ambitious *Zuiderzeeplan*, which would create many thousands of hectares of much needed agricultural land in the near future, was finally accepted by parliament in 1918 (Brugmans 1969: 498). The government participated in the establishment of a number of 'basic industries' which were to make the Dutch economy less dependent on imports. Two new companies, Hoogovens (basic metals) and Nederlandse Zoutindustrie (salt) were established. The railway companies were consolidated and reorganized into a single company (Van den Broeke 1989). A number of social reforms was finally introduced (see Chapter 4). All in all, it was an important departure from the laissez-faire stance of the prewar period.

The financing of these measures, of the mobilization of the army and the distribution apparatus became increasingly costly as the war went on. In spite of the introduction of a number of war taxes government deficits went up from 0.1 percent of GDP in 1913 to 9.1 percent in 1915, then stabilized at 5.3 percent in 1916 and 1917, and reached a peak of 13.5 percent in 1918 (Van der Bie 1995). During the first years of the war the government could easily find the required funds on the capital market, because domestic and foreign investments were at low ebb and money was cheap. However, in 1918 this became more difficult and the boom of the following years led to a tight capital market and sharply rising interest rates. The result was an increase in the short-term debt of the government, which undermined its solidity and contributed to the inflation of these years (Keesing 1947: 55 ff). After 1920 these problems would become even more pressing (see next section).

One of the features of industrial growth in the 1910s was a strong 'deepening' of the structure of industry. Throughout the nineteenth century mining and the metal industry had been the 'weak', underdeveloped parts of the industrial structure. During the growth spurt that began in the 1890s heavy industry moved ahead at a fast pace, a process that was accelerated by the war. The growth of employment was particularly rapid in shipbuilding, engineering and electrical appliances. In the metallurgic industry employment grew by more than 60 percent between 1909 and 1920, whereas in the rest of industry employment increased by 'only' 21 percent (Oomens and Den Bakker 1994). The establishment of Hoogovens in 1918, the first modern blast furnace in the Netherlands, further contributed to this trend.

Even more rapid was the expansion of coal mining in Limburg, made necessary by the large demand for fuel during the war which could no longer be satisfied by large-scale imports from Germany and Britain. The output and employment of the mines more than doubled between 1913 and 1920 (Kreukels 1986: 552, 559).

Another aspect of the 'deepening' of the industrial structure was the strong growth of large enterprises. Table 6.4 presents figures on the distribution of employment in industry based on data from the industrial accidents insurance. This source is not perfect, because before 1921 part of the workers was not insured, but it gives a good impression of the magnitude of the changes. The table shows that employment in small firms relatively declined; in fact, in absolute terms employment in firms with less than 10 employees was almost constant. The share of the large firms

Table 6.4 Structure of employment in industry, 1913 and 1920 (percent)

|  | 1913 | 1920 |
|---|---|---|
| *Enterprises with* | | |
| 0–4 employees | 14.2 | 10.9 |
| 5–9 | 9.4 | 7.3 |
| 10–49 | 23.7 | 21.8 |
| 50–199 | 22.1 | 22.2 |
| 200–499 | 13.3 | 13.7 |
| 500–999 | 7.4 | 10.3 |
| > 1,000 | 9.9 | 13.7 |
| *Total* | 100.0 | 99.9 |

*Sources*: CBS, *Jaarcijfers*, 1917, 1925

increased rapidly (and total employment in firms with more than 1,000 employees almost doubled), which testifies to an important shift in the industrial structure. At the same time, the share of the self-employed in total employment fell from about 25 percent in 1909 to 19.8 percent in 1920 (Van der Bie 1995; Den Bakker and Van Sorge 1996). After 1920 the share of the self-employed more or less stabilized; it even increased a little to 21.3 percent in 1930 (and 20.5 percent in 1939). Breaks in the statistics of the industrial accidents insurance make it impossible to compare trends throughout the early 1920s, but between 1925 and 1940 there were no comparable changes in industrial structure. The continued rise of a few large multinationals, documented in Chapter 3, did not much affect the structure of industry as a whole.

Both processes – the 'deepening' of the industrial structure and the growth of large entreprises – were interrelated. In 1920 the metal industry and coal mining were by far the most concentrated branches with between 30 percent (shipbuilding and engineering) and 67 percent (mining) of the workers in firms with over 1,000 employees. Only public utilities had a comparable share of employment in large firms; in the rest of industry firms were generally much smaller (CBS, *Jaarcijfers*, 1925).

The sector that was probably changed most by the events of the 1910s was banking. Until 1910 Dutch banks had been relatively small and catered mostly to the needs of international trade by supplying short-term credit. Mixed banks, which attracted large amounts of deposits and gave long-term credit to industry, had failed to arise in spite of a number of attempts to introduce this type of business. The main cause of the relative stagnation of the banking sector was the efficiency of the capital market, especially the *prolongatie* system, which made it possible to invest surplus cash in monthly loans on the stock exchange, thereby bypassing the banks (Jonker 1996). The interest rates offered by banks on deposits were generally lower than the interest rate on the *prolongatie* market, which meant that the banks had great difficulty in attracting deposits.

The creation of the Robaver in 1911, the result of a merger of three smaller Rotterdam banks, signalled the start of a process of concentration in the banking sector, which accelerated during the war years. The closure of the Amsterdam Stock Exchange in July 1914 clearly revealed the drawbacks of the *prolongatie* system for lenders, and rendered many averse to further investment in this system (Vissering and Westerman Holstijn 1928: 80). As a result deposits began to flow to the banks. Moreover, the NOT required every entrepreneur who wanted to import goods to come up with a written bank guarantee, which greatly enhanced the role of banks in the international trade of Dutch business (DeMonchy 1928: 120). The banks reacted swiftly to the new opportunities and in a few years they intensified relations with industry. One of the indications for the 'revolution' in the banking sector is the fact that the number of non-executive directorships of

Dutch bankers in other (large) firms increased from 200 in 1910 to 431 in 1923 (Jonker 1989). Industry profited most from the increased attention from bankers. The Robaver, which had in a way set off the entire process, was by far the most dynamic and increased its number of directorships in other firms from 30 (1910) to 127 (1923). The non-executive directorships of bankers were a means to control their long-term investments in industry and to cement the mutual relationship (Jonker 1989).

During the war and the boom that followed these investments were quite secure, since profits in industry soared to continuously high levels. Van der Bie (1995: 158) estimates that between 1915 and 1919 profits were about 40 percent higher than before the war, the result of strong increases in the price level and stagnating wages. The share of wages in income declined sharply during the first years of the war (from about 44.4 percent in 1913 to 37.4 percent in 1916) which contributed to the social tensions of the war years. Until 1918 nominal wages, another aspect of the same process, lagged behind the increase in prices, which caused real wages to decline by about 10 percent (Kuijpers 1996).

The boom of 1918 to 1920 and the fall in the price level after 1920 suddenly changed the picture: real wages went up by almost 50 percent between 1918 and 1921 and income inequality declined sharply as a result. The net effect of the large swings in income inequality and real wages during the 1910s was decidedly positive: real wages went up substantially and, as Jan de Meere (1983) has shown, after 1920 the inequality of income distribution was much lower than before 1914.

This brings us to a final assessment of economic development during the period between 1914 and 1921. Compared with other neutral countries the Netherlands did quite well: the economy grew substantially, unemployment was kept at a fairly low level, income inequality (which had been virtually stable in the nineteenth century) experienced a strong downward trend after 1918, and even the rate of inflation was relatively modest despite the sometimes chaotic distribution policies. The cost of living almost doubled between 1914 and 1920, but inflation was higher in almost all other European countries, neutral and otherwise. The depression of 1921–3 would, however, show that the remarkable performance also had its weak points.

## PROSPERITY IN THE 1920s

The favourable development of the Dutch economy during the 1910s was first of all the result of its neutral status. Yet, overexpansion during the war period could lead to a prolonged depression in the afterwar years, as especially the Scandinavian countries discovered. Two forces were behind the economic difficulties of a number of neutral countries: overextension of the banking system led to major banking crises in Norway, Denmark, and

Sweden in the 1920s, and the forced return to gold at the prewar parity had strong deflationary effects on the economy at large (Haavisto; Nordvik 1995 and Jonung 1995). Britain, which took the lead in the attempts to restore the gold standard, made the same mistake and its economy also had great difficulty as a result. In many ways developments in the Netherlands were similar: the early 1920s witnessed a grave banking crisis and the monetary authorities also aimed at restoring the gold standard at the prewar parity (De Vries 1989). But somehow the real economy managed to overcome these strains: GDP continued to grow, even at the worst of the depression of 1921–3, and unemployment remained relatively low – much lower than in the Scandinavian countries and Britain (Den Bakker and Van Sorge 1996). While the neutral countries generally had problems in adapting to the postwar economy, the Netherlands did quite well in the 1920s.

This does not imply that the downturn after 1920 did not have serious consequences for the economy. First, it put an end to the experiment with mixed banking. After 1920 a number of banks got into serious trouble when clients went bankrupt, share prices went down, and the fragility of the new structure became apparent. A few smaller banks had to close down and the Robaver, the most aggressive representative of the concentration movement during the preceding decade, could only be rescued through intervention by the Central Bank (which needed government guarantees to save it because the liabilities were so large) (De Vries 1989: 203 ff). Confidence in the banking system declined sharply between 1920 and 1924, but was finally restored by the actions of the 'lender in last resort' (Van Zanden 1997).

Behind this banking crisis was a huge decline in profits, the result of falling prices and more or less constant nominal wages. In consequence investments in machinery and equipment dropped sharply, from their very high level in 1919–20 (Den Bakker et al. 1987: 67). However, a number of forces counteracted the fall in investment demand. In the first place, ambitious efforts to modernize the housing stock, begun immediately after the war, were now yielding results and construction peaked in the early years of the international depression (in 1922, to be precise) (CBS 1959). Second, consumption stepped up as well due to the sharp increase in real wages. Third, government deficits were quite substantial in 1921 and 1922, which helped to dampen the downturn of the economy. Finally, exports grew at an astonishing rate of about 12 percent per year between 1920 and 1923. As a result GDP continued to grow during the 'depression' of 1921–3, albeit at a more modest rate (4.7 percent in 1922 and 1.4 percent in 1923), and, more remarkably, unemployment remained constant at about 7 percent (for all data: Den Bakker et al. 1987; Den Bakker and Van Sorge 1996).

International developments certainly help to explain this development.

C.L. Holtfrerich (1980) has shown that the rapid reconstruction of the German economy in the early 1920s – made possible by the strong monetary impulses it received – encouraged the international economy. The Dutch were clearly aware of the strategic importance of that country for their own prosperity and tried to contribute to it by supplying Germany with much needed international credit. In 1920 the government made available a loan of 200 million guilders at the request of big business, which was intended to stimulate international trade between the two countries (De Vries 1989: 295). As other capital markets (i.e. London and Paris) were closed for the former 'aggressor', German business began to make much use of the Amsterdam market, which stimulated the growth of international banking (Houwink ten Cate 1995).

In the early 1920s the tension was greatly relieved by the reorganization of government finances. Deficits had been relatively large in the afterwar period and, combined with the huge increase in investment in 1918 to 1920, this led to a widening gap in the balance of payments and rising interest rates. After 1920 the downturn of the price level caused a fall in tax income and deficits increased even more, which forced the government (for the first time in the history of the Netherlands) to turn to foreign capital markets to finance them. In 1921–2 it issued a number of dollar loans on the New York market, all of which were successful (Keesing 1947: 60).

It was clear that a thorough reorganization of government finances was necessary, and in 1921–4 this was implemented by successive Ministers of Finance (De Geer and Colijn). In 1922–3, after a slight decline in interest rates (from 7 percent in 1920 to 6 percent), the short-term debt was consolidated, all budgets were cut by 17 percent, salaries and social transfers were lowered and the various separate 'crisis' funds, established during the war to finance war-related expenditure, were abolished (Stevers 1976: 126). Expenditure on social issues (housing, social security) went down most. Colijn, the financial 'strong man' of the early 1920s, especially detested the many social programmes that had been introduced during the 1910s and had, in his view, increased tax levels beyond proportion (Fritschy 1994). The reorganization of public finances partly undid the progress that had been made in these fields. As a result of these measures the deficit disappeared. In the second half of the 1920s the budget showed a small surplus which was used to redeem public debt and lower some of the most 'oppressive' taxes.

The reorganization of government finances also restored confidence in the economy. The exchange rate to the dollar, which had declined by 30 percent in 1919–20, slowly went up and reached the prewar parity in 1923 (helped by the inflow of German capital which tried to escape the hyperinflation at home). At the same time, the large deficit on the balance of trade disappeared as exports grew far more rapidly than imports. A return to gold at the prewar parity became a possibility, but the Central Bank wanted to coordinate its decision with the British and therefore had to wait until 1925 (De Vries 1989: 303 ff). Unlike the British and the Scandinavians, it did not have to deflate the economy in order to reach this goal. During the 1910s prices had increased much less in the Netherlands than in Britain (or Denmark, Sweden and Norway), which made possible a very smooth return to gold. In fact, strong confidence in the guilder and an ample gold cover made it possible to precede the return to gold by two reductions in the base rate in an attempt to help the British (Van Zanden 1997).

After 1923 the economy began to grow at an unprecedented rate. Exports increased by 6.8 percent per year between 1923 and 1929, private investments boomed at a rate of 8 percent per year in the same period, and consumption grew at almost 3 percent per year (Den Bakker *et al.* 1987: 67). The Dutch economy had never seen anything like this before and these rates still compare favourably with those of the 1950s and 1960s.

Part of the explanation is the very rapid growth of exports, industrial exports in particular. In the nineteenth century the strong development of agriculture and international services was already highly dependent on the international market; both were excellent examples of export-led growth. Yet industry lagged behind, working mainly for the domestic market. There were, of course, some exceptions to this rule, such as the cotton industry, the agro-based industries and margarine factories. In the 1920s things seem to have changed. Exports from a broad range of industries – such as aircraft production (Fokker), electrical appliances (Philips), shipbuilding, artificial fibres (AKU) and pig iron (Hoogovens) – also grew rapidly (Brugmans 1969: 473 ff). The share of Dutch exports in international trade, which had gone down in the course of the nineteenth century, moved up in the early 1920s and remained at about 120 percent of the 1913 level during the rest of the decade (as internal absorption increased during the ensuing boom) (see Graph 7.2).

The strong growth of exports could be achieved in spite of a large increase in real wages during the preceding decade. In fact, business responded to this change by heavily investing in mechanization, which led to an increase in installed horsepower per worker, and by introducing all kinds of measures to rationalize the production process (Van Zanden and Griffiths 1989: 118). Taylorism made some progress as a result of the pressure to cut costs (Bloemen 1988). Moreover, after 1923 real wages stabilized and profits climbed to new record levels in the late 1920s. There were certainly no 'internal' problems that contributed to the downturn after 1929.

Agriculture was equally dynamic (Knibbe 1993: 171 ff). The growth of agricultural exports was only slightly slower than the increase in industrial exports. Moreover, because the pull from the growth of industrial employment was strong, the labour force in agriculture hardly increased at all (Table 6.5). The growth of output therefore resulted in an almost equal

Table 6.5 Structure of the labour force, 1909, 1920, 1930, 1947
(thousands of men and women)

|      | Agriculture and fisheries | Industry and mining | Services | Total |
| --- | --- | --- | --- | --- |
| 1909 | 618     | 788     | 838     | 2,244   |
|      | (27.5)  | (35.1)  | (37.3)  | (99.9)  |
| 1920 | 639     | 1,025   | 1,057   | 2,721   |
|      | (23.5)  | (37.7)  | (38.8)  | (100.0) |
| 1930 | 640     | 1,230   | 1,301   | 3,171   |
|      | (20.2)  | (38.8)  | (41.0)  | (100.0) |
| 1947 | 718     | 1,354   | 1,794   | 3,866   |
|      | (18.6)  | (35.0)  | (46.4)  | (100.0) |

Sources: Oomens and Den Bakker 1994; Den Bakker and Van Sorge 1996: 155

growth in labour productivity. In fact, labour productivity in agriculture grew more than in industry, which is another 'modern' feature of economic growth in this period. In the nineteenth century, the growth of labour productivity in agriculture lagged behind industry, whereas after 1950 this pattern was reversed. However, after 1925 the price of agricultural products on the international market began to fall and consequently incomes declined sharply. The years 1927 and 1928 were quite difficult with negative incomes for many farmers, which induced the government to start a large-scale inquiry into the economic backgrounds of the problem. Bumper crops in 1929 and 1930 temporarily reversed the trend, but agricultural incomes remained depressed (Knibbe 1993: 180–5).

The international services probably expanded even more rapidly than the other sectors of the economy. Shipments of goods through Dutch harbours, that were dominated by transit trade with the German hinterland, grew at a staggering rate of 16 percent a year between 1920 and 1929, only interrupted by the two (German) recessions of 1923 and 1928 (Van Zanden and Griffiths 1989: 122–3). After the fat years between 1918 and 1920 international shipping had to compete much more vigorously in the 1920s, as freight rates fell down from their 1920 peaks. The sector continued to expand despite meagre profits (Van Zanden and Griffiths 1989: 122). The government contributed much to the establishment (in 1919) and growth of the KLM (Royal Dutch Airlines), mainly because of the strategic importance of direct connections with Indonesia. KLM was relatively successful in developing its own network of connections (Bouwens and Dierickx 1996).

The banking sector returned to the orthodoxy of the prewar period. Investments in industry were liquidated and the relationships between banks and industry became looser once again, as can be seen from the decline in the number of non-executive directorships of bankers (from 431 in 1923 to 167 in 1931) (Jonker 1989). Especially small and medium-sized firms therefore had more difficulty in attracting capital than before 1920. Moreover, the concentration process in banking, which continued into the 1920s, led to the disappearance of many local banks that had been quite important to small and medium-sized enterprises.

In the second half of the 1920s government policy had almost returned to the benign neglect of the nineteenth century. There was some concern about the rise of protectionism, which was clearly disadvantageous to the Dutch economy, but the government could do little to stem the tide. In 1924 Colijn actually introduced a moderate increase in tariffs, primarily for fiscal reasons but – off the record – also to have something with which to negotiate in further international discussions on the topic (Blaisse 1952: 94–8). Pressures from agriculture to increase protection for this sector were unsuccessful, as were complaints from entrepreneurs who saw the Dutch share in Indonesian imports decline rapidly. But as long as exports were growing at about 8 percent per year and the economy boomed, there were no good reasons to reconsider these issues. Even the crash on Wall Street in October 1929 was no reason for great concern, because American stock markets had always been highly volatile. In the past such a crisis would have been followed by an economic downturn of one or two years, succeeded by a new upswing. Moreover, the healthy state of the Dutch economy made it likely that it would be able to overcome the international depression rather easily – just as it had during the downturn of 1921–3. The optimism seemed well founded. During the 1920s economic growth – with the strong performance of industrial exports and the large increase in total factor productivity – had been impressive and foreshadowed the 'golden years' of the 1950s and 1960s.

In short, during the 1910s and 1920s the economy had had the best of both worlds: it had profited more than other neutral countries from being outside the war, and in the 1920s it had not paid the price which other neutral countries had to pay for overextension of the banking system and the return to gold at the prewar parity. In a way the Netherlands had twice been extremely lucky – but now it was to run out of luck.

# 7

# THE LONG STAGNATION
# 1929–1949

## MACROECONOMIC PERFORMANCE

At the beginning of the 1930s the Netherlands lost the good fortune that had given the country the best of both worlds in the 1910s and the 1920s. During the first years of the Great Depression the economy did rather well, as it had in the early 1920s, but in 1931 – when Britain left the gold standard and the Germans introduced foreign exchange controls – the international downturn and loss of confidence hit the economy very hard. Whereas in most European countries the Depression hit rockbottom in 1932 and the recovery began in 1933, the Dutch economy continued to perform poorly in 1934 and 1935 (Table 7.1). As will be shown in the next section, the Dutch continuation of the Great Depression was largely caused by its monetary policy, i.e. that it stuck to the gold standard until September 1936.

In a way it was just bad luck that the Netherlands was not thrust off gold in 1931 and that its gold reserves were so ample that a forced devaluation was out of the question. In fact, during the crucial months in the autumn of 1931 large capital flows into the country (partly made up of the withdrawal of funds from Germany and Britain) strengthened the position of the guilder even more. When the Scandinavian countries returned to the gold standard in the 1920s they introduced the gold exchange standard and kept a large part of their reserves in pounds. The devaluation of the pound in September 1931 therefore forced them to follow the British example. The Dutch Central Bank, officially still a private company, had only kept part of its reserves in pounds. This share was large enough to cause huge losses for the bank (which had to be compensated for by the government) but too small to force a devaluation of the guilder (De Vries 1989; Van Zanden 1997). Consequently, the guilder remained firmly attached to gold and its defence became one of the priorities of government policy in the 1930s. Only after Switzerland left the gold standard in September 1936 – one day after the devaluation of the French franc – did the Netherlands follow suit

*Table 7.1* Development of GDP and unemployment in the Netherlands and its main trading partners, 1929–1939

| | Growth GDP | | | Unemployment | | |
|---|---|---|---|---|---|---|
| | *Neth.* | *Partn.* | *Diff.* | *Neth.* | *Partn.\** | *Diff.* |
| 1929 | 2.4 | 2.6 | −0.2 | 1.7 | 4.6 | 2.9 |
| 1930 | −1.1 | −1.2 | 0.1 | 2.3 | 7.6 | 5.3 |
| 1931 | −4.6 | −5.2 | 0.6 | 4.3 | 11.8 | 7.5 |
| 1932 | −0.9 | −3.5 | 2.6 | 8.3 | 14.8 | 6.5 |
| 1933 | 0.4 | 3.3 | −2.9 | 9.7 | 13.1 | 3.4 |
| 1934 | −1.1 | 5.4 | −6.5 | 9.8 | 10.6 | 0.8 |
| 1935 | 2.7 | 4.5 | −1.8 | 11.2 | 9.5 | −1.7 |
| 1936 | 5.4 | 4.9 | 0.5 | 11.9 | 7.5 | −4.4 |
| 1937 | 5.7 | 5.6 | 0.1 | 10.5 | 5.7 | −4.8 |
| 1938 | −3.2 | 3.1 | −6.3 | 9.9 | 6.4 | −3.5 |
| 1939 | 7.7 | 3.8 | 3.9 | − | − | − |

*Sources*: GDP: Den Bakker *et al.* 1987, Unemployment: Maddison 1991.
\* Unweighted average of Germany, UK and Belgium

(Griffiths 1987). There soon followed a strong upturn of the economy, but this could not compensate for the stagnation of the first half of the 1930s.

Extravagant gold and foreign exchange reserves, the reputation as a haven for foreign capital, and rigid government policies to defend the guilder led to the long stagnation of the 1930s (Keesing 1947; Drukker 1990; Van Zanden 1996a). In the 1940s the Netherlands was equally unlucky: this time the Germans decided to invade the country in their offensive against the French and Belgian forces. After a short campaign, there began a period of five years of occupation during which the Germans exploited the country very efficiently. In the final year (1944–5), when large parts of Western Europe had already been liberated, the population of the western part of the country was cut off from its food supply, which caused the disastrous 'hunger winter'. At the same time the Germans took away large parts of the capital stock and destroyed even more. The economic collapse during the war and the loss of human lives and capital goods was therefore more severe in the Netherlands than in most other countries in Western Europe (with the obvious exception of Germany). Postwar reconstruction started from a lower level than in Belgium or the Scandinavian countries.

The estimates in Table 7.2 exemplify the long stagnation of the Dutch economy during the 1930s and 1940s. In 1947 GDP was only slightly higher than in 1929, whereas the population had increased by 24 per cent (or almost 2 million people). Per capita growth rates of GDP were negative in both periods, contrasting markedly with the rest of Western Europe. Total factor productivity declined considerably (as the capital

*Table 7.2* Growth of GDP in the Netherlands and North West Europe, 1929–1947

|  | GDP | | GDP per head | | Real gross hourly wages | |
|---|---|---|---|---|---|---|
|  | *Neth.* | *NW Eur.* | *Neth.* | *NW Eur.* | *Neth.* | *NW Eur.* |
| 1929–38 | 0.33 | 1.54 | −0.89 | 0.80 | 0.2 | 0.7 |
| 1938–47 | 0.72 | 1.20 | −0.43 | 0.18 | −0.3* | 1.2* |
| 1929–47 | 0.52 | 1.37 | −0.66 | 0.49 | −0.1** | 0.9** |

*Source*: Van Ark and De Jong 1996: 201, 218
\*   1938–1950
\*\* 1929–1950

stock and especially the stock of R&D continued to rise), which provides further proof of the poor performance of the economy (see Table 6.2). The development of real wages followed exactly the same pattern: stagnation in the Netherlands as against a continued increase elsewhere.

The economic stagnation also gave rise to a number of structural problems. The stagnation of employment in industry and services led to a renewed increase in the agricultural labour force; total employment in the primary sector continued to grow until about 1947 (Table 6.5). This prompted the splitting up of farms and the creation of a group of very small farms that were inefficient and harboured a great deal of under-employed labour. After World War II the 'small farmers question' (*kleine boeren probleem*) was identified as a source of inefficiency in Dutch agriculture, which had to be solved in order to restore its competitiveness (De Groot and Bauwens 1990: 151–2).

A reduction of the agricultural labour force was one of the solutions to the problem. However, the long stagnation meant that levels of investment had been low (during the 1930s) or even negative (during the war). The existing stock had therefore become small and obsolete, and large-scale investments were necessary to create new employment opportunities for the growing population. These supply-side problems had to be faced by policymakers after 1945.

This is, however, just one part of the story of the 1930s and 1940s. Beneath the surface some of the same forces that had contributed to the economic dynamism of the decades before 1929 were still alive and kicking. In Chapter 3 we have seen that the growth of Dutch multinationals continued and probably even accelerated in the 1930s and 1940s (see also Bloemen *et al.* 1993b). The output of patents (issued to Dutch inhabitants in the USA and Germany) boomed in the 1930s and reached record levels in the late 1940s and early 1950s, which have not been surpassed since, at least in relative terms (see Chapter 3). The annual report of Philips NV for 1945 explained that during the war much progress was made in the development of new techniques and products (Lakeman 1991: 143). More-over, the economic hardships of the 1930s and the German occupation forced employers and unions (temporarily) to forget the old ideological differences and work more closely together. This mood led to the formation of the Stichting van de Arbeid in 1945, which made possible the pacifica-tion of labour relations and the introduction of the guided wage policy after the war (see Chapter 5). Other important institutional changes would follow in the second half of the 1940s and set the stage for the growth spurt of the 'golden years' after 1949.

## THE GREAT DEPRESSION 1929–1939

The openness of the Netherlands made it inevitable that the chain of events that started with the Wall Street crash of October 1929 would have a tremendous impact on the Dutch economy. Share prices on the Amsterdam market declined rapidly in the final months of 1929, soon followed by a fall in exports and prices (especially for agricultural commodities). But con-sumer expenditure as well as public and private investments still went up substantially in 1930, which resulted in a very small decline of GDP in 1930 (Den Bakker *et al.* 1987).

Therefore, 1930 was not a bad year, but this was to change in 1931. Table 7.1 traces the Dutch version of the Great Depression in more detail. After a more or less 'normal' contraction of the economy during the first years of the Depression, when the economy even performed a little better than its neighbours, the downward trend continued in the years between 1933 and 1935, when the Netherlands performed much worse than its trading partners. The evolution of employment presents the same picture, which is reinforced by the relatively strong growth of the labour force in the Netherlands (Drukker 1990). Until 1933 unemployment remained below international standards but continued to grow thereafter, whereas elsewhere a decline was already apparent. In the Netherlands unemploy-ment peaked in 1936 as against 1932 in most other European countries.

From the start the debate about the causes of the economic stagnation between 1932 and 1936 has been dominated by the work of the monetary economist Keesing (1947), who put the blame largely with the govern-ment's choice to stick to the gold standard. This resulted first of all in an unfavourable development of international competitiveness and, second, in a long string of deflationary measures aimed at lowering prices and wages, which further contributed to the sluggish economic performance. In the 1970s Peter Klein (1973) has attempted to modify this interpretation by focusing on the structure of the economy as the main explanation for the long stagnation during the 1930s. For example, the heavy dependence on agricultural exports was considered to be a major reason for its vulnerability (Klein 1973). This interpretation has, however, not been able to stand up to close scrutiny (see Drukker 1990; Van Zanden 1996a).

Recent research into the development of international competitiveness has certainly vindicated the first part of Keesing's analysis. In Graph 7.1 various ways to calculate the (real effective) exchange rate of the guilder are shown. The upper line represents the development of the weighted exchange rate (the weights are derived from the share of the various trading partners in Dutch exports in 1929–30), the other lines are real effective exchange rates (calculated on basis of the same weights) estimated by means of data on nominal wages, wholesale prices, and cost-of-living indices. All series have 1913 as the base year. The graph shows that compared with the main competitors the value of the guilder was already higher in the 1920s than in 1913 (as was the level of nominal wages), but also that it increased rapidly between 1932 and 1935, when all series peak. The overvaluation of the guilder declined in 1936 – as a result of the devaluation in September of that year – and 1937, but in 1938 there occurred another (relatively small) increase in its value.

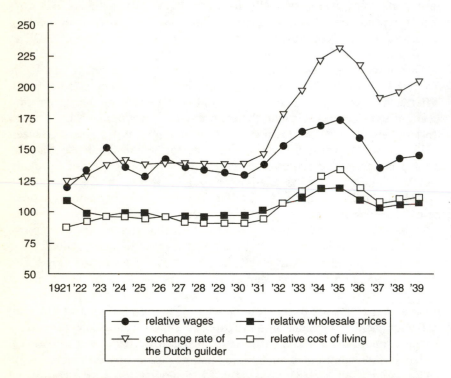

*Graph 7.1* Development of relative prices and wages in the Netherlands and weighted exchange rate of the Dutch guilder (compared with major competitors with the exception of Germany), 1921–1939 (indices 1913 = 100)
*Source*: Van Zanden 1988a

Attempts to calculate the share of Dutch exports in world trade show some of the consequences of the strong overvaluation of the guilder between 1932 and 1935 (Graph 7.2). During the 1920s this share was much higher than in 1913, which makes clear that the increase in the (real) effective exchange rate between 1913 and 1921 did not really harm the economy. The series of export shares appears to peak in 1931. This perverse reaction to the onset of the Depression is probably a sign of the strong competitiveness of Dutch industry (see Chapter 8). But after 1931 there followed a disastrous fall in the export share, which almost perfectly mirrored the increase in the real effective exchange rate. This analysis shows that the upward trend in export shares was interrupted by overvaluation of the guilder between 1931 and 1936 that brought about a sharp decline in Dutch exports (Van Zanden 1996a: 126).

The weak performance of exports was certainly one of the reasons for the slow recovery after 1932. Between 1929 and 1932 exports fell much more than any other component of effective demand (by about a third; even investment fell by 'only' 27 percent) and it stayed on a low level until 1936 (Den Bakker *et al.* 1987). Since foreign economic policy tended to

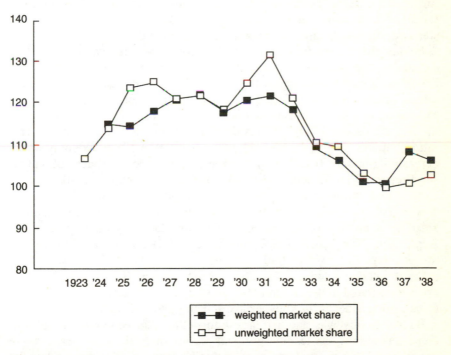

*Graph 7.2* Development of the weighted and unweighted market share of Dutch exports, 1923–1938 (indices 1913 = 100)
*Source*: Van Zanden 1988a

111

favour agricultural exports (see below), these fell by less than the exports of industry, which were almost 40 percent below the 1929 level between 1932 and 1935.

The second part of the interpretation of Keesing, i.e. that sticking to gold made necessary a string of deflationary measures which depressed the economy, is somewhat less obvious. First, until Belgium left the gold standard in March of 1935, the Central Bank hardly had to defend the currency because of its overwhelming reserves. Interest rates were low, because the demand on the capital market was slack and supply was abundant (now that (foreign) investment outlets were closed off), and the base rate of the Central Bank fluctuated between 2.5 and 3 percent (De Vries 1994: 120 ff). The Belgian devaluation ended this period of tranquillity, and in the following eighteen months the Central Bank often had to use its base rate to stem speculative movements against the guilder. A political crisis that lasted for three days and speculation against the French franc were among the disturbances that caused great swings in the official rates of the Central Bank (Keesing 1947: 199–200). The measures were quite effective in showing the strong will of the monetary authorities to resist speculation against the guilder (Van Zanden 1997), but they had little impact on interest rates on the capital market at large. Interest rates remained at a historical low, which means that the defence of the gold standard did not deflate the economy to any extent.

Behind the successful defence of the gold standard was the fact that deficits on the balance of payments were often more than offset by the inflow of capital. Especially in 1932 and 1933 these deficits were relatively large, but this hardly affected the gold reserves of the Central Bank. Moreover, in 1935 a surplus reappeared on the balance of payments (for the first time since 1930), as a result of the strong decline in imports. This fall in imports was partly caused by the contraction of the economy which depressed imports, but also by a largely spontaneous process of import substitution (Van Zanden 1996a: 124). When its export markets were closing and world market prices were dropping dramatically, industry was rather successful in capturing a larger slice of the internal market, aided by a number of protectionist measures taken in the course of the Depression (Van Schaïk 1986). The net effect of all this was that neither the development of the gold reserves nor the state of the balance of payments necessitated a devaluation of the guilder. If the Gold Bloc had not disintegrated in the autumn of 1936 (due to the instability of the French franc), the guilder would never have left the gold standard.

Budget policy was another means to deflate the economy. There was consensus among the leading political parties that prices and wages were too high and that the budget deficit had to be reduced, in order to adapt the economy to the new circumstances. Balancing the budget was almost an obsession for right-wing politicians in the 1920s and 1930s, and almost every 'ordinary' budget that was submitted to parliament gave evidence of such an outcome. It was almost impossible to combine this strict rule with the huge budgetary problems of the 1930s, when tax revenues fell dramatically as a result of the Depression and politicians were under strong pressure to introduce a host of new programmes to protect agriculture, shipping, parts of industry, and to increase spending on public works, unemployment benefits, etc. (see below). The solution to these contradictory pressures was that parts of expenditure were moved from the ordinary budget to the capital budget, where a deficit was largely accepted, and separate funds were created to finance the new programmes (i.e. for agriculture, public works, etc.) (Stevers 1976: 133–8). These new funds were also allowed to run large deficits, but these remained outside the control of parliament. The result of this combination of de jure financial orthodoxy (the ordinary budget as presented to parliament was balanced) and de facto large deficits was that almost all observers lost track of the country's financial situation, as an almost inaccessible jungle of financial transactions was created between the various separate funds and the two regular budgets. The net effect was that in spite of attempts to lower the overall deficit, it remained quite large throughout the 1930s. In a few years (1931, 1933, 1935) the economy was probably boosted by these demand impulses, but in other years (especially in 1934 and 1936) the effect was highly negative (Van Zanden 1996a: 128–9). The overall effect of budget policy between 1931 and 1936 was probably small but positive.

Naturally, this does not mean that the government did not cut its budget and generally tried to make ends meet. When it became clear, after the failure of the London conference in 1933, that no reconstruction of a multilateral trading system should be expected in the near future, a series of harsh budget cuts was introduced, including measures to lower salaries, wages, and benefit levels. These measures were not without effect, but fell short of adapting the price level to world market levels. Moreover, this *aanpassingspolitiek* (policy of adaptation) was thwarted by almost every other measure aimed at protecting parts of the economy against the worst effects of the Depression. For example, policies to protect agriculture led to a substantial increase in food prices above those on the world market; in 1935 agricultural protection was estimated to increase the cost of living by 7 to 8 percent (Blaisse 1952: 198). The government also failed to lower sticky rents, as it did not want to interfere directly in the markets for agricultural land and housing, which also contributed to the failure of the *aanpassingspolitiek*. Keesing (1947) made a big point of these inconsistencies in government policies in the 1930s, but it is difficult to imagine a truly consistent *aanpassingspolitiek*, given the political realities of the day.

The obvious solution to these problems was to devalue, but this was out of the question. Colijn, the most prominent policymaker, believed that a voluntary devaluation was immoral, because it meant that the government broke its promise to guarantee the value of the currency. Moreover, he hoped that the Gold Bloc could form a stable nucleus for a restructured international trading system. If these countries would also leave the gold standard, the result would be total chaos. Fear of another inflationary wave, comparable with what had happened in Germany in 1923, also played a large role (De Vries 1983: 123–4).

It is important to note that all major political parties, the trade unions, and employers' organizations – in fact, all political groups of some importance – officially supported these views (Griffiths 1987). Behind this facade there was some resistance against the monetary policy, and prominent businessmen (from Shell, Philips, Unilever, Hoogovens) urged the government to reconsider, but public criticism was almost a taboo since it might lead to speculation against the guilder. In 1934 a separate pressure group was established consisting (mainly) of economists and businessmen who favoured devaluation, which organized a few unsuccessful petitions to press its case (Griffiths and Schoorl 1987: 139 ff). The Belgian devaluation of March 1935 again brought up the subject; the Catholic Minister of Economic Affairs Steenberghe believed that the Netherlands should follow this example, which eventually led to his resignation. Trip, the President of the Central Bank, and Colijn remained adamant.

Between 1931 and 1936 the Dutch economy found itself in a paradoxical position. On the one hand, it was obvious that the currency was overvalued, that exports were extremely depressed, and that the price level was under strong pressure as a result of low prices on the world market. The real economy stagnated and unemployment continued to rise. On the other hand, from a strictly monetary perspective the situation was basically sound: gold reserves were ample, interest rates low, and after a few years of deficits on the balance of payments a surplus returned in 1935. This low-level equilibrium might have persisted for a number of years after 1936, had the Gold Bloc not collapsed in that year.

Government policy was not restricted to the *aanpassingspolitiek*. In Chapter 4 some attention has already been paid to the agricultural policies that came into existence after 1930. Starting in 1932 the shipping sector received subsidies to improve its competitiveness (De Hen 1980: 86). Policies towards industry were much less liberal, but after 1933 a large number of protectionist measures was introduced to increase the share of Dutch industry in the domestic market (Van Schaik 1986). In 1934 a new programme of public works (the *Werkfonds*) was introduced to do at least something about the enormous rise in unemployment (Wieringa and Zijp 1979). These measures were inadequate relative to the magnitude of the problems, but together they formed a radical break with the long tradition of non-intervention in the economy.

In the field of international economic policy the government was equally unsuccessful. Until 1933 the government vested its hope on the success of international trade conferences to turn the rising protectionist tide. It committed itself to the results of the Geneva Conference (1927) and was one of the members of the Treaty of Oslo (1930), an attempt by a number of small (Scandinavian and Benelux) countries at least to keep intact their mutual trade (Klemann 1990: 113). After both initiatives had failed – the failure of the Oslo convention could partly be blamed on the change in Dutch policy towards the agricultural sector – the government hoped to restore part of its credibility by concluding the Ouchy convention with Belgium and Luxemburg (in 1932), which would create a zone of relatively liberalized trade in the region. This convention was, however, blocked by the UK, which did not want to abstain from its rights as 'most favoured nation' (Blaisse 1952: 212–16).

The failure of the World Economic Conference in London in 1933 made it necessary to review bilateral trade relationships. Protectionism on the Indonesian market was introduced unilaterally, which raised the Dutch share in Indonesian imports from 12.4 percent in 1933 to 16.7 percent in 1936 (largely at the expense of Japanese imports) (Blaisse 1952: 293–7). It proved far more difficult to deal with its other main trading partners, Germany and the UK.

The fundamental problem in the relationship with the eastern neighbour was that German demand for Dutch products (and for the products of its colonies) was more expansive than Dutch demand for German products. The *Sonderkonto*, an account in which both trade flows were offset against each other since the trade agreement of 1932, had growing German deficits. This necessitated a new round of negotiations in August 1934, in which the Dutch negotiators gave preference to the liquidation of German debts (including the *Sonderkonto* balance) and to keeping agricultural exports on a relatively high level. The result was a strong decline in Dutch exports, since their value was now determined by the low level of Dutch imports minus the sums needed to liquidate the German debts. Industrial exports were depressed most because they had been given low priority by the policymakers (Klemann 1990: 153 ff).

Negotiations with the British were not very successful either, in part because the government had already granted important concessions to the Germans (for example, the preferential supply of coal to the Dutch market). The lack of clear results in the field of international trade policy obviously contributed to the loss of market share of Dutch exports during the 1930s.

The development of the different sectors of the economy was affected by the degree of government protection and by sectoral dependence on inter-national markets. Agriculture had already gone through rough economic weather in the second half of the 1920s and was the first, and in a way the only one, to receive a comprehensive system of protectionist measures. As early as November 1930 minimum prices for wheat were introduced at twice the level of the world market price. In the following years other parts

115

of the sector (dairy, meat) were brought into a protectionist regime and in 1933 a comprehensive *Landbouwcrisiswet* (Agriculture Crisis Law) was introduced to streamline the system. It was quite effective in that the incomes of farmers, which had declined to disastrously low levels in 1930–2, rapidly recovered and returned to normal levels in 1934. One of the peculiar characteristics of the agricultural sector is that the enormous fall in the price level (by about 50 percent between 1928 and 1932) hardly affected output and productivity: value added at constant prices did not decline at all in the early 1930s, apart from the fluctuations in harvest results (Knibbe 1993: 292). The relatively flourishing state of agriculture after 1933 led to an increase in the labour force of this sector. After the devaluation of the guilder, when protectionist measures were relaxed, incomes continued to increase. The final years of the 1930s were probably the most prosperous period for agriculture since 1921 (Knibbe 1993: 180 ff).

On the other hand, large parts of industry had great difficulty in adapting to the new circumstances. The metal industry, which had been central to the previous industrialization drive, did not surpass the 1929 level of output and productivity until 1938 (Seegers 1987: 208). As a result of the continued depression in international trade, shipbuilding hardly recovered at all. In general the recovery of the capital goods sector came very late (after 1935) and was only partial. The consumer goods industry, however, profited from the much more stable development of its demand (consumer expenditure never fell below the 1929 level and only decreased slightly in 1934) and from the introduction of import quotas (Van Schaik 1986; Seegers 1987). The markets of export industries such as cotton textiles, artificial fibres or electrical appliances were closed and consequently fared much worse than sheltered sectors working for the internal market.

Most service industries that worked for the domestic market did quite well, helped by the almost continuous growth of consumer demand. After the reorganization of the banking system in the early 1920s the banks had become very cautious and had loosened their ties with industry. There was therefore no second banking crisis. Only one major bank, the NHM, had to be reorganized (in 1934) as a result of its large losses in Indonesia, but this did not lead to a loss of confidence in the banking system (De Vries 1994: 61). In fact, the biggest problem that faced the banks was their excess liquidity: the liquidation of foreign investments, speculative capital movements into the Netherlands, and the low level of investments resulted in the accumulation of savings for which they could not find profitable investment opportunities. As a result interest rates on the capital market were very low, which made possible a major conversion of government debt (Keesing 1947: 197).

International services were, of course, hit very hard by the Depression. The shipping industry was one of the first to receive some protection in the form of subsidies to lower the wage bill, but these were far too small to have much effect on the huge losses of the big shipping lines. After a large decline in international transport during the first years of the Depression, in the second half of the 1930s the big port cities began to profit from the strong recovery of the German economy.

The failure of the government to develop a consistent set of policies towards the industrial sector led to a number of initiatives to stimulate industrial development. In Limburg an institute to further the industrialization of the province was set up in 1931. Other provinces followed this example in the hope of attracting new industries or creating employment in existing enterprises (De Hen 1980: 148 ff). Critics of government policy pointed out that small and medium-sized industries found it difficult to attract (venture) capital (in a period in which the banks had great difficulty in investing their surplus savings). The government responded by establishing the Mavif (Society for the Financing of Industry) in September 1936, but its activities remained small-scale (De Hen 1980: 245–8). The best documented 'alternative' for the policy of adaptation was proposed by the socialist party, which presented the *Plan van de Arbeid* (Labour Plan) in 1935. It mainly consisted of a policy to give the economy a demand impulse via a number of large-scale public works, which through the multiplier effect would create about 120,000 new jobs (Jan Tinbergen did the econometric work for it) (Abma 1977). In order to prevent another depression, the plan also wanted to reorganize the economy according to socialist principles (however, not by nationalizing industry, but by introducing planning and coordination). Colijn responded that the government had already carried out the useful suggestions of the plan (De Rooy 1979: 149).

On the 27 September 1936 the government finally decided to leave the gold standard. The special fund that was created to monitor the development of the exchange rate, was instructed to aim at a devaluation of 22 percent, which was just enough to bridge the gap in wholesale prices with Great Britain (Vlak 1967). The discussion then centred on the continuation of the official policy of balancing the budget. Critics argued that the need to increase defence expenditure and the desire to stimulate the economy should lead to more inflationary policies. The economy recovered quickly in the final months of 1936 and 1937, which caused an increase in tax income, and made it possible to begin with the reorganization of the complex budgetary system (Van Zanden and Griffiths 1989: 160).

The optimism of these years did not last long: the short depression of 1938 hit the economy quite hard. Public works were stepped up and a few other measures were taken to inflate the economy, but their impact remained fairly small. Employment in public works never exceeded 55,000 (De Rooy 1979: 265).

The final years of the decade were characterized by the threat of war and the related preparations. Already in the summer of 1937 the first plans were made to restructure agriculture in the event of a blockade of the country.

By reducing the numbers of pigs and poultry, which were heavily dependent on imported fodder, and by extending arable land, it was hoped that the Netherlands could become largely self-sufficient in food. A detailed system of distribution was set up and stocks of foodstuffs were built up to be better prepared than in 1914 (Trienekens 1985: 10 ff). The beginning of hostilities during the 'phoney war' of 1939 brought the same problems that had occurred during World War I: how many products could the Netherlands still import overseas and how much could it export to Germany? This time the government conducted the negotiations and was rather successful in securing large imports to increase stocks for the years to come. It actually gave guidelines to its officials on how to act in times of war and occupation. However, these plans were almost all based on the assumption that the Netherlands would once again be neutral (or, in the case of the guidelines to government officials, that at least part of the country would remain unoccupied). Therefore, the Netherlands was quite well prepared for another World War I, but this illusion ended during five days in May 1940 when the German army conquered the country.

## OCCUPATION AND EXPLOITATION 1940–1945

Although war preparations had been going on for a number of years, the German attack and invasion of 10 May 1940 still came as a surprise. The country was overrun by German forces, the royal family and the cabinet fled to London, leaving behind the secretary-generals (the heads of the departments) as the highest civilian authorities. No plans had been made for such a disaster and almost the entire production apparatus fell into German hands intact. Only the greater part of the merchant fleet was able to escape (De Jong 1970: 427, 501–2).

All citizens in an occupied country are faced with difficult dilemmas. Should you cooperate with the enemy to keep things going as usual? Or should you resist the occupier if he orders goods for his war economy? Government officials who drew a clear line were replaced by Germans or by members of the NSB (the pro-Nazi political party), which generally made matters worse. Entrepreneurs often decided to work for the Germans in order to keep their employees at work; the unemployed were forced to work in the German war industry. But in the early months of the war, when fighting in France was still in progress, Dutch arms manufacturers already accepted German orders, the railway system was put at the disposal of the German authorities so that trains could run directly to the French border, and the city of Amsterdam was rebuilding Schiphol Airport – all against the explicit instructions of General Winkelman, the highest authority in times of war. Moreover, at the Ministry for Social Affairs, Secretary-General Verwey was already making plans to 'induce' unemployed workers to go to work in Germany. For him, the 'new order' brought the final solution for this enormous social problem (De Jong 1972: 191 ff).

The Dutch had the dubious honour of being regarded as a fraternal nation, destined in the end to merge into the New Order of the Nazis. Reichscommissioner Seyss-Inquart was ordered to restructure Dutch society according to fascist principles, but before this was done the Dutch economy was expected to contribute to the war effort. Furthermore, he received two specific guidelines from Hitler. The first was that the Dutch standard of living should not fall below the German level (*Gleichberechtigung*). Second, Dutch business should merge with German industry (*Verflechtung*) (De Jong 1972: 375).

Not all Dutchmen had to be won for the New Order. The Jewish population, which was particularly large in Amsterdam, was repressed from the start and gradually isolated from the rest of the nation. In February 1941 the deportations to concentration camps began and more than 100,000 Jews would follow, most of them to die in the Nazi gas chambers. The attitude of the Germans towards the rest of the populations was ambivalent; as long as the war went on, it became increasingly difficult to continue the policy of *Gleichberechtigung*. When economic problems mounted in 1942 and Speer began to reorganize the German war economy, the Germans changed course and began to exploit the economy as much as possible (Klemann 1997).

This exploitation demanded a certain degree of control over decision-making. A centralized administration for the distribution of foodstuffs and raw materials had already been set up before the war, which made the implementation of German demands much easier. To begin with, they could take away the large stocks of raw materials and foodstuffs that had been built up. After protests from Hirschfeld (Secretary-General for Economic Affairs), only part of these stocks was claimed. The two organizations that had been set up, i.e. for foodstuffs and raw materials, were headed by strong administrators, S.L. Louwes and H.M. Hirschfeld, who held key positions in negotiations with the Germans (Barnouw and Stellinga 1978: 65, 81; Trienekens 1985: 68 ff). As long as a large part of the German wishes was fulfilled, they preferred to use their services, and the 'fascist' organizations that had been set up to reorganize agriculture and industry remained powerless. But as the war dragged on both administrators began to obstruct the more extreme German demands and were constantly compromising between these requests and their own desire to secure the supply of food and to keep the economy working. Only in two important fields could the occupiers easily dictate matters: the Ministry for Social Affairs was too well prepared to cooperate and in Finance they appointed their own puppet, Rost van Tonningen (De Vries 1994: 280).

Control of financial policy became complete after the Germans announced the abolition of exchange controls between the two countries in April 1941. The measure exposed the Dutch economy to the full force of the overheated German war economy (where the money supply had already run far ahead of production since 1936) and made it a favoured shopping place for German businessmen and bureaucrats. The president of the Central Bank L.J.A. Trip resigned in protest, to be replaced by Rost van Tonningen (De Vries 1994: 279). From May 1940 the Central Bank was forced to accept German *Reichskreditkassenscheine* as a legal means of payment; after April 1941 the occupier could just pay with Reichsmark to supply his needs.

One method of measuring the degree of exploitation of the economy is to analyse the development of the foreign exchange reserves (i.e. the reserves of Reichsmarks) of the Central Bank. These data certainly underestimate the exploitation, since large amounts of Reichsmarks were paid out to the German treasury to pay for the occupation of the country. When this is taken into account, the total amount of Reichsmarks that flowed to the Central Bank between March 1941 and May 1945 was about 6,300 million guilders (compared with a GDP of almost 6,000 million guilders in 1939). The loss of goods on the clearing account with Germany before March 1941 can be estimated at about 300 million guilders for a total of 6,600 million (Van Zanden and Griffiths 1989: 170). Roughly spreaking, 80 percent of this amount was related to the purchase of goods and services, and 20 percent to the purchase of stocks, bonds, and real estate (CBS 1947: 196–7). These are all minimum estimates, because in the final years of the war the occupier often did not pay at all for requisitions.

Data on the development of international trade with Germany present us with a comparable picture. The deficit on the balance of trade in the late 1930s disappeared immediately in 1941. Until July 1944 (after which statistics are no longer available) exports to Germany were much higher than ever before, whereas other destinations almost disappeared and imports began to dwindle rapidly (CBS 1947: 148–54). For example, Dutch exports of foodstuffs, which had covered about 5 percent of German consumption before the war, rose to about 11 to 12 percent in 1940 to 1941, to fall off again to 8 to 9 percent in 1942 to 1943 and 5 percent in 1944 (Milward 1987: 262).

Statistics of the orders given by the Zentral Auftragstelle (ZAST), an organization set up to coordinate German orders for Dutch industry, suggest that already in the second half of 1940 large orders were given to Dutch industry – generally because most orders of the Dutch government were directly continued. Metal working, shipbuilding and electrical appliances especially profited from German orders during the rest of the war (Van Zanden and Griffiths 1989: 172–4). Actual deliveries of goods, however, were much lower, as a result of long production periods, scarcities of raw materials and energy, and the slowing down of production and (other) attempts at sabotage. Nonetheless, industrial supplies from the Netherlands matched about 2 to 3 percent of German armaments productions in 1943, when they peaked (De Jong 1976: 148).

Besides acquiring goods and reorganizing the production apparatus for that purpose, the Germans could also exploit the Netherlands by deporting its means of production. They were especially interested in the large labour reserves, but the Dutch workers were less keen on acquiring their own place in the New Order. Measures to induce the unemployed to go to work in Germany included the suspension of unemployment benefits, which resulted in a sharp reduction in the number of registered unemployed. At the end of 1941 about 150,000 labourers were working in Germany according to official statistics, which was much less than the Nazis had hoped for. After the invasion of Russia in 1942 the principle of free choice was abandoned completely and the hunt for workers was on. Industries were systematically searched for (surplus) labourers, which almost doubled the number of deported workers. However, this search led to many complaints from entrepreneurs that work on the orders of the ZAST was stagnating, which brought some relief to the search for workers. At the end of 1944 about 400,000 people, or about 13 percent of the total labour force, was forced to work in Germany (CBS 1947). These workers represented about 1 percent of the total German labour force (Sijes 1966: 317).

In short, the exploitation of the Dutch economy was rather successful and until the second half of 1944 the Netherlands had contributed significantly and in an orderly fashion to the German war economy. The fact that the country was relatively well prepared for the transformation into a war economy helps to explain this phenomenon. Yet, in another way the Dutch were completely unprepared for war and certainly for an occupation. There was a strong tendency to obey authority – even if it was foreign – which contributed to the efficient operation of the system of distribution and exploitation (the more so as the Germans cooperated with Louwes and Hirschfeld) (see in another context: Blom 1989: 149).

The 'positive' side of cooperation with the Germans was that the economic downturn was delayed and that, especially during the first four years of the war, the system of distribution could function quite well. To begin with, the agricultural sector was completely restructered to secure the food supply. Numbers of pigs and poultry were reduced dramatically, pasture was broken to increase the acreage available for potatoes and cereals, and even the number of cattle declined as a result of fodder shortages. Between 1940 and 1943 arable and horticultural production went up by about 30 percent despite an increased shortage of fertilizer and pesticides. Livestock production fell steeply during the first years of the war when numbers of livestock were radically reduced, but recovered somewhat after 1942 (Table 7.3). According to Trienekens (1985) the diet probably became even better as a result of these changes – vegetables and bread partly replaced meat and fat – and the food supply was certainly distributed

121

*Table 7.3* Indices of production in major sectors of the economy (1938 = 100)

|      | Manu-facturing | Mining | Const-ruction | Trade | Trans-port | Agriculture arable and horticulture | Live-stock | Total |
|------|------|------|------|------|------|------|------|------|
| 1939 | 113 | 97  | 96 | 114 | 97 | 111 | 109 | 106 |
| 1940 | 105 | 92  | 42 | 111 | 68 | 101 | 96  | 94  |
| 1941 | 82  | 105 | 33 | 92  | 81 | 100 | 84  | 88  |
| 1942 | 61  | 96  | 23 | 78  | 84 | 140 | 61  | 91  |
| 1943 | 53  | 97  | 18 | 67  | 94 | 144 | 69  | 98  |
| 1944 | 32  | 67  | 14 | 46  | 61 | 119 | 74  | 89  |

*Sources*: CBS 1947: 7; Van Zanden and Griffiths 1989: 177; Klemann 1997

more evenly among the population as a result of the introduction of rationing (of course, this levelling off was partly undone by the black market that sprang to life for rationing cards and all kinds of products). In his view there is no doubt that the system worked quite well until the second half of 1944 (Trienekens 1985).

Industrial production went down more rapidly as some industries were quickly deprived of work (construction, for example), while others found it increasingly difficult to acquire raw materials, coal, and other inputs. Naturally, some industries continued working. Food production went on, sometimes producing substitutes for coffee, tea, and other imported commodities. The manufacture of ships, armaments, electrical machinery, and iron and steel boomed during the first years of the occupation, because these branches received large orders (and the necessary raw materials) from the Germans. The high demand for coal led to attempts to increase the output of mining, but it proved difficult to stimulate the workers to increase productivity (CBS 1947). The CBS figures of industrial production presented in Table 7.3 probably exaggerate the true decline because (a large part of) the production for the Germans was not covered by the statistics and unregistered black market output undoubtedly increased considerably. In a recent study Klemann (1997) draws the conclusion that before the autumn of 1944 the decline in industrial production must have been fairly modest, but he cannot as yet provide more detailed estimates of its magnitude.

Opposite the decline in production stood an excessive growth in the money supply, the result of huge German orders (i.e. a large surplus on the balance of trade) and large government deficits (Barendregt 1993: 18–27). Already in May 1940 all prices, wages, and rents were frozen at their prewar level. There was some increase in the price level during the first years of the war, partly because (agricultural) prices were increased to the German level. After 1942 price and wage policies became more effective, although there continued to exist a certain measure of wage drift. All in all, the cost of living increased by 50 percent between 1938 and 1939 and the first half of 1944, and real wages declined by 13 percent (CBS 1947: 264, 292).

The decline in the level of economic activity was persistent but certainly not disastrous during the first years of the occupation. The intensification of exploitation in 1942, leading to the mass deportation of workers, produced a further fall in economic activity, but the economy could have done much worse, certainly compared to many other countries that were occupied by the Germans (but did not profit from being regarded as a fraternal nation). All this changed in the final months of 1944. In November 1944 the southern part of the country was liberated, but the Allied offensive failed to cross the rivers. During the campaign the government in exile had ordered the railways to strike in order to obstruct the German defence. The Germans retaliated by cutting off all transport to Holland, which completely broke down the food supply (De Jong 1981: 17–19).

At the same time the hunt for workers intensified and massive round-ups took place to deport all men of working age who were not directly necessary for the war effort. Shortages of energy intensified as the northern part of the country was now cut off from the Limburg mines (and German supplies). Consequently much of the industry that had still been working in 1944 was closed down. In an attempt to increase productive capacity in the German heartland, factories were dismantled and taken away. Capital goods that could not be removed (harbour installations, for example) were destroyed to make certain that the Allies could not use them (De Jong 1981).

The population of the western part of the country had to endure a long 'hunger winter': food supplies were totally inadequate and many trekked to the countryside to try to find something to eat; coal was extremely scarce and almost all timber was used for heating and cooking. Massive starvation was the consequence of the German blockade of the transport system and the severe winter that followed. According to De Jong (1981: 218–19) about 22,000 people died as a result of hunger and malnutrition. In February 1945 the official food ration was down to 500 kcal. per day (whereas an average adult needs about 2,400 kcal.). From then on the situation improved slightly as domestic transport resumed and food aid from Sweden and Switzerland arrived. In March the new offensive against the Germans began, which resulted in the liberation of the eastern part of the country in April and the end of war on 4 May 1945.

## RECOVERY AND RECONSTRUCTION

The new cabinet that was installed in June 1945 first of all had to oversee the recovery of the economy. The lack of food, coal, and raw materials, especially in the western part of the country, had to be solved and transport systems and industrial capacity had to be repaired and put into operation.

Most of the required goods had to be imported and the provision of foreign exchange therefore became one of the most urgent problems. Yet the cabinet wanted to do more than just restore the economy to prewar status. The reform of society, according to ideas developed before and during the war by social democrats and other social reformers, was high on the agenda. In fact, the cabinet was headed by W. Schermerhorn, one of the most outspoken representatives of the movement to 'break through' the pillarized structure of prewar society (De Liagre Böhl *et al*. 1981: 27ff). Finally, the cabinet had to adapt the economy to the new conditions of the afterwar period: population growth had been strong in the preceding decade, but productive capacity had actually decreased as a result of war damage, and the increase of employment in agriculture had led to a decline in its efficiency. The rebuilding of industrial capacity would also contribute to the huge external deficit. First estimates of the balance of payments revealed that it would be very difficult to close that deficit. As a result, long-term policies for restructuring the economy and increase of international competitiveness were also needed (De Liagre Böhl *et al*. 1981: 131 ff).

First attempts to estimate the extent of the war damage showed that the Dutch economy was badly hurt – probably more than most other European countries. On aggregate, about 40 percent of the capital stock was lost according to the 1945 figures (and as long as there was still some discussion on German war reparations, there was no reason to lower these estimates) (Van Zanden and Griffiths 1989: 185). Moreover, the disastrously high figures warranted a policy of restraint – wage and price controls – to try and overcome the enormous fall in the productive capacity of the economy.

Newer and better informed estimates pointed to a much lower level of war damage. In 1948 the CBS could present a more detailed picture which showed that about 29 percent of the 1939 capital stock was lost during the war. Losses in the transport sector were highest (61 percent), followed by industry (29 percent, including an 85 percent reduction in stocks), while agriculture had been least affected (a 14 percent loss of capital goods) (Van Zanden and Griffiths 1989: 186). However, these estimates neglected the fact that in certain industries – metal working, and shipbuilding – German orders and finance had made possible large-scale investments. Productive capacity (and employment) in these industries had increased markedly between 1939 and 1946. When this is taken into account, the decline in the capital stock was probably less than 10 percent (a recent study suggested 7 percent) (Van Ark and De Jong 1996).

Another legacy of the war was the inflated money supply, the result of the exploitation of the economy by the Germans. Whereas the supply of goods had shrunk by more than 50 percent during the occupation, the money supply had grown to more than four times the prewar figure (Table

Table 7.4 Money supply and national income, 1938–1951 (in million guilders)

|  | Money supply (1) | National income (2) | Ratio (1)/(2) |
|---|---|---|---|
| 1938 | 2,480 | 5,400 | 46 |
| 1945, May | 10,908 | 3,000 | 300–400 |
| 1945, Dec. | 4,100 | 8,000 | 51 |
| 1946 | 5,410 | 9,930 | 54 |
| 1947 | 6,470 | 12,070 | 54 |
| 1948 | 7,190 | 14,230 | 51 |
| 1949 | 7,337 | 15,960 | 46 |
| 1950 | 7,267 | 17,750 | 41 |
| 1951 | 6,984 | 19,560 | 36 |

Source: Lieftinck 1973: 14

7.4). Already during the war plans had been made for a currency reform, but these were delayed because the new money first had to be printed. As an immediate measure, on 9 July 1945 all banknotes of 100 guilders were declared void. The population was asked to return the notes; their counter-value would be deposited on a blocked bank account. The second tranche of the currency reform followed in September when all other notes were withdrawn from circulation. Every household received ten guilders of the new money in return to cover expenses during the first week. Popular belief has it that for once all the Dutch were equally poor during the week of 26 September (Barendregt 1993).

There are many ways to implement a currency reform. Often the aim of reducing the money stock is realized by 'punishing' people who happen to have a lot of money (banknotes, deposits in banks), whereas the possession of goods – from stocks and bonds to real estate – is left out of considera-tion. A trade-off between efficiency (how to realize a smooth and fast reduction in the money supply) and equity (how to distribute the implicit burden equally among the population) was at stake. Most currency reforms seem to opt for an efficient solution and, in a way, spare the speculator who has turned his money into goods (Barendregt 1993: 89 ff).

Dutch policymakers, and especially the social democrat Pieter Lieftinck who headed the operation as Minister of Finance, chose a rather different kind of currency reform in which considerations of equity predominated. All money that was handed in was deposited in blocked bank accounts. Next, two capital levies were introduced to share the burden of the war as equally as possible. The first, the *Vermogensaanwasbelasting*, rigorously taxed any increase in wealth between 1940 and 1946. If the increase was the result of legitimate activities, the tax rate varied between 50 and 70 per-cent. Illegal activities (black market trade and working for the Germans) were taxed at 90 percent. The second, the *Vermogensheffing ineens*, was a

125

tax on the level of capital wealth in 1946, with progressive rates ranging from 4 to 20 percent (Barendregt 1993: 172–80).

The basic idea of the currency reform was that all inhabitants first had to pay these taxes (as well as the large arrears of the normal income tax of the war years) before the accounts into which their money had been deposited could be unblocked. This meant that (a) a lot of money (i.e. the proceeds of the taxes) was taken out of circulation; (b) that unblocking would take time to levy all these taxes, during which the economy could recover and the supply of goods could return to the prewar level. The final aim was to restore monetary equilibrium, which was defined as the prewar relationship between money supply and national income (see Table 7.4).

The big dilemma was, of course, that this complex currency reform should not obstruct the recovery of the economy, which was essential for its very success. New money should be available to entrepreneurs for the payment of wages and salaries as well as raw materials, to households for the purchase of basic necessities, to the government for continuing its operations, etc. To ensure that the taxes on wealth could be levied and that speculators would not radically move into other assets, capital markets were restricted in their operations; the stock market was closely watched and became almost paralysed (Barendregt 1993: 156–60). Two different circuits developed: one of 'blocked money', subject to many restrictions and increasingly complicated rules, and one of new money. The costs of the currency reform were substantial in terms of: (a) the enormous bureaucratic apparatus that implemented it; (b) the many restrictions on the functioning of the economy (especially the capital market). Unblocking was done in a number of phases and continued until 1952. The liberalization of the Amsterdam Stock Exchange also took a number of years (De Vries 1976: 201 ff). In essence, this was the price paid by the population for a relatively equitable currency reform.

In some respects it was an immediate success: it contributed to the popularity of the new cabinet (though not with every inhabitant), and lowered the money supply by more than 60 per cent. In 1946 and 1947, however, the continued unblocking of deposits and large government deficits led to a renewed increase in the money supply (large deficits on the balance of payments notwithstanding) (Table 7.4). Consequently, a total liberalization of the economy (as had happened in Belgium after the currency reform of 1944) was not yet considered. This would have led to a strong increase in prices (and wages), which would undermine the efforts at recovery. The system to control the price level – the distribution apparatus of the war economy – was therefore kept in place.

But in spite of growing criticism of the inefficiency of the system, economic recovery was quite spectacular. At the end of 1945 industrial production was at 38 percent of the prewar level; it doubled in the next two years, with a brief interruption during the winter of 1947. Agricultural production, which had fallen less, recovered more slowly, mainly because it took time to rebuild the stocks of cattle and horses (CBS 1955: 314). In 1946 and 1947 recovery was well under way.

Increasingly the real bottleneck in the recovery process became the deficit on the balance of payments. In 1946 only 37 percent of imports was covered by exports, and the resulting deficit accounted for 14 percent of GDP (see Table 7.5). The enormous expansion of (pent-up) demand to rebuild the economy was partly to blame. Another contribution to the problem was that incomes from foreign investments were much lower than before the war, largely because of the disorganization of the Indonesian economy and the sale of foreign securities to finance the deficit. Finally, the government needed huge funds for the 'liberation' of the colony. In the years to come, the refusal to recognize the new Republic of Indonesia would draw heavily on Dutch government finances and currency reserves.

During 1946 emergency measures, such as the forced sale of foreign securities and the negotiation of American (short-term) loans, made it possible to finance the huge trade deficit. More than 50 percent of the deficit was with the dollar area – especially with the USA, while the sterling area contributed another 10 to 20 percent of the deficit (Van Zanden and Griffiths 1989: 192). However, at the end of 1946 the government had to scale down its recovery programme as a result of the dollar gap. The original plan, prepared by the Central Planning Bureau (CPB) to buy almost 2 billion guilders of goods in the dollar area, had to be lowered by almost 60 percent, as it proved impossible to find sufficient funds. The economy was certainly heading for a slower recovery as a result of the balance of payments problem.

A number of measures was taken to speed up exports. For example, firms which mainly produced for foreign markets were given preferential access

Table 7.5 Imports, exports, income from abroad, and Marshall Aid as a share of national income (percent) 1938–1951

|  | 1938 | 1946 | 1947 | 1948 | 1949 | 1950 | 1951 |
|---|---|---|---|---|---|---|---|
| Imports | 24.2 | 22.9 | 33.5 | 32.7 | 31.0 | 42.0 | 42.8 |
| Exports | 19.9 | 8.7 | 16.9 | 19.6 | 23.6 | 30.6 | 35.9 |
| Balance of trade | −4.3 | −14.2 | −16.6 | −13.1 | −7.4 | −11.4 | −6.9 |
| Services and income from abroad | 6.2 | 0.0 | 1.7 | 2.4 | 5.3 | 4.8 | 5.2 |
| Balance of payments | 1.9 | −14.2 | −14.8 | −9.2 | −2.0 | −6.6 | −1.7 |
| Marshall Aid | – | – | – | 5.0 | 8.4 | 6.9 | 2.5 |

Source: Van Zanden and Griffiths 1989: 191

127

to raw materials, labour and unblocked money. Large corporations such as KLM and Philips profited greatly from these measures (and from preferential treatment by the government) (Bakker and Van Lent 1989: 109–10). As a result, exports went up dramatically, more than doubling in 1947. Yet despite the favourable development of exports, the relative rise of export prices, and the large cuts in the dollar-spending programme, the import gap actually widened in 1947, reaching an all-time high of one-sixth of GDP (Table 7.5).

The announcement of a programme to assist European recovery by George Marshall in 1947 therefore received a warm welcome in the Netherlands. The cabinet immediately consulted the Belgian government in order to formulate combined plans (because Marshall had made closer European cooperation one of the conditions for its implementation). The two countries began to inject new life into the virtually moribund plans to form a Benelux economic union to show their willingness (Van der Eng 1987: 35). In the forthcoming negotiations the Dutch had the advantage that the magnitude of the dollar gap was one of the criteria for distributing the funds. The Netherlands could outperform almost all other European countries in this respect. As a result, it received a fairly large share of the funds of the Marshall Plan – more than most other European countries (Milward 1984: 104–7). These funds contributed enormously to the closing of the balance of trade deficit between 1948 and 1951 (Table 7.5). The gradual increase in income from international services and the continued strong growth of exports also helped to narrow the external gap.

The Marshall Plan had important consequences for reconstruction. Large amounts of foodstuffs (breadgrains), raw materials (cotton and tobacco), and machines for the rapidly growing metal working and chemical industries, could be financed (Van der Eng 1987: 173). Payment for these goods in guilders was deposited in a counterpart account, and the money was used to fund a number of large-scale government investments and to liquidate part of the government debt. Finally, the programme signalled the beginning of European cooperation; the OEEC was founded to administer the funds and in 1950 the EPU (European Payments Union) was set up to liberalize intra-European exchange. The Benelux countries had particularly asked for such an initiative to improve the conditions for international trade.

A final measure that contributed to the restoration of external equilibrium was the devaluation of the guilder vis-à-vis the dollar. Already in 1944 the government in exile had devalued by 30 percent, but the huge dollar gap showed that this had not been enough. In 1947 about 5 percent of dollar imports was covered by exports, and notwithstanding the continuous growth of exports in the following year, this share hardly increased (it was 15 percent in 1949). Already in August 1949 the cabinet discussed the possibility of another devaluation, albeit without taking a decision. This was more or less forced upon them by the devaluation of the pound sterling in September of that year, soon followed by the Scandinavian currencies. The Dutch government chose the same degree of devaluation as the British, namely 30 percent. Exports to the dollar area shot up immediately: in 1950 30 percent of imports was covered by exports to the dollar zone, which increased to 42 percent in 1952 (Van Zanden and Griffiths 1989: 196).

The development of the German economy had always been of vital importance to the Netherlands. As long as the Allies did not agree on a policy of economic reconstruction and the German economy remained as disorganized as it was in 1945, the Dutch economy would be cut off from its most important export market. The share of Germany in Dutch exports had declined from 14.6 percent in 1938 (already much lower than during the 1920s) to 3.1 percent in 1947. Similarly, imports from Germany had declined from 21 percent of total imports in 1938 to less than 3 percent in 1946 and 1947 (CBS 1979: 112–18). The rapid recovery of the German economy after the currency reform and its liberalization in 1948 brought new hope for a revival of Dutch–German trade. In September 1949 one of the last acts of the Allied authorities was to grant the Netherlands a new agreement which implied a complete liberalization of mutual trade. Dutch exports to the booming German economy sky-rocketed: its share in total exports climbed from 5.9 percent in 1948 to 20.6 percent in 1950 (CBS 1979: 112–18). This signalled the beginning of a return to 'normal' international trade relationships.

The decision to join the Schuman Plan to form a European Community for Coal and Steel was also dominated by concerns over the future development of the German economy. For obvious reasons the Dutch welcomed any plan that would stimulate the integration of Germany into Western Europe and on that score even the relatively 'interventionist' Schuman Plan met the test (Griffiths 1990).

The beginning of the Marshall Plan in 1948 and the sharp rise in export earnings (temporarily) solved the balance of payments problem. But before a complete liberalization of the economy could be realized other internal imbalances had to be corrected. The currency reform of 1945 had sharply reduced the money supply, but the gradual unblocking of accounts and large government deficits resulted in a renewed increase, which outpaced even the fast recovery of the economy (Table 7.4). The large government deficits had a number of causes: the immediate needs of recovery and reconstruction, the military actions in Indonesia, and the maintenance of a costly bureaucratic apparatus to control the economy and implement the currency reform (Lieftinck 1973).

Moreover, government debt had increased enormously during the war and interest payments took a large share of the budget. A major problem was to consolidate the huge short-term debt, which would be strongly inflationary once the economy was liberalized. The afterwar situation of extreme capital scarcity and the enormous demand for funds by the government to finance its deficit and consolidate its short-term debt would normally have resulted in a strong rise in interest rates, which would have crippled government finances even more. To counter these problems Lieftinck introduced his 'cheap money' policy (De Vries 1994: 471–3). Credits were rationed: banks had to ask advance permission for giving credits over 50,000 guilders, and the Central Bank had to see to it that the only credits granted were those 'essential' for the reconstruction. Moreover, holders of blocked money could buy 3 percent government bonds to earn at least some interest. Through these and a number of other devices Leiftinck kept interest rates at a low level (Meade *et al*. 1964: 147–50). By rationing private demand for credit the government could in fact monopolize the capital market and dictate interest rates.

Marshall Aid was also fundamental in easing the inflationary threat to the economy in 1948 and 1949. The crediting of large sums on the counter-value fund meant that this money was (temporarily) withdrawn from circulation. As a result, the money supply stabilized after 1948 and the ratio between money supply and national income began to fall to the prewar 'equilibrium' (Table 7.4). Moreover, the government managed substantially to lower the deficit in 1948 and 1949, mainly because of the decline in expenditure on reconstruction and the final acceptance of the independence of Indonesia.

External pressures also contributed to the liberalization of the economy in 1949. The newly founded Benelux (see Chapter 8) remained a 'paper tiger' as long as the domestic economy was dominated by planning and distribution. The USA made liberalization of the economy one of the conditions of the Marshall Plan. These pressures helped the Minister of Economic Affairs J.R.M. van de Brink to push through the almost complete liberalization of the economy in 1948–9. The distribution system was dissolved and price controls were relaxed – only coffee remained subject to rationing until 1951. Simultaneously, import quotas for a large number of goods were ended (in the middle of 1950 as much as 65 percent of imports was completely liberalized) and the rationing of credit was relaxed (Clerx 1986: 59 ff).

There were however important exceptions. To keep down the cost of living, agricultural products remained strictly controlled and rents were frozen at the 1941 level and the guided wage policy kept wage restraint in place.

This rather sudden liberalization of the economy resulted in a modest increase in price levels. According to the cost-of-living indices inflation, which had been 3 to 4 percent in 1947 and 1948, accelerated to 6 percent in 1949 and about 10 percent in 1950 and 1951; wholesale prices increased even more (Lieftinck 1973: 26). In 1950–1 this inflation was, however, partly imported because prices on the world market shot up during the first months of the Korean War.

Imports also increased sharply during 1948–9 (see Table 7.5). In combination with a deterioration of the terms of trade as a result of the Korean boom on world markets, this resulted in a renewed increase in the balance of payments deficit. At the beginning of 1951 the cabinet had to announce a number of measures to counteract overheating of the economy.

The liberalization of the economy in 1949–50 signalled the end of the period of recovery. The economy had grown almost without interruption between 1945 and the end of 1950. Industrial production had regained the prewar level in 1947 and was already 40 percent above this level by 1949–50. Only coal mining did not yet surpass prewar production levels. In agriculture recovery was also completed by 1950, when the 1939 level of production was reached for the first time. Moreover, agriculture had made an impressive contribution to the solution of the balance of payments problems, since between 1946 and 1950 about 45 to 50 percent of exports consisted of agricultural products (Fortuyn 1980: 474). International services expanded more slowly, mainly as a result of the stagnation of the German economy until 1948. The merchant fleet was again at its prewar level in 1949, but port activities and international river transport were still relatively depressed. Finally, estimates of GDP show that already in 1948 it surpassed the 1939 level; GDP per capita followed in 1950 (CBS 1955: 292).

The first postwar cabinet not only aimed at economic recovery and reconstruction, but also wanted to reform society at large. In this attempt it could build on the desire to 'break through' the prewar pillarized structure of society, a desire widespread in academic and political circles, and on two traditions of social reform proposals of the Catholics and the social-democrats. During the interwar period Catholic thinkers had developed ideas for a corporatist restructuring of the economy in which 'labour' and 'capital' would cooperate with each other. At the same time, the social-democrats had more or less abandoned their proposals for the nationalization of the means of production and instead began to advocate the introduction of planning and demand management as a way to guarantee full employment and growth.

Broadly speaking, both traditions merged into the economic programme of the first cabinet. In September 1945 Hein Vos, Minister of Economic Affairs (co-author with Jan Tinbergen of the 1935 *Plan van de Arbeid*), announced the founding of the Centraal Planbureau. This was to be an independent government agency, which would advise government on the effects of policies on the basis of an economic (and econometric) understanding of the economy. Tinbergen became its first director (Fortuyn 1980: 173 ff).

Vos announced the next and far more daring plan in December 1945: an ambitious plan for the corporatist restructuring of the economy. He hoped to reconcile the socialist ideals of a 'managed' economy with the Catholic notions of cooperation between employers and employees. The plan started with the introduction of a strict restructuring of the economy, more or less in line with the distribution agencies (*rijksinkoopbureaus*) that had managed the war economy. Every branch of industry would be given its own organization to regulate almost every aspect of production and distribution, and would severely restrict the independence of individual businessmen. The central authority in each organization would be a government appointed commissioner, while other members were to be chosen by employers and employees (Fortuyn 1980: 195 ff; De Liagre Böhl *et al.* 1981: 62 ff).

The plan met with considerable criticism, as many feared that it would give government an almost complete control over the economy. Employers' organizations, right-wing liberals, and the confessional parties all strongly opposed the proposed law. Even the Stichting van de Arbeid, the official representative of 'labour' and 'capital' and itself perhaps the most prominent result of the desire for real socio-economic change, published a strong criticism of the plan, nicely spelling out that Vos had consulted neither unions nor employers' organization in its making (Van Bottenburg 1995: 108).

The first elections after the war in 1946 proved to be a test case for these ambitious plans. In a sense, the Labour Party lost the elections (because it received a much smaller share of the votes than it had expected), whereas the Catholic Party regained its strong middle position and could dominate negotiations about the formation of the new government. It demanded that Vos would be succeeded by the conservative Huysmans and that the plan for restructuring the economy would be radically changed. Moreover, employers and trade unions would be closely consulted about all new plans.

The new plan that was introduced in 1948 was completely different. It stressed the voluntary nature of the new organizations, only to be set up at the request of a branch, as well as their limited influence. Above the branch organizations there would be a Sociaal–Economische Raad (SER) (Social–Economic Council), which had to become the official advisory board of the government on all social and economic issues (Van Bottenburg 1995: 109). Unions and employers' organizations would each appoint a third of the members of the SER, the remaining third would consist of independent members selected by the government. The plan was made into law in 1950, which signalled the end of the discussion on the economic restructuring. Little came of the voluntary branch organizations afterwards; only in (heavily organized) agriculture did they play a role of some importance.

Another part of the institutional 'rebuilding' of Dutch society was the nationalization of the Central Bank in 1948. Already in 1945 the Minister of Finance received the authority to give guidelines to the bank. However, the banking law of 1948, which announced its nationalization, created a number of guarantees for its independence (De Vries 1994: 480 ff).

During the interwar period the lack of venture capital for small and medium-sized industries had generally been regarded as a bottleneck. The establishment of the Herstelbank in 1945 was aimed at solving the problem. A number of private banks participated in the project, but the government bore most of the risk. Starting in 1946 the Herstelbank supplied capital to (industrial) firms under a guarantee from the government (Posthuma 1955). The bank was a real success during the first decade; later the other banks more or less took over its role.

The importance of these attempts at rebuilding the institutional structure of the economy must not be exaggerated. The CPB (Central Planning Bureau), a creation of the socialist Vos, remained rather isolated during the first years after the war, but slowly built up its prestige and influence (Passenier 1994: 81 ff). During the 1950s its predictions began to play a role in attempts to manipulate the demand side of the economy. The SER did not suffer from these initial problems, but its recommendations were rarely unanimous, which made it possible for cabinets to do whatever they had already intended. The nationalization of the Central Bank did not really change its status or its policies in the long run. The Stichting van de Arbeid, the symbol of the historical compromise between labour and capital, was perhaps the most important change of all, certainly in the first years after the war. It made possible the implementation of the guided wage policy which was important for long-term economic performance (see Chapter 8).

One of the side effects of the attempts at institutional renewal was the end of the debate on the future structuring of the economy. The sharp ideological differences of the interwar period (and before), in which socialists and to a lesser extent Catholic reformers proposed radical changes in economy and society, disappeared after 1950. It seemed almost as if an end had come to all ideology and that the major parties shared a consensus about the desirability of economic growth, industrialization, and the extension of the welfare state. The SER, in which the 'social partners' (trade unions and employers' organizations) discussed economic and social policies with the government, symbolized this new consensus. In its first advice of 1951 it formulated the goals of economic policy that were shared by all parties: full employment, a balance of payments in equilibrium, a stable price level, economic growth, and an equitable distribution of incomes. In order to realize these goals new instruments had been developed to everyone's satisfaction, namely the wage policy and the industrialization policy (see Chapter 8). After twenty years of stagnation – in 1950 per capita GDP only just surpassed the level of 1929 – the Netherlands was ready for a new period of strong economic growth.

# 8

# THE GOLDEN YEARS 1950–1973

## MACROECONOMIC PERFORMANCE

The quarter of a century between the liberalization of the economy in 1948–9 and the oil crisis at the end of 1973 was a unique period of fast and stable economic growth. The economy expanded at an (unprecedented) average rate of almost 5 percent per year, and only in 1958 did there occur a minor contraction of GDP. Unemployment fell to less than 2 percent of the labour force. During the 1960s the economy was almost constantly in a state of 'overemployment', with demand for labour in excess of supply. However, in comparison with the rest of Western Europe the growth rate of GDP was not exceptionally high, and the relatively rapid increase in population kept the growth of per capita GDP around the average (Van Ark and De Jong 1996).

An important reason for the strong performance was the favourable development of the world economy. A number of American initiatives to form a stable system of international economic relations had been highly successful and these were supplemented with European plans to reorganize and liberalize intra-European trade (see pp. 155–7). As a result, international trade expanded enormously during the 1950s and 1960s and there began a process of 'catching up' which narrowed productivity differences between Europe and the USA (Maddison 1993).

There was also a national dimension to the story of the 'golden years'. One of the most interesting questions is to what extent national economic policies contributed to the 'Dutch miracle' of the period, i.e. to what extent the guided wage policy or the industrialization plans of the 1950s were fundamental to the rapid economic growth of the period (Griffiths 1996b). This question will be returned to in the next section. It was, however, certain that the enormous expansion of Dutch exports was helped by the guided wage policy. Exports were indeed the most dynamic part of demand during this period. Their volume increased at almost twice the rate of total GDP (Table 8.1). This result is remarkable given the relatively unfavourable composition of Dutch exports, with its large share of agricultural

134

*Table 8.1* Growth of GDP and its components, 1951–1973
(average annual growth rates)

|                     | *1951–63* | *1963–73* | *1951–73* |
|---------------------|-----------|-----------|-----------|
| GDP                 | 4.4       | 5.5       | 4.9       |
| Private consumption | 4.9       | 5.3       | 5.1       |
| Govt consumption    | 4.3       | 2.6       | 3.5       |
| Private investment  | 6.1       | 7.4       | 6.5       |
| Govt investment     | 6.9       | 2.8       | 5.0       |
| Exports             | 8.3       | 10.4      | 9.3       |
| Imports             | 8.5       | 9.8       | 9.1       |

*Source*: CBS, *Nationale Rekeningen*, 1958–1973

products. Especially during the 1950s, favourable supply-side forces (low wages and prices) seem to offer a better explanation than the average growth of exports (see pp. 149–50).

Apart from exports, investments were the dominant force in the growth of GDP (Table 8.1). The extension and modernization of industrial capacity was stimulated by the industrialization plans of the 1950s and by the high level of profitability in the economy. Whereas private investment even accelerated during the 1960s, the growth of public investment (and public consumption) fell (despite a strong increase in taxation, which was mainly used to increase social transfers). Finally, the growth of consumption was more or less in line with the general expansion of GDP (Table 8.1).

The demand side of the economy was dominated to a large extent by the rapid expansion of exports and investments. The supply side shows a small increase of labour input, the result of a modest growth in the labour force and a strong decline in working hours, and a much greater expansion of the capital stock and the stock of R&D (Table 6.2). The human capital stock also increased fairly quickly at almost 1 percent per year. About half of the growth of GDP can be explained from these increases in inputs; the other half resulted from the growth of productivity. In short, the fundamental supply-side forces behind the economic miracle of the period were capital formation and technological change that resulted in higher levels of productivity.

The economic expansion was distributed unequally among the various sectors of the economy. Judging from the growth of production and productivity the industrial sector was the engine of growth during the 1950s. Moreover, industrial employment increased rapidly during this decade (Table 8.2). The situation changed after 1963. Industrial output growth fell slightly, whereas the growth rate of production increased in all other sectors. The increase in employment stagnated because productivity growth accelerated in almost every sector. At the same time the growth rate of investments went up, which indicates that capital formation was increasingly aimed at 'deepening' the capital stock and at replacing labour.

135

*Table 8.2* Growth of output, employment and labour productivity in six sectors of the economy, 1953–1973 (average annual growth rates)

| | Output | | Employment | | Labour productivity | |
|---|---|---|---|---|---|---|
| | *53–63* | *63–73* | *53–63* | *63–73* | *53–63* | *63–73* |
| Agriculture | 2.1 | 4.5 | −2.9 | −3.3 | 5.0 | 7.8 |
| Industry | 6.8 | 6.4 | 1.7 | −0.7 | 5.1 | 7.1 |
| Energy | 5.1 | 12.3 | −0.5 | −4.5 | 5.6 | 16.8 |
| Construction | 2.6 | 3.5 | 2.8 | 1.1 | −0.2 | 2.4 |
| Tertiary | 5.0 | 5.1 | 2.1 | 1.3 | 2.9 | 3.8 |
| Quarternary | 3.2 | 3.9 | 2.9 | 4.9 | 0.3 | −1.0 |
| *Total* | 4.9 | 5.9 | 1.4 | 0.5 | 3.5 | 5.4 |

*Source*: CPB 1986: 268–71

Both trends, the deceleration of industrial output growth and the increase in productivity growth, led to a decline in industrial employment after 1965, but because employment in services and construction underwent strong growth this was not yet considered a problem.

Table 8.1 shows that the growth of the Dutch economy accelerated during the 1960s in contrast to most other European countries. This (modest) acceleration is remarkable for a number of reasons. First, international competitiveness – as measured by real effective exchange rates – definitely declined during the late 1950s and early 1960s. Especially the introduction of the five-day work week and the revaluation of the guilder in 1960–1 led to a strong rise in relative wage costs. This temporarily slowed down the increase in exports, but after 1966 there began a renewed strong growth in the share of Dutch exports in world trade, even though Dutch international competitiveness was much weaker (see below). Profits on exports (and on production in general) declined, because entrepreneurs continued to conquer new foreign markets despite cost pressures at home. The share of 'other income' in GDP (at factor costs) – a rough indicator of profit income – increased during the 1950s, peaked in 1960, but declined rapidly thereafter (until the late 1970s) (Graph 8.1). Real share prices on the Amsterdam Stock Exchange displayed an almost identical development: a strong increase during the 1950s, a peak in 1961 (indicating perhaps that share prices lagged behind the real development of profits), and followed by an almost continuous decline until 1982. Only between 1966 and 1969 was the trend in both indicators interrupted by an upturn in (anticipated) profits. This was also related to international competitiveness, because during these years wage costs in the rest of Europe increased even faster than in the Netherlands (see also Armstrong *et al.* 1984: 241 ff). This short interlude ended in 1970 and during the short boom of 1971–3 real share prices fell once again.

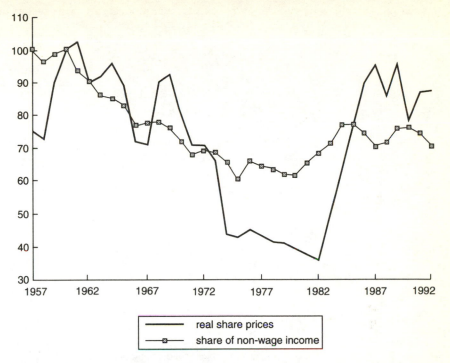

*Graph 8.1* Real share prices and share of non-wage income in total net income
(at factor costs), 1957–1992 (indices 1960 = 100)
*Sources:* CBS 1994 and Graph 3.1

The paradox of the 1960s is that exports and investments grew even more rapidly than during the preceding decade in spite of the declining profitability of industry. This contributed to an intensification of the boom, the continuation of overemployment on the labour market, and the acceleration of the rate of inflation. In short, the decline in profits did not relax the economy and decrease growth rates, as standard economic theory predicts.

Part of the explanation is that the direction of investments in industry changed. Graph 8.2 shows the relationship between industrial employment and investments in machinery and equipment. During the 1950s investments were aimed at widening the industrial basis of the economy and they resulted in a strong increase in industrial employment. However, the relationship between investment and employment growth changed during the 1960s: investments continued to rise, but employment stagnated and even declined slowly after 1965. The year 1970 was a second turning point after which investments began to decline in real terms, which led to a very strong fall in industrial employment.

In the long run the change in the direction of investment in response to

137

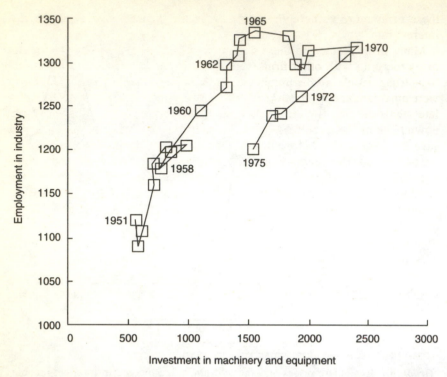

*Graph 8.2* Employment (thousands of manyears) and investments in machinery
and equipment in industry (in 1953 prices), 1951–1975
*Sources*: CBS 1951–1975

rising wage costs resulted in the rise of (structural) employment. In the
short term the demand effects of the renewed investment drive seem to
have stimulated growth and contributed to the overexpansion of the 1960s.
Moreover, falling profits and the need to step up investment to save wage
costs led to a growing imbalance in the financial structure of enterprises.
During the 1950s more than 70 percent of private investment was financed
out of retained profits, encouraged by government policies (i.e. profit tax
rebates for investments) (Dercksen 1986: 135–7). In the 1960s falling profit
rates made it increasingly necessary for firms to attract loans to finance
their investments. This made them more dependent on contacts with banks
and other financial institutes. The share of equity capital in the total assets
of the largest industrial enterprises fell from 54 percent in 1965 to 38 percent in 1973 and 32 percent in 1979; short-term loans increased sharply
from 25 percent (1965) to 37 percent (1979) (CBS 1984: 87). This did not
undermine profitability so long as real interest rates were low – and lower
than real earnings on total assets – but the decline in solvent assets made

these firms more vulnerable to changes in the business cycle and the real interest rate.

Many firms reacted to these pressures by trying to diversify production or by merging with other firms. During the 1960s a merger movement led to a strong decline in the number of large industrial enterprises when many were amalgamated or, in some instances, taken over by foreign firms. In the late 1960s the first big industrial firms (especially in textiles) had to close down. One of the main reasons for the merger movement was to cut costs, save on overhead, and profit from economies of scale, for example, by introducing large computer mainframes. Diversification into other – and hopefully more profitable – activities was another basic reaction to the combined pressures of rising (wage) costs and increased international competition. As will be shown, the standard response of the government to declining industries was also to try and merge the remaining firms and diversify their operations.

A general expansion of the role of the government in the economy added to the tension as it resulted in a strong increase in taxes and social security premiums. This is in stark contrast with the (early) 1950s when there occurred a slow reduction in the share of government in total GDP. Although the various cabinets were aware of the risks of overly expanding the government sector and tried to cut a number of budgets, the pressure to expand the welfare state was irresistible (see Chapter 4).

A final feature of the change in the macroeconomic development of the golden years was the increase in the rate of inflation. In Chapter 9 more attention will be paid to the shift in the Phillips curve that occurred in the early 1970s. Between 1950 and 1970 this curve had been relatively stable: low unemployment was associated with high inflation, and vice versa. The first sign that things were changing was probably the relatively high rate of inflation in 1969 (see Graph 8.3). In 1970 a temporary price stop (of six months) appears to have contained the problem somewhat, but in the next few years inflation as well as unemployment increased spectacularly, and the new phenomenon of stagflation was born. A typical feature of the change in the inflationary expectations that lay behind the shift in the Phillips curve was the introduction of wage indexation in almost every CAO of the late 1960s (Windmuller and De Galan 1979: II, 163). At the same time conditions on the labour market deteriorated (Chapter 5).

Superficially, the golden years between 1950 and 1973 seem to have been a homogeneous period of very rapid growth, driven mainly by increase in exports and investments. However, a close look at various indicators of macroeconomic performance shows the important shifts that were taking place. The economic 'eldorado' of the 1950s, a period of rising profits and rapid industrialization, disappeared as a result of its very success. But the declining profits of the 1960s did not cool down the economy – in fact, investment and exports grew at an even higher rate,

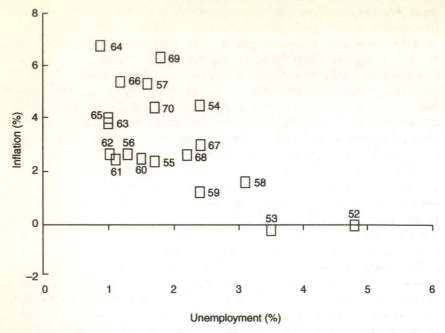

*Graph 8.3* Relationship between unemployment and inflation, 1952–1970
*Source*: CPB 1969, 1971

which resulted in a serious 'overheating' of the economy. Wages began to outgrow productivity in the 1960s, inflation accelerated, especially after 1970, and the financial structure of enterprise was undermined.

In the economic literature on the causes of 'structural' unemployment in the 1970s and 1980s much attention has been paid to the 'wage explosion' of 1963–4 as the decisive turning point in postwar economic development. This analysis does not corroborate that view: the decline in profits and international competitiveness predates the 1963–4 events; the 'first' wage explosion of 1960–1 seems to have been much more decisive. Moreover, after 1966 – or shortly after the second wage explosion of 1963–4 – there is a short reversal of trends, probably caused mainly by the fact that wage costs in the rest of Europe rose even more strongly during these years. In most other European countries the events of 1967 to 1970 led to a sudden fall in profits and, after some delay, in investment (Armstrong *et al*. 1984: 245–7). The fall in profits in the Netherlands already had begun in 1961, but the boom of the 1960s was extended and intensified by the relatively favourable developments of the years after 1966. The year 1970 marked the end of this phase: investment in industry started to fall and at the same time there began an outward shift of the Phillips curve.

The result was that the 'exogenous' shocks of the 1970s – i.e. the oil

140

price hike and the downturn of the international economy that followed – struck an economy that had become quite vulnerable. The supply side of the economy had been undermined by the increasingly imbalanced financial structure of enterprise, high wage costs and rapidly rising level of taxation. It is therefore evident that there was a national dimension to the economic problems of the 1970s and 1980s which was very much unlike the situation of the 1930s, when the Depression was entirely 'imported'.

## AGRICULTURE, INDUSTRY AND SERVICES

There was perhaps no sector of the economy that changed so fundamentally during the golden years as agriculture (Douw 1990). Throughout the nineteenth and first half of the twentieth century the primary sector had already contributed to economic development in many ways, even though it faced large structural problems, such as a slow growth of final demand, a continuous increase in its labour force, and the predominance of relatively small and rather inefficient family farms. The long boom of the 1950s and 1960s did much to alleviate these problems, first and foremost by causing a large outflow of labour that made possible an enormous increase in labour productivity (Table 8.2). The process was, however, spurred on by a number of government policies aimed at the rationalization of the farm structure. Large-scale projects to consolidate holdings (*ruilverkavelingen*) were vigorously promoted and heavily subsidized in order to solve the 'small farmer's problem'. As a result the number of farms declined sharply – by almost 50 percent in livestock and arable farming between 1950 and 1974 – and their average size grew accordingly (Douw 1990). Employment in agriculture declined even more as the class of agricultural wage labourers shrunk in size. The fall in labour input was compensated for by a strong rise in mechanization, initiated by the imports of tractors paid for by the Marshall Aid.

The strong performance of agriculture was to a large extent caused by the fact that the family farms were embedded in a tight infrastructure of agricultural research, education, and extension services, which gave a continuous impulse to change production techniques and – in the horticultural sector – develop 'new' products. This system of research, education, and extension dated back to the beginning of the twentieth century, but as (European) markets for agricultural products expanded and demand diversified it was able to fulfil its role in an optimal way (Post 1990: 122). At the same time the importance of 'agro-business' increased rapidly. Rural banks supplied agriculture with the capital it needed. Cooperatives and commercial firms, which specialized in the supply of inputs (such as fodder and fertilizer) or the processing of output, developed into sizeable and even multinational companies. Around 1970 the share of 'agro-business' in GDP surpassed the (declining) share of agriculture itself (Ministerie van Land-bouw 1977).

After 1958 the old problem that supply tended to outgrow demand was temporarily 'solved' by the creation of a protected European market for agriculture. Exports expanded rapidly, much more than domestic consumption, and as a result of its favourable food balance the Netherlands profited considerably from the Common Agricultural Policy. However, the performance of agriculture was especially strong in sectors that received little or no protection; bulbs and flowers, the most dynamic part of horticulture, were a telling example (Ministerie van Landbouw 1977).

The growth of industrial employment and output became one of the priorities of government policy during the 1950s. Chapter 7 has told the story of the failure of the plans of Hein Vos to restructure and 'plan' the postwar Dutch economy. But this story did not end with the elections of 1946 or with the liberalization of the economy by Van den Brink in 1948–9. In 1947–8 schemes had to be made for future expenditure in order to acquire funds from the Marshall Plan. During this exercise it was acknowledged that, even though the economy recovered rapidly, its long-term economic problems were not yet solved. According to the predictions of 1947–8 structural unemployment would rise rapidly as a result of the acceleration of the growth of labour supply and the deficit on the balance of payments seemed to run out of control. The only solution that could be offered was a further acceleration of industrial growth; industries that exported a large part of their output had to be given a special stimulus. This would create employment and in the long run (after the end of the Marshal Plan) it would solve the external problem (De Liagre Böhl 1981: 196–212).

These problems were widely discussed in 1947–8. Politicians from the Labour Party attacked the Minister for Economic Affairs for not taking action and they fell back on the still rather popular ideas of the *Plan van de Arbeid*. Since the Labour Party took part in the cabinet, Van den Brink could not completely ignore the criticism of his partner in government. His solution, the industrialization plan of 1949, was brilliant. The proposal he put forward set out the desired development of Dutch industry between 1948 and 1952, with detailed targets for employment, exports, and output. At first sight it was an impressive and ambitious scheme to solve the major problems of the economy. But when it came to specific measures its contents were meagre: the starting point of the plan was that government would not interfere with the autonomy of private enterprise. Policies would be restricted to the creation of a favourable climate for investment and growth; for example, tax reductions for investing firms were augmented. As a matter of fact, apart from some tax cuts no new measures were suggested (Van Zanden and Griffiths 1989: 243–5).

Industrial policies between 1949 and 1963 – when the official policies were terminated – were a typical product of Dutch policymaking. They were a compromise between the Labour Party (or at least its left wing) which persisted in its demands for a more active, 'planning' government, and the other parties which resisted any interference with private enterprise. Industrial policies were implemented by Ministers for Economic Affairs (Van den Brink, Zijlstra) with a strong preference for the free market economy. As a result actual policies were restricted to financing the expansion of no more than two large companies, to regional subsidies (aimed at industrializing the 'underdeveloped' parts of the country), to the encouragement of technical education, and to the modernization of the supply of electricity (De Liagre Böhl *et al.* 1981).

The two firms that received substantial direct capital transfers were Hoogovens, which was able to enlarge its operations and set up an integrated steel mill, and the new firm Koninklijke Nederlandse Soda Industrie (Royal Dutch Soda Industry), which became part of AKZO in 1969. One of the reasons for investing in these firms was that they were 'basic industries', which made the Dutch economy less dependent on imports of semimanufactures.

Cheap energy was used as an instrument to stimulate the creation of a Dutch aluminium industry. During the early 1960s the government promised to supply cheap gas (with which equally cheap electricity was generated) to a new firm (Aldel) – a joint enterprise of Hoogovens and Shell-subsidiary Billiton – which was created to build a large aluminium plant in the northern part of the country. The cheap gas was set apart from the rest of the gas reserve in order to stimulate the industrialization of this part of the Netherlands, where the huge reserves were found. In 1967 the large French aluminium firm Péchiney received almost the same privileges for the start of another plant in the province of Zeeland (Dankers and Verheul 1993: 280–97).

At the local and regional level government became much more involved with the encouragement of industrial development than before World War II. Every province set up an institute for economic development (*economisch technologisch instituut*) after the model developed during the 1930s, with the explicit aim to increase industrial employment in the region. The development of the port of Rotterdam was stimulated by ambitious schemes to attract new industries (oil refining and chemical processing) and to enlarge the harbour (De Goey 1990). Schiphol, which was designated as the national airport in 1945, profited from large loans by the state to increase its facilities and improve its position vis-à-vis other continental airports (Bouwens and Dierickx 1996). Both in Rotterdam and Schiphol municipal bodies were responsible for the rapid development of infrastructure and the efficient organization of international services in a highly competitive environment. In 1958 Schiphol became a joint stock company (because the city of Amsterdam could no longer afford to finance the investments necessary for its development) with national government and Amsterdam as the main shareholders (De Ru 1981: 68). The long-term success of the two 'public enterprises' turned out to be lasting: in the 1990s they are still counted among the main engines of economic growth in the western part of the Netherlands.

In the public mind the industrialization plans of the years between 1949 and 1963 became far more important than they were in practice. The discussion in the 1970s and 1980s about the causes for the decline of Dutch industrial employment breathed new life into the myth that the recovery and growth of the Dutch economy after the war should be attributed to the beneficial effects of this policy (Griffiths 1986). The reason why the industrialization plan made such a big impact on the public mind is that it changed the traditional definition of the nation's identity. The Dutch used to think of themselves as a nation of farmers and merchants that prospered by virtue of a large colonial empire. In 1949 this idea was shattered by the independence of Indonesia. At the same time Van den Brink formulated a new 'destiny' for the Dutch nation: to become an industrial economy (a process which had in reality started way back in the nineteenth century). The industrialization plan of 1949 was therefore important in that it helped to foster a new identity (De Liagre Böhl *et al.* 1981).

In 1963 the industrialization policy was officially terminated: balanced growth became the government's new aim. In the same year industrial employment peaked; after 1965 there began a slow but consistent decline, which was concealed until 1975 by the strong expansion of tertiary employment. After 1963 industrial policy switched towards the problems of the declining industries – textiles, leather, shipbuilding, and mining. A period with brilliant industrialization plans but no real guidance of industrial development was followed by years without a plan but with many sometimes far-reaching interventions in the development of the declining industries.

Perhaps the most radical decision was taken in 1965, when the socialist Minister for Economic Affairs Den Uyl decided gradually to close down the Dutch coal mines over the next ten years. With ample subsidies from the proceeds of gas exploitation the state mines were converted into a large chemical company, DSM (see Chapter 3) (Messing 1988).

On a smaller scale the government became involved with other declining industries. The main goal of policy became the restructuring of these activities in order to create larger, more competitive firms and to close down surplus capacity. In 1972 the Nehem (Netherlands Reconstruction Company) was created as an independent body to carry out this policy (Vrolijk 1982). During the late 1960s and early 1970s subsidies for declining industries grew rapidly; shipbuilding profited most from these new programmes.

Roughly speaking these were two forces behind the sharp differences in growth performance of the various branches of industry: specialization in response to the gradual opening up of the international economy and the strong rise in wage costs. The latter was the main cause behind the (relative) decline in labour intensive industries, such as textiles, shoes and apparel (as well as coal mining), especially after about 1965. The loss of market share in the 1960s was quite dramatic; for example, the share of the textile industry in domestic demand fell from 72 percent in 1958 to 39 percent in 1973 (CPB 1976: 165). In these branches the loss of market share was not restricted to the lower segments of the market, where low-cost producers had a clear advantage. The higher market segments were also taken over by foreign firms, because Dutch enterprises were often unable to follow fashions and develop new designs.

Capital intensive industries were less vulnerable to rising wage costs. There were nonetheless large differences in performance within this group. Two groups of industries were least affected by the deterioration of international competitiveness during the 1960s. To begin with, the highly capital intensive processing industries that were dependent on a strategic position close to the Dutch harbours (oil refining, chemicals, steel, aluminium, and paper) performed rather well (CPB 1976). The supply of cheap energy (gas) often stimulated their growth, but also made them more vulnerable to changes in the price of energy. Another strong sector was the foodstuffs industry that was partly related to the dynamic agricultural sector and was dominated by a few large multinationals (Unilever, Heineken). However, large parts of the metal industry – shipbuilding, engineering – that had been at the heart of the industrialization drive of the 1950s were faced with increasing difficulties which points to weaknesses in the industrial structure. Attempts by the government to create larger firms and increase international competitiveness met with little success (see Chapter 9).

The service sector generated the greater part of the increase in employment. It can be argued that the constant high demand for labour from this sector not only forced up wages but also crowded out industrial employment and was therefore partly responsible for the de-industrialization after 1965. Traditionally, the Dutch economy was specialized in international services, which can be observed in the large contribution of service income to the balance of payments. However, judged by this standard the degree of specialization declined as strong growth in the imports of services – tourism in particular – outstripped the continued expansion of service income from abroad (CBS 1979: 164).

The evaluation of developments in the service sector varied greatly. Some foresaw the advent of the post-industrial society, the logical successor of the industrial economy of the nineteenth and first half of the twentieth centuries. The main reason for the growth of employment in services was believed to be a change in the pattern of consumption that accompanied the increased welfare of the population. The demand for industrial products declined relative to the demand for services, just as the rise of industrial society had once been brought about by a relative fall in the demand for foodstuffs and an increase in the demand for industrial products. Moreover, these developments were appreciated: labour in the service sector was generally of a high quality and did little harm to the environment.

The opposite view contended that the service sector was at the root of all economic problems in the 1960s and 1970s. A large part of the service sector worked for a sheltered market, where international competition did not compel enterprises to reduce costs. Moreover, the strongest growth occurred in sectors in which government subsidies largely replaced the market mechanism, e.g. health care and education, which led to an 'abnormal' growth of demand and inefficiencies in supply. As a result, tertiary labour productivity increased only slowly, which meant that the strong rise in wage costs led to comprehensive increases in the price of services (or the level of government subsidies) (Driehuis 1975). The resulting inflation drove up wage costs and in the end crowded out sectors that had to compete internationally. The result would be an economy dominated by services with a very slow growth of productivity. According to this view, services were an important source of inflation and economic stagnation, which was fed by the enormous expansion of the welfare state in the 1960s and 1970s.

The most important objection to this view of the service sector is that it is treated as a homogeneous entity, which obviously it is not. About half of the sector consisted of activities that were geared towards (increasingly) competitive markets and were able to improve their productivity quite considerably.

In trade – the most important branch – labour productivity increased by almost 4 percent per year during the 1950s and 1960s (see Table 8.3). In retail trade the rise of chain stores and the decline in small retail shops help to explain this strong performance. In wholesale trade the rapid expansion of international exchange led to the amalgamation of firms and the realization of economies of scale, which resulted in a huge increase in turnover per employee (CPB 1976: 351 ff).

Developments in the transport industry were more diverse. After a strong start during the late 1940s and 1950s the big ship-owning companies were faced with severe international competition and loss of market share as a result of the rise of aviation. Shipping companies increasingly hired low-wage personnel from Third World countries and moved abroad. As a result, the Dutch share in the world merchant fleet fell sharply after 1960 and the country almost stopped being a seafaring nation (Flierman 121ff).

Aggressive policies to capture a large slice of the intercontinental aviation market resulted in the expansion of KLM, which to some extent

*Table 8.3* Growth of output and employment in the service sector, 1953–1973
(average annual growth rates)

| | Output | | Employment | | Employment in 1973 |
|---|---|---|---|---|---|
| | *53–63* | *63–73* | *53–63* | *63–73* | *(thousands)* |
| Trade | 6.4 | 5.5 | 2.5 | 1.7 | 735 |
| Shipping and aviation | 3.3 | 4.2 | 1.3 | −4.8 | 35 |
| Other transport | 6.0 | 5.6 | 1.6 | 1.0 | 270 |
| Other services | 3.5 | 4.9 | 2.1 | 3.2 | 975 |
| Banking | | 7.7 | | 5.1 | 85* |
| Insurance | | 5.3 | | 3.1 | 63* |
| Business services | | 4.5 | | 3.6 | 240* |
| Health care | | 5.6 | | 4.9 | 233* |
| Catering | | 2.3 | | 0.5 | 94* |
| Entertainment | | 6.0 | | 1.5 | 22* |
| Other | | 2.3 | | 1.7 | 281* |

*Source*: CPB 1976: 188, 380–82
* In 1975.

compensated for the decline in international transport. The government heavily subsidized this growth industry and financed almost every large infrastructural project that was involved (such as the new Schiphol Airport) (Bouwens and Dierickx 1996). Perhaps even more important was the growth of international truck transport. During these years Dutch enterprises began significantly to dominate international freight traffic in Western Europe, due in part to the strong position of Rotterdam in the supply of cargo. At the same time international river transport – traditionally a strong sector of the economy – had difficulty in competing with this relatively new means of transport.

The dynamic development of international trade and transport was closely related to the strong performance of Rotterdam – which became the largest port of the world – and Schiphol airport, and it made a sizeable contribution to the economic growth of the 'golden years'. The growth of port-related processing industries – oil refining, chemicals, etc. – was heavily dependent on the modern infrastructure and the efficient transport sector.

The development of international trade and transport could build upon existing patterns of specialization. Yet the (renewed) rise of the banking sector during the 'golden years' can be seen as a process of catching up. After about 1960 industry increasingly needed to attract external capital and the big banks were prepared to fill the gap. At the same time the concept of 'retail banking' was introduced and the large banks began to set up affiliates in almost every village and district, in order personally to service their customers (Barendregt and Visser 1997). This resulted in an enormous increase in employment (Table 8.3); the share of banking and insurance in total employment almost doubled between 1947 (1.8 percent) and 1975 (3.3 percent). In the 1960s there arose a merger movement in banking and insurance in order better to meet the demands of (big) business and to face international competition, which resulted in a sharp concentration in the financial sector.

The pessimistic analysis of the economic performance of the service sector applies especially to the 'quarternary' sector, which was almost completely subsidized by the government. A large part of this sector consisted of the medical services, where the growth of (measured) labour productivity was indeed very small (Table 8.3). Demand continued to grow, in spite of rising costs, which resulted in a enormous increase in the share of medical services in national income (from 3.5 percent in 1953 to 8.3 percent in 1974) (CBS 1984). At the same time, average life expectancy increased slightly and sick leave doubled (from 4.1 percent of the number of working days in 1953 to 8.5 percent in 1973) (CBS 1984: 36). The expansion of education – another sector for which the improvement of productivity is hard to estimate – undoubtedly contributed much to the long-term performance of the economy. The growth of demand for this branch was also unhampered by rising costs, and its share in GDP more than doubled during the 1950s and 1960s (CBS 1984). A similar story can be told about the development of other parts of the quarternary sector.

The development of the service sector therefore shows a mixed picture: international services, the financial sector, and business services were largely working for competitive markets and contributed much to economic expansion. Demand-related forces were behind the enormous growth of the 'quarternary' sector, while the welfare state, which supplied these services almost for free, did much to accelerate their growth. In sum, the expansion of the service sector neither led to the post-industrial utopia, nor was it at the root of all economic evil.

## GOVERNMENT POLICIES: INTERNATIONAL COMPETITIVENESS AND DEMAND MANAGEMENT

One of the primary aims of postwar economic policy was to improve the international competitiveness of Dutch industry. To that purpose a number of policies was introduced. Already in 1944 the guilder was devalued against the dollar; a second devaluation followed in 1949 (see Chapter 7). Because the currencies of neighbouring countries (Belgium, Germany) were devalued less rigorously, the effective exchange rate fell rapidly.

In a number of ways the government tried to turn the Netherlands into a country of low wages and low prices. First, the prices of foodstuffs and rents were controlled to keep down the cost of living. The Germans had already frozen rents at the 1941 level, and this measure was continued after

1945. As a result the share of rents in working-class budgets fell from 16.6 percent in 1936 to 7 percent in 1951 (Van Zanden 1986). At the same time agricultural price policy was used to keep the price of foodstuffs below world market prices. As a result the cost of living in the Netherlands increased by 'only' 100 percent between 1938 and 1947, which was much less than in the neighbouring countries (for example, in Belgium the increase was 250 percent) (Van Zanden 1996b: 189).

The guided wage policy was used for the same purpose: to keep wages and consumption down in order to increase exports. Calculations of real effective exchange rates on the basis of the development of the cost of living and the rise in nominal wages in industry show a remarkable improvement in competitiveness until the mid-1950s (Graph 8.4). Compared with the wage development of the trading partners – corrected for changes in exchange rates – nominal wages declined relatively by about 25 percent between 1938 and 1949 and this downward trend continued until 1953. The introduction of 'welfare' wage increases after 1953 resulted in a gentle rise in relative wage levels, but until the late 1950s they remained

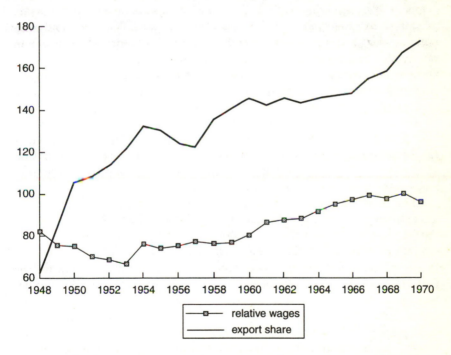

*Graph 8.4* Relative wages in industry (compared with major competitors and corrected for changes in exchange rates) and market share of exports in world trade, 1948–1970 (1938 = 100)

*Sources*: 1948–1962: Van Zanden 1996b; these estimates were then linked to the CPB series, CPB 1984

149

low (by prewar standards). A large part of the success of the guided wage policy should be attributed to the policy to keep down the cost of living as the decrease in relative prices was almost as large as the decline in relative wages (Graph 8.4).

As a result of these developments the Netherlands became a country with very low prices and wages. For example, contemporary OECD estimates showed that in 1950 the Belgian price level was 43 percent higher than in the Netherlands (in 1955 the difference was still 32 percent); differences in wage levels were about the same (Van Zanden 1996b: 191). Exports expanded accordingly. In the mid-1950s the share of Dutch exports in world trade had increased by about 20 percent since 1938, even though the structure of exports was relatively unfavourable. In years of recession – 1952–3 and 1957–8 – the gain in market share was especially large, because in these years domestic consumption stagnated and industry could profit from its high degree of competitiveness to undercut high-cost producers abroad. This anti-cyclical development of exports contributed to the stabilization of the economy during recession years (Van Zanden 1996b: 192).

One of the preconditions for the success of these policies was the system of stable exchange rates, introduced after the war. The price and wage policies were a complicated method to achieve an undervalued exchange rate, which could persist by virtue of the stability of the Bretton Woods system. The 'overheating' of the economy during the 1960s should be seen from this perspective. A system of flexible exchange rates would probably have resulted in a continued rise in the exchange rate already in the (late) 1950s, and would have helped to 'cool down' the economy. Now the only way to restore 'equilibrium' (besides changes in the exchange rate) was to raise prices and wages. The inflationary pressures that built up in the late 1950s and 1960s were therefore to some extent the price the country had to pay for the success of its low-wage policy during the 1950s.

Until 1958 the guided wage policy had been supported by coalition governments that were dominated by the Labour Party and the Catholic Party. However, the latter had become increasingly critical of its rigid nature and when the coalition fell apart a major revision of policies seemed to be at hand. For the first time since 1945 the Labour Party did not participate in the new government that was inaugurated in 1959. Its primary goal was to liberalize what were considered to be the remains of the interventionist policies of the 1940s: the guided wage policy, the agricultural policy, and the housing policy. However, its attempt to decentralize wage policies and introduce a system of branch-specific wage controls was highly unsuccessful as it resulted in a sharp increase in wages in all branches of industry (see Chapter 5). The liberalization of agricultural policy was also a failure. During these years the newly formed EEC began to formulate its Common Agricultural Policy, which was to some extent a copy of the Dutch agricultural policy of the 1950s (see Chapter 4). The CAP soon replaced the agricultural policies of the member countries. The extensive housing policy that had been introduced after the war was a consequence of the freezing of rents during the 1940s. Because real rents had fallen by more than 50 percent during the decade, the construction of houses had to be subsidized to restore production. No cabinet in which the Labour Party participated had dared to return rents to a market equilibrium level, which would have meant a strong increase in the cost of living and would have undermined the guided wage policy. But in 1959 the new 'right-wing' cabinet thought that is was time to liberalize the housing market and it began a series of relatively large rent increases and created more incentives for private constructors (Van der Schaar 1987: 112 ff). However, this attempt at liberalization failed as well. Although the private sector increased its output, it was not enough to compensate for the decline in subsidized construction. Moreover, the housing shortage that had persisted since 1945 was now considered to be the major problem of the population, and a government whose only solution was to try and liberalize the market came under strong attack for its lack of action. As a result, all major parties proposed the renewed increase in heavily subsidized housing during the elections of 1963 (Van der Schaar 1987: 118).

The de facto liberalization of wage policy, the attempts to deregulate the housing market, and the formation of the EEC (which brought agricultural prices more in line with those of the neighbouring countries and pushed up food prices) all contributed to the change in relative prices, wages, and profits that occurred around 1960–1 (see first section). Given the undervaluation of the guilder, it was also quite natural for the Netherlands to follow the German example in 1961 and revalue the guilder (by a modest 5 percent). But this remained an incident which was not really able to affect matters much. The combination of these developments led to a strong decline in international competitiveness between 1958 and 1966; at the same time the share of exports in international trade stabilized (Graph 8.4).

The most paradoxical developments are to be found in the years between 1966 and 1973: exports boomed while competitiveness – as measured by real effective exchange rates – underwent a sustained (though somewhat slower) decline. In other words, in spite of strong domestic cost pressures, relative export prices declined and the share of Dutch exports in world trade increased by almost 30 percent (Graph 8.4). One of the explanations for this development might be the (changing) composition of exports. The paradox can be solved if the export drive was concentrated in a few capital intensive industries with a strong growth of labour productivity (and a decline in wage costs as a result). Yet, this does not seem to have happened, as is suggested by CPB figures of cost increases and sales growth (Table 8.4). A comparison between the first two columns of the table shows that all industries tended to increase the price of the output they sold on the

*Table 8.4* Increase in sales prices, volumes and costs per unit of output in agriculture and industry, 1963–1973 (average annual growth rates)

| | costs per unit of output | Sales prices | | Sales volumes | |
|---|---|---|---|---|---|
| | | domestic | exports | domestic | exports |
| Agriculture | 3.0 | 3.5 | 1.5 | 4.5 | 6.5 |
| Foodstuffs | | | | | |
|   Animal origin | 5.0 | 5.5 | 4.5 | 1.5 | 8.0 |
|   Other foodstuffs | 3.5 | 3.5 | 4.5 | 4.0 | 8.0 |
| Beverages/tobacco | 3.5 | 4.0 | 1.0 | 3.5 | 13.5 |
| Textiles, clothing | 3.5 | 3.5 | 2.5 | −3.0 | 7.5 |
| Construction materials | 3.5 | 3.5 | 3.5 | 6.0 | 10.5 |
| Paper, printing | 7.0 | 7.5 | 2.5 | 1.0 | 11.5 |
| Chemicals | 0.5 | 1.5 | −0.5 | 6.5 | 18.5 |
| Basic metals | 2.5 | 2.0 | 3.0 | 6.5 | 11.5 |
| Metal products | 3.5 | 3.5 | 3.5 | 5.0 | 11.0 |
| Electronic equipment | 1.5 | 2.5 | 0.0 | 8.0 | 11.5 |
| Transport equipment | 3.5 | 3.0 | 3.5 | −1.0 | 11.0 |
| Oil refining | 2.0 | 4.0 | 1.0 | 4.5 | 13.5 |
| Industry | 3.0 | 4.0 | 2.0 | 3.5 | 12.0 |

*Source*: CPB 1986, 460–7

domestic market more or less in accordance with the increase in their costs. In fact, profit margins of products sold on the domestic market must have gone up by an average of 1 percent, which contributed to the inflation. This strong increase in domestic sales prices must have stimulated the erosion of market shares. Sales on the international market increased far more rapidly (see columns 4 and 5 of Table 8.4) as a result of a different pricing policy. In most industries the increase in the sales prices on the export market was lower than the growth of prices on the domestic market and often much lower than the increase in costs per unit of output. Pricing policy on the export market had almost no relationship with cost increases but seems to have been motivated by the desire to capture export markets – even at a (short-term) loss. As a result, exports increased at a much higher rate than sales on the domestic market. Perhaps entrepreneurs only assigned marginal costs to their exports, or they considered raising their market shares abroad as an investment in future growth. The result was: (a) that they had more and more difficulty defending their position on the (probably more profitable) domestic market; (b) that an increased share of output consisted of exports whose proceeds grew at a lower rate than their costs.

An alternative interpretation is that transaction costs on export sales were falling very rapidly to make up for the difference in price policy. As a result of the formation of the EEC and the abolition of tariffs, general tariff reforms in the 1960s, and the decline in transport costs that accompanied the improvement of transport systems, the costs of selling a certain amount of goods on a foreign market must have declined sharply. The way 'national accountants' measure export prices (fob, at the border) and cost increases probably does not take into account (some of) these 'transaction costs'. The 2 percent difference in the increase in domestic and foreign sales prices can therefore perhaps also be interpreted as a quantitative measure of the economic value of trade liberalization – the formation of the EEC (see also final section where it will be shown that the boom in exports was especially directed towards the EEC market).

For reasons of completeness some attention must be paid to the budget policy of the 'golden years'. In the public image the stability of growth in the postwar period is often associated with the rise of Keynesian demand management. This link has been the subject of a number of studies. Already in 1963 the CPB published a detailed account of the effects of demand management during the 1950s, which concluded that in many cases policies had in fact been pro-cyclical (Van den Beld 1963). The first 'Keynesian' attempt at demand management occurred in 1951, when the overexpansion of the economy led to a number of harsh measures to cut demand: nominal wages were increased by only 5 percent causing a decline in real terms of almost the same magnitude, investment subsidies were cut and government expenditure was severely reduced. However, when these measures became effective in 1952 the economy was already in a recession and was actually pulled down by them (Graph 8.5). The second *bestedingsbeperking* (demand cut) of 1958–9 fared no better. Once again it came too late, mainly as a result of complicated negotiations between the government parties, and the cuts lasted too long (Graph 8.5). Moreover, during the boom years between 1953 and 1957 the government reacted to the rapid growth in tax incomes by lowering tax rates, which led to large pro-cyclical demand impulses. Although a number of politicians from the Labour Party warned against this effect, the package of tax reforms was too popular to stop (Ter Heide 1986: 290–7).

These largely negative experiences with demand management during the 1950s led Zijlstra, Minister of Finance between 1959 and 1963, to introduce a more stable system of government expenditure. The starting point was the estimated long-term growth of the economy and the growth of tax revenues that was somewhat higher as a result of the progressive nature of most taxes. Every year it had to be decided how to use the expected growth in taxes: to reduce tax levels or to increase expenditure. In his view this would result in an automatic stabilization of total expenditure: in years of recession tax income would grow less than the long-term trend and a deficit would be created, which would disappear as soon as the economy began a new upswing. Boom years would automatically result in surpluses on the budget, which would help to stabilize the business cycle. The extreme fluctuations in government expenditure of the 1950s, which

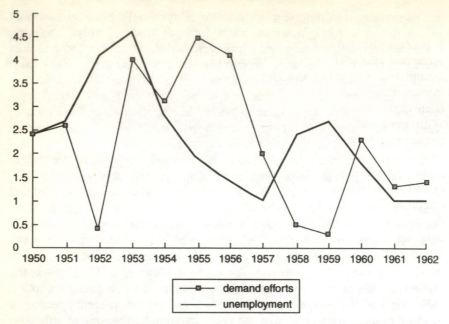

*Graph 8.5* Demand effects of budgetary policies (as a percentage of national income) and level of unemployment (as a percentage), 1950–1962
*Source*: Van den Beld 1963: 23

had contributed to economic instability, disappeared with this system (Sterks 1982: 140 ff). Moreover, Zijlstra also hoped to strengthen the position of the Minister of Finance, because negotiations in the cabinet would no longer deal with the level of total expenditure, which was determined by the growth of tax income, but only with their distribution. However, already in the first years the 'structural budget norm' (as it was called) was exceeded by actual expenditure. Moreover, the share that was used for tax cuts declined rapidly (Van Wijngaarden and Van der Griend 1971: 59–71). As a result the 'structural budget norm' also contributed to the renewed growth of public expenditure in the 1960s, although it brought more stability to budget policy, (Sterks 1982: 222–3).

More recent studies have shown that the effects of budget policy were pro-cyclical as often as they were anti-cyclical during the period from 1952 to 1980 (Sterks 1984). This was no improvement compared with the interwar period (before the Keynesian revolution), when the score was about the same (Van Zanden 1996a: 128). Monetary policies did not do any better (Post 1973). It should therefore be concluded that demand management did not contribute to the stability of growth during the post-war period.

## FOREIGN ECONOMIC POLICY

It is somewhat paradoxical that there emerged a movement for European economic cooperation during the 1950s. After the war governments had assumed almost complete responsibility for national economic performance. Especially in the Netherlands, where economic liberalism had been quite strong in the 1930s, the changes of the 1940s were radical. With interventionism at its height, supported by Keynesian and social-democratic ideas, there began a movement towards greater European cooperation which was to undermine the basis for the 'nationalist' economic policies. With every international treaty that abolished tariffs and other restrictions on international trade and the more so with any treaty that established a supra-national organization such as the ECSC and the EEC, the margins for government intervention in the economy narrowed. Moreover, these policies contributed to increased openness and dependence on international economic forces, which also meant that national policies became increasingly ineffective. In the end, the interventionism of the postwar period was therefore bound to disappear or be replaced by interventionism on a European scale.

The Benelux offers an interesting case study to answer the question why governments decided to embark on this path (see Bloemen 1992). During the war the Dutch government in exile had concluded two treaties with Belgium to form a customs union when hostilities ended (as Belgium already had an economic union with Luxemburg, a group of three countries would be formed under the name of Benelux). It was hoped that this would strengthen the position of the two countries vis-à-vis the other allies and that it would lay a basis for cooperation after the war (Kersten 1982). But the enormous problems that confronted the Dutch government in 1945 precluded any attempt to realize a measure of free trade between the two countries in the near future, and thus postponed the implementation of the Benelux plan. The Belgians, who were able to restore their economy far more rapidly, pressed for further negotiations. In the end the Dutch complied with some further steps in the direction of a customs union, in return for loans to finance the substantial deficit on mutual trade. In 1947 the formation of Benelux received a new impulse from the Marshall Plan, which encouraged European cooperation (see Chapter 7). The outcome was a customs union that came into effect in 1948.

A number of developments complicated this experiment in European economic cooperation. Whereas the Netherlands was a low-cost producer with an undervalued guilder, especially after the devaluation of 1949, Belgium had become a country with high prices and wages, the more so because the Belgian franc was devalued by only 12.3 percent against the dollar in 1949 (Van Zanden 1996b). The rapid recovery of the Belgian economy, which made it one of the few countries with sizeable export surpluses in Europe directly after 1944, partly explains this development. In the 1950s there were large differences in price and wage levels between Belgium and the Netherlands, which led to a great deal of tension in the Benelux.

During the international downturn of 1951–2, when domestic demand was slack, Dutch industry considerably increased its exports to Belgium; the gap in mutual trade, which had been very large in 1950 (almost 50 percent), declined to less than 15 percent in 1952. A number of labour intensive industries in the region of Flanders were especially hurt by the Dutch export drive, which led to renewed negotiations to set limits to Dutch exports of 'sensitive' products (i.e. products that competed too much with the output of certain labour intensive Belgian industries) (Meade *et al.* 1964: 128–35). These limits were introduced in 1953 and seriously undermined the whole concept of a customs union.

One of the conditions of Belgium during the negotiations of 1947 had been that agricultural trade would be left out of the customs union, which allowed them to continue the protection of their agriculture at an even higher level than the Dutch. The problems in this sector were comparable with those in industry. Prices in the Netherlands were much lower than in Belgium, and a liberalization of mutual trade would have resulted in a strong decline of prices in Belgium, which was unacceptable for political reasons (Mommens 1992).

In spite of these problems, trade within the Benelux expanded rapidly. The share of Dutch imports from the BLEU (Belgium–Luxemburg) went up from 11.7 percent in 1938 and 12.2 percent in 1947 to 18.4 percent in 1950, after which it stabilized at about this level (CBS 1984). Exports going to the BLEU amounted to 10.6 percent of total exports in 1938, but increased at a higher rate than other exports (the share rose to about 15 percent in the 1950s and 1960s).

Although the Benelux contributed to a relatively strong growth of trade between its partners, these persistent problems undermined its success. During the negotiations leading up to the Treaty of Rome it was regarded as a classic example of an unsuccessful attempt at economic integration (Boekestijn 1992: 163). Sicco Mansholt, the Minister of Agriculture, concluded from the problems with the Benelux that he would never allow trade in agricultural products to be left out of another customs union. He became very active in the promotion of plans to form a European market for agricultural products, comparable with what the ECSC was doing for coal and steel. These plans ended up in the famous section of the Treaty of Rome in which a Common Agricultural Policy was announced that would create the European market which Mansholt wanted (Milward 1992: 300 ff).

The formation of the EEC in 1958 immediately led to a sharp upturn in trade with the other member countries (with the notable exception of the

BLEU). The share of Dutch exports going to EEC countries went up from 41.5 percent in 1957 to 54.2 percent in 1963 and 64.9 percent in 1972 (CBS 1984). The share of France and Italy in exports more than doubled and the German share increased by more than 80 percent. Changes in the structure of imports were somewhat less dramatic – the share of the EEC increased from 41.1 percent in 1957 to 55.5 percent in 1972 – but still demonstrated the enormous growth of intra-EEC trade (CBS 1984).

On the whole attempts to estimate the static welfare effects of the EEC have come up with rather low results. Especially for the Netherlands, which had relatively low external tariffs before 1958, the negative welfare effects of trade diversion were probably rather large, which tends to lower the estimated economic importance of the EEC even further (Davenport 1982; Pelkmans 1986). However, there is substantial evidence that the dynamic effects have been quite large indeed. One of the main reasons why during the 1960s exports and investments continued to expand in spite of falling profit rates was that the European market offered growing opportunities (see previous section). However, it is almost impossible to quantify these dynamic effects.

The discussion of the formation of the Benelux and Dutch involvement in the agricultural section of the Treaty of Rome shows some of the considerations behind Dutch support for these steps in the process of European economic integration. The bottom line is that policymakers tried to use international negotiations to solve problems that resulted from government intervention in the economy. In most cases their basic aim was to promote exports and secure export markets, and in return they had at times to relinquish a certain degree of freedom in domestic economic affairs. The very fact that after 1945 government intervention was so intense and varied created a lot of problems that could only be dealt with through international agreement. The force behind the Dutch drive for a Common Agricultural Policy – the overproduction of its agriculture and the need to finance export subsidies – is a case in point. Moreover, this generation of politicians thought in terms of planning and intervention by government agencies as the best way to approach these problems. To solve the problems that resulted (at least in part) from government intervention in the national economies, they set up supra-national agencies such as the ECSC and the EEC. These institutions proved to be highly durable and in the long run began to develop their own policies, while trying to reduce the power of national governments. This basically explains the paradox with which this section began. As a matter of fact, in many ways this brief excursion into the history of the EU shows that it was to a large extent a legacy of the interventionism of the postwar period.

# 9

# 1973–1995: FALLING BEHIND AGAIN?

## MACROECONOMIC PERFORMANCE

The early 1970s witnessed the end of a long period of stable and rapid growth. The long-term growth rate of GDP fell from almost 5 percent during the 1960s to about 2 percent between 1973 and 1994. In the Netherlands this deceleration of economic growth was somewhat steeper than in the rest of Western Europe, so that during the 1980s the increase in per capita GDP fell behind that of most other OECD countries (Table 9.1).

Three different periods can be distinguished. Between 1973 and 1979 growth was still marginally higher than in the rest of Western Europe as a result of relatively expansionary policies and the growth of private consumption. The depression of the early 1980s, however, hit the Dutch economy particularly hard and between 1979 and 1987 growth clearly lagged behind the rest of Western Europe (and the OECD). After 1987 this changed once again and the growth of GDP accelerated markedly, especially in comparison with neighbouring countries (Table 9.1). The relatively good performance after 1987 was the result of a strong growth of labour input combined with a modest increase in GDP per hour (Table 9.1, final columns). In this respect growth after 1987 was quite different from that during the previous decades, when the increase in labour pro-

Table 9.1 Macroeconomic performance of the Netherlands compared with North West Europe, 1973–1994 (average annual growth rates)

|  | GDP | | GDP per capita | | GDP per hour | |
|---|---|---|---|---|---|---|
|  | Neth. | NW Europe | Neth. | NW Europe | Neth. | NW Europe |
| 1960–73 | 4.83 | 4.52 | 3.57 | 3.63 | 4.39 | 4.80 |
| 1973–79 | 2.68 | 2.26 | 1.93 | 2.05 | 3.45 | 2.81 |
| 1979–87 | 1.22 | 2.01 | 0.67 | 1.74 | 2.56 | 2.16 |
| 1987–94 | 2.54 | 1.76 | 1.83 | 1.13 | 1.50 | 2.10 |

Source: Van Ark and De Jong 1996: 201

ductivity had been relatively high in the Netherlands (and the increase in the labour input relatively slow).

Growth accounting confirms this picture: the rise in the number of people employed was rapid after 1987, mainly as a result of increased female labour participation (see Chapter 5) (Table 9.2). The number of part-time jobs also experienced a strong rise, which led to an ongoing decline in the number of hours worked per person. These estimates also show that the growth rate of capital accumulation fell sharply after 1973 (from almost 6 percent before 1973 to about 3 percent between 1973 and 1994). The stock of R&D, measured as the cumulative number of patents issued to Dutch citizens in the USA during the preceding 30 years, continued to grow rather quickly. However, statistics on the actual expenditure on R&D show a much sharper break in the 1970s (Minne 1995). The 'residual' – the growth of total factor productivity – slowed down considerably after 1973 which continued into the 1980s (Table 9.2). The sudden slackening of productivity growth after 1973 occurred everywhere in the OECD (Maddison 1991), but the continued decline of the residual seems to have been a typically Dutch feature.

This development is still one of the mysteries of the period: why did the growth of total factor productivity decline so much after 1973? A large number of explanations has been put forward. The most popular one is perhaps the deceleration in the rate of technological change after 1973 (Maddison 1991), although it does not seem to agree with the perception of most people of what happened during the 1980s and (early) 1990s (when, for example, the advance in computer technology revolutionized work in many sectors of the economy). In the next section it is argued that a number of exogenous shocks, such as the sharp increase in the wage bill and the price of oil as well as the introduction of environmental legislation, led to a sudden reduction in the value of the capital stock and the scrapping of

*Table 9.2* Growth accounting for the post-1973 period (growth rates of GDP, inputs and the residual)

|  | GDP | Persons employed | Hours per person | School per person | Capital stock | R&D stock | Total factor productivity (residual) |
|---|---|---|---|---|---|---|---|
| 1947–73 | 5.07 | 1.51 | −0.89 | 0.98 | 4.52 | 4.74 | 2.50 |
| 1973–79 | 2.68 | 0.92 | −1.38 | 0.88 | 3.85 | 4.92 | 1.10 |
| 1979–87 | 1.22 | 0.56 | −1.85 | 0.03 | 2.31 | 2.56 | 0.74 |
| 1987–94 | 2.54 | 1.73 | −0.69 | 2.55 | 2.80 | 3.14* | 0.16 |

*Sources*: Van Ark and De Jong 1996: 211, except for the data R&D stock: the output of R&D is measured as the number of US patents granted to inhabitants of the Netherlands; the service life of R&D is estimated at 30 years (source: *Annual Report Patents*, 1947–1993).
* 1987–1993

obsolete equipment. These changes also induced supplementary investments to save energy and reduce levels of emission to keep the capital
stock in operation. As a result estimates of the growth of the capital stock,
which generally assume unchanging rates of depreciation and do not take
into account these exogenous shocks, are biased upwards. Moreover, after
1973 (and especially after 1980) a significant part of investments was not
directed at increasing output but at accommodating for these changes. The
real increase in the capital stock was therefore much smaller than the
official statistics suggest, and this probably helps explain part of the slower
growth rates of total factor productivity (which is measured on the basis of
the official capital stock estimates).

The remarkable development of the Dutch economy after 1973 can also
be seen in data on the level of unemployment. According to the standar-
dized unemployment rates of the OECD, which probably underestimate the
true level but give a rather accurate picture of its development, unemployment increased to about 5 percent of the total labour force during the first
depression (1974–5) and then remained stable until 1980. In that year it
was still somewhat below the EC average, but this changed between 1980
and 1983 when unemployment more than doubled. From the peak level of
about 12 percent in 1983–4 there began a consistent fall in unemployment,
which was much steeper than in the rest of Europe (Hartog and Theeuwes
1993: 2). In fact, in 1992 in the EC unemployment was only marginally
smaller than during the depth of the 1983 depression, whereas in the
Netherlands the decline had been substantial (from 12.0 percent in 1983
to 6.7 percent in 1992) (OECD 1995). However, the average duration of
unemployment increased sharply during the 1980s – in 1988 almost half of
the unemployed had not held a job for over 12 months – which means that a
further fall could hardly be accomplished (Hartog and Theeuwes 1993: 16).
Moreover, the recession of 1993, which was comparatively modest in the
Netherlands, did cause a renewed increase in unemployment.

Another part of the macroeconomic performance is the story of the
inflationary wave of the period. During the 1960s strong inflationary forces
had been unleashed, largely by the tight nature of the labour market (and
the cumulative effects of wage indexation). The inflationary boom on the
world market between 1970 and 1973 further accelerated these tendencies,
when the price of almost all foodstuffs and raw materials soared, culminat-
ing in the oil price hike of 1973–4. As has been shown in the previous
chapter, it brought about an outward shift in the Phillips curve, which
points to a structural change in inflationary expectations and in the 'natural' (or non-accelerating wage) rate of unemployment. In the Netherlands
the appreciation of the guilder after 1973 (see below) and the sharp
increase in (real) interest rates after 1979 were the two brakes on the
inflationary trend. The outward shift of the Phillips curve had already
ended in 1975, but at the expense of a sharp upturn in unemployment

160

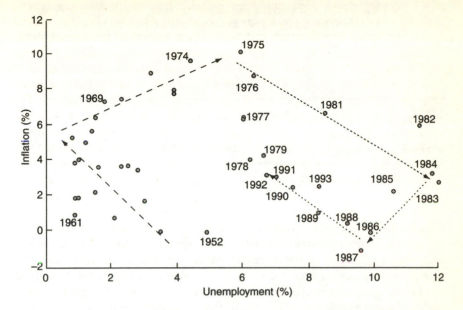

*Graph 9.1* Development of the Phillips curve, 1952–1993
*Source*: CBS 1994

(Graph 9.1). After 1982 the rate of inflation fell to a level which had been more or less normal during the 1950s and early 1960s. During the mid-1980s the Phillips curve shifted inward and the rate of inflation and unemployment declined between 1984 and 1987. After 1987 a new Phillips curve seems to have been established with a non-accelerating wage rate of unemployment at least twice that of the 1950s (Graph 9.1).

One of the surprising features of economic growth after 1973 was its sectoral composition. Dutch agriculture was not hindered by the problems of the 1970s and 1980s: it was able substantially to increase the growth rates of output and productivity (Table 9.3). Employment in the sector stabilized as a result of its continuing strong performance (after the sharp fall in agricultural employment during the preceding period). This success story cannot simply be attributed to the protection offered by the EC. First of all, in the rest of the EC agricultural growth was much less spectacular with average growth rates between 1 and 2 percent. Moreover, Dutch success was concentrated in sectors that received little or no protection: horticulture (flowers, bulbs, vegetables), pigs, and poultry in particular, whereas its share in the production of grain and sugar beet was more or less constant (Landbouweconomische verkenning 1986: 37). The crisis that erupted in the EC in the early 1980s as a result of the sharp increase in the costs of agricultural policies did affect parts of Dutch agriculture, but

161

*Table 9.3* Growth of value added and labour productivity in agriculture and manufacturing, 1960–1992 (average annual growth rates)

| | Real value added | | | Real value added per person employed | | |
|---|---|---|---|---|---|---|
| | *Agric.* | *Manuf.* | *Services* | *Agric.* | *Manuf.* | *Services* |
| 1960–73 | 3.0 | 6.4 | | 6.9 | 6.4 | |
| 1973–79 | 3.6 | 0.0 | 3.7 | 3.3 | 1.9 | 2.4 |
| 1979–87 | 4.2 | 1.6 | 1.7 | 3.8 | 3.0 | 0.9 |
| 1987–94 | 5.1 | 1.8 | 2.8 | 5.1 | 1.9 | 0.9 |

*Sources*: Van Ark and De Jong 1996: 215; CBS, 1980–1995 (*Nationale Rekeningen*)

the ensuing attempts at liberalization did not harm the long-term growth of the sector. More important were the growing environmental costs of the unlimited expansion of the horticultural and intensive livestock sectors. The huge surpluses of manure that resulted from the enormous growth of pig breeding in certain parts of the country became one of the most acute environmental problems of the 1980s, the more so because the Ministry of Agriculture continued to deny its urgency. On a somewhat smaller scale comparable problems arose in horticulture (where enormous amounts of pesticides and herbicides were used).

The industrial sector, on the other hand, was the real problem child of the period: output stagnated in the 1970s and grew very slowly in the 1980s, and the growth of labour productivity was generally rather sluggish (although this can also been seen as a response to the low-wage policy of the period) (Table 9.3). The depression of the 1970s and early 1980s hit parts of the industry particularly hard. The already declining textile, clothing, and shoemaking industries underwent an almost continuous fall in output; employment fell by about 70 percent between 1970 and 1984, after which it more or less stabilized (CPB 1986). The oil industry, on the other hand, and related basic chemical industries, which had been major engines of growth during the preceding decades, were suddenly confronted with a sharp rise in prices and a fall in output (CPB 1986). They too contracted sharply until the middle of the 1980s. The chemical industry rapidly recovered afterwards, but the oil industry continued to develop rather slowly. The most stable part of industry was food processing, which remained one of the strong branches, partly due to its relationship with the agricultural sector. Metalworking and electrical engineering did relatively well with the exception of shipbuilding.

The result of the shrinking industrial basis of the economy was that the share of the labour force occupied in this sector declined sharply (Table 9.4). The growth of employment after 1985 was concentrated almost

*Table 9.4* Structure of employment, 1950–1994 (percent)

|                      | 1950  | 1973  | 1987  | 1994  |
|----------------------|-------|-------|-------|-------|
| Agriculture          | 13.5  | 5.2   | 5.3   | 4.8   |
| Manufacturing        | 27.9  | 26.0  | 18.8  | 16.6  |
| Other industry       | 11.1  | 11.1  | 8.7   | 7.9   |
| Market services      | 26.1  | 31.1  | 36.4  | 40.7  |
| Non-market services  | 21.4  | 26.8  | 30.8  | 29.8  |
| *Total*              | 100.0 | 100.0 | 100.0 | 100.0 |

*Sources*: Van Ark and De Jong 1996: 214; CBS 1995

completely in the services sector. In this respect two different periods can be distinguished: during the 1970s and first half of the 1980s the growth of employment in non-market services was almost as rapid as in market services. But the constant budget cuts of the government in the 1980s put an end to the strong rise of non-market services; their share in total employment fell after 1987. Between 1987 and 1992 employment in industry began to rise again, but this increase disappeared completely during the recession of 1992–3. In the longer run market services were therefore the only 'engine' of employment growth in the late 1980s and 1990s (see also Chapter 5, pp. 88–90 where the contours of this process have been sketched).

## EXOGENOUS SHOCKS AND DOMESTIC REACTIONS: THE 1970s

The radical change in economic performance during the 1970s can probably best be understood by analysing the nature of and reaction to the different 'exogenous shocks' that struck the Dutch economy during the decade. Four shocks can be distinguished:

- the disintegration of the Bretton Woods system and the resulting appreciation of the guilder;
- the acceleration in the increase in wage costs, stimulated by the inflationary boom of the early 1970s;
- the enormous increase in energy prices during the two 'oil crises' of 1973–4 and 1979;
- the introduction of environmental legislation during the early 1970s

A fundamental change was the disintegration of the Bretton Woods system. Until 1971 the international financial system was based on constant exchange rates between the different currencies and the dollar, which in turn was fixed to gold. The system was managed by the IMF, which had to supervise monetary policies. Changes in exchange rates were only allowed when countries faced structural problems in their balance of payments. The system had already come under stress during the late 1960s as a result of American overspending and the related deficits on the balance of payments, which led to a gradual loss of confidence in the dollar and to a fall in American gold reserves. In August 1971 this resulted in the decision by Nixon to suspend the convertibility of the dollar into gold, which marked the beginning of a period of radical changes in exchange rates.

Two attempts were made to stem the tide. The 'Smithsonian agreement' of December 1971 tried to introduce a new system of fixed exchange rates after a thorough appreciation of the European and Japanese rates against the dollar. Already in the spring of 1973 it was clear that this attempt had failed and it was replaced by a 'system' of floating exchange rates. On a European scale attempts were made to reintroduce fixed exchange rates: in 1972 the EC began to coordinate monetary policies and introduced the 'snake', a system which allowed for limited fluctuations in the exchange rates of the participating countries. A number of countries was unable to continue its participation; the UK (1972), Italy (1973) and France (1974) had to return to a floating currency fairly quickly, but for a few 'core' countries (Germany, the Netherlands, Belgium) it was relatively successful (Swann 1988: 185–6).

Dutch policymakers responded to these changes by reorienting monetary policy. Already in 1961 the Netherlands followed the German example and revalued the guilder (although they did not do so during the second German revaluation in 1969). In view of the increased importance of Germany for the Dutch economy and the growing role of the eastern neighbour in the EC, it was only natural to try and maintain a close link with the Deutsche Mark. Moreover, the balance of payments showed healthy surpluses during the greater part of the 1970s, partly as a result of the increased value of the exports of natural gas. At the recurring reassessment of exchange rates within the 'snake' – in 1976, 1978, 1979 – the guilder had to yield a little to the Deutsche Mark, but in comparison with almost every other currency it continued to increase in value. The result was a sharp increase in the effective exchange rate of the guilder. According to different calculations, it increased by 30 to 40 percent between 1971 and 1979 (Szász 1981).

The second 'shock' that can be distinguished was the strong and continued rise in real wage costs. The Central Planning Bureau manoeuvred itself into a central position in the debate on the economic problems of the decade, and it considered the 'wage explosion' of 1963–4 and the following continued increase in wage costs as their main causes. In a famous paper by Den Hartog and Tjan (1974, 1976) the CPB presented a vintage model which showed that the increase in (structural) unemployment of the early 1970s could be explained from the scrapping of older series of capital equipment with a lower labour productivity – in response to rising wage costs (Passenier 1994: 220–2). After discussion among economists (Drie-huis and Van der Zwan 1978) the results of the model were largely accepted. Its diagnosis that high wage costs were the fundamental cause of increased unemployment became a matter of common knowledge.

A number of causes was behind the continued rise in wage costs: tension on parts of the labour market, lags in the response of trade unions to changes in the labour market, the system of wage leadership in wage negotiations (Chapter 5, pp. 82–4), strong increases in minimum wages under the Den Uyl cabinet, and increases in taxes and social security premiums which were largely shifted to non-wage incomes. Moreover, the indexation of wages was considered an established right by the trade unions, which meant that the sharp rise in import prices in the early 1970s and especially the oil price hike of 1973–4 spurred on the increase in wage costs. In general the position of the unions remained strong during the 1970s. In 1973–4, when complaints about the negative effects of strong wage rises were mounting, the unions adopted a policy of income redis-tribution in favour of the lower incomes; rather than demand given per-centage wage rises they asked for a lump sum wage round, which would favour the lowest incomes. This met with strong opposition from the employers' organizations (Windmuller and De Galan, 1979: II, 167 ff). To complicate matters even further, the government often intervened in wage negotiations because it became convinced that the economic pro-blems could not be solved without the moderation of wage increases. It tried to set ceilings to wage rises, but in general these interventions were not very successful (Van Hulst 1984).

In practice the 'scrapping' of obsolete capital equipment implied that a number of declining industries had to be reorganized and partly closed down. The government developed an industrial policy to manage the restructuring of industry which involved postponing harsh decisions and granting large subsidies to create (larger, more capital intensive, diversi-fied) firms that would be able to withstand international competition, particularly in 'sensitive' regions and industries.

The combination of large increases in wage costs and the rise in the effective exchange rate led to a sharp deterioration of international com-petitiveness. After having been a 'low-wage' country during the 1950s, the Netherlands suddenly became a country with (very) high wage costs during the 1970s. This undermined the profitability of Dutch enterprise and after 1975 led to a decline in export shares (Smits 1979). After 1976 the combination of domestic overspending (see below) and the relative stagna-tion of exports led to the disappearance of the surpluses on the balance of payments.

In the final years of the 1970s there arose discussion among economists about the effects and desirability of the monetary policies of the Central Bank, but this did not really affect policies (Szász 1981). The President of the Central Bank, Zijlstra, clearly preferred the battle against inflation – which was fought by increasing the effective exchange rate of the guilder – to any policy that would allow for a devaluation of the guilder against the Deutsche Mark. Moreover, it was expected that devaluation would result in more inflation, so that the short-term effects on growth and employment would soon disappear. However, it is very clear that these monetary policies contributed to the economic problems of the 1970s by undermining the profitability of the open sector of the economy.

In the long run the battle against inflation was highly effective: between 1969 and 1973 inflation in the Netherlands was slightly above that of neighbouring countries (with the exception of the UK), but this changed after 1973. The rate of inflation did not accelerate markedly in the Netherlands, whereas elsewhere (with the exception of Germany) prices shot up (Table 9.5). After 1979 the margin between the Netherlands and its most important trading partners became even more favourable, as a result of which the real effective exchange rate began to fall. Two factors were behind the relatively 'favourable' development of the rate of inflation: the increase in the exchange rate held down the import of inflation, and the growth of unemployment 'solved' the most fundamental cause of the inflationary boom of the 1960s, that is, the tight labour market.

A third shock that hit the economy was the radical change in the price of energy. The literature has paid little attention to the effects of the 'oil crises' on the long-term development of the Dutch economy, probably because the role of the Netherlands as a large exporter of energy was supposed to have limited the net effects. I will argue, however, that because of the recent exploitation of gas reserves, the effects on the economy were substantial.

*Table 9.5* Rate of inflation in the Netherlands and its most important trading partners, 1968–1973 to 1985–1994

| | *Prices of private consumption* | | | |
|---|---|---|---|---|
| | *1968–73* | *1973–79* | *1979–85* | *1985–94* |
| Germany | 4.6 | 4.7 | 4.1 | 2.4 |
| France | 6.1 | 10.7 | 9.9 | 2.7 |
| UK | 7.5 | 15.6 | 8.5 | 4.7 |
| Italy | 5.8 | 16.1 | 15.3 | 5.7 |
| Belgium | 4.9 | 8.4 | 6.7 | 2.3 |
| USA | 5.0 | 8.5 | 6.1 | 3.5 |
| Trading partners* | 5.3 | 8.4 | 6.8 | 3.0 |
| Netherlands | 6.9 | 7.2 | 4.4 | 1.7 |

*Sources*: OECD, 1987, 1995
* Weighted average of Germany (43%), Belgium (20%), France (14%), UK (11%), Italy (7%) USA (5%).

During the 1960s it was considered optimal to use the reserves of natural gas as quickly as possible, because it was expected that in the long term gas would not be able to compete with oil and nuclear energy. As a result, the government started a programme to maximize the consumption of natural gas and to use cheap energy as an instrument of industrial policy (Lubbers and Lemckert 1980: 88–90). For example, a new aluminium industry was established on this basis (Dankers and Verheul 1993: 289 ff), cheap energy was supplied to the booming chemical industry, and the state company that ran the coal mines was transformed into a large chemical entreprise (DSM) with the proceeds from gas exploitation. Moreover, cheap gas was supplied to the horticultural sector to replace the more polluting fuel oil as a source of heating. As a result, the energy intensity of the economy increased markedly between 1963 and 1973 (see Graph 9.2), which is exceptional because the relationship between energy and GDP was already on the decline in most other industrial countries (Maddison 1991). In the early 1970s the Netherlands was one of the most energy intensive economies in the world, with a much higher ratio between GDP and energy consumption than the rest of Europe (Darmstadter *et al.* 1977: 7, 31).

The Dutch economy was therefore quite vulnerable to the enormous rise in the price of oil in 1973–4 and again in 1979. In terms of the 'vintage' approach adopted by the CPB to analyse the impact of the rise of wage costs, it seems clear that the cheap energy policies of the 1960s had made the most recent vintages of the Dutch capital stock relatively energy

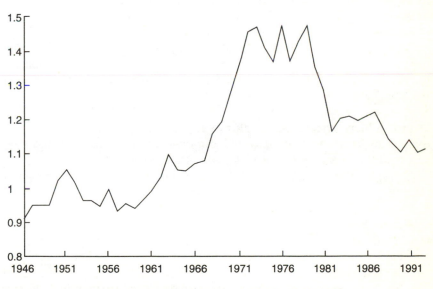

*Graph 9.2* Energy intensity of GDP, 1946–1993
*Source*: CBS 1994

167

intensive (or inefficient), so that they rapidly became obsolete. In other words, the profitability of these vintages must have been depressed heavily by the high energy prices. This meant that either a part had to be scrapped or that supplementary energy saving investments were needed to keep them in operation. The rise in energy prices therefore had two consequences for the Dutch capital stock: it lowered its value (and probably made the most energy inefficient parts redundant) and it increased the need for new, energy saving investment. Both processes resulted in a long-term decline in energy intensity after about 1980.

Lags in the price setting of natural gas and related government policies mitigated the effects of the radical change in energy prices. However, this changed during the second oil crisis when the government began to push for a full rise in the price of gas following international oil prices (Lubbers and Lemckert 1980: 106). Moreover, these hidden subsidies met with resistance from Brussels (as in the case of the supply of cheap gas to horticulture). That the energy intensity of output did not start to fall before 1980 (in contrast to what was happening elsewhere) emphasizes the delayed response to the change in relative prices (Graph 9.2).

Some parts of the economy profited from the high energy prices. The government and the few companies that participated in the joint venture that exploited the gas fields (Shell, BP, DSM), reaped enormous profits. The extra funds acquired by the government were used to finance the ambitious policies of the left-wing cabinet of Den Uyl, which aimed at the redistribution of income, knowledge and power, and tried to stem the downturn of 1974–5 with classical Keynesian instruments (spending more to boost employment) (Lubbers and Lemckert 1980: 102).

Finally, the large exports of natural gas supported the balance of payments. The exports of the manufacturing sector became increasingly depressed as a result of the decreased competitiveness of Dutch industry, but the expansion of the proceeds from natural gas sustained the surplus on the balance of payments. In this way, by backing the policy of the Central Bank to create an overvalued guilder (in order to maintain the link with the Deutsche Mark) the increased value of exports of natural gas 'crowded out' exports of goods and services and diminished employment in the open sector of the economy (the well-known 'Dutch disease').

A supplementary shock of perhaps lesser importance was the fundamental changes in the legislation concerning the environment. Until the late 1960s growth had been largely unrestricted by environmental concerns, but this changed fundamentally as a result of the rise of the environmental movement after about 1965. A series of laws against various forms of pollution was introduced between 1969 and 1979, which demanded measures to reduce levels of emission (Van Zanden and Verstegen 1993: 146). The effects were twofold: part of the existing capital stock lost its economic potential and had to be scrapped and supplementary investments in the reduction of pollution were needed. The importance of these investments increased rapidly: in 1975 about 2.6 percent of total investment by industry aimed at reducing emissions, which went up to 3.4 percent in 1980 and 5.9 percent in 1990 (CBS 1994b: 307).

In view of the strong pressures exerted on the Dutch economy – high wage costs, high taxes and social security premiums, an overvalued currency, enormous rises in energy prices, and the introduction of environmental policies – it is almost a miracle that it performed fairly well (by international standards) until 1979. A comparison with OECD Europe can shed some light on this performance (Table 9.6). Two elements of final expenditure seem to cause the divergence. Private and public consumption increased much more rapidly in the Netherlands than elsewhere.

The favourable development of private consumption was partly related to the ongoing increases in real wages and the strong expansion of the market for consumer credit. Real interest rates were negative between 1972 and 1976 and remained low until the end of the decade, which boosted consumer credit. Moreover, fuelled by low interest rates and intended as a hedge against inflation, the price of real estate went up, which stimulated consumer expenditure through the expansion of the market for 'second mortgages'. Enterprises had the same reaction to the low real interest rates and financed a large part of expansion with outside capital (although this further undermined their solidity). Looking back, it is surprising that the Central Bank, focused as it was on the battle against inflation, allowed the ongoing expansion of the money supply that went along with these processes. After an almost continuous fall in the ratio between money supply and national income between 1946 and 1972, the ratio went up again between 1972 and 1977, without provoking a response from the Central Bank until May 1977 (Compaijen and Den Butter 1991: 130).

The left-wing cabinet of Den Uyl (1973–7) reacted to the economic downturn of 1974–5 in a classical Keynesian way: in view of the surplus on the balance of payments it decided to boost demand. More money was

Table 9.6 Growth of GDP and components of expenditure in the Netherlands and OECD Europe, 1973–1979 and 1979–1985 (average annual growth rates)

|  | Netherlands | | OECD Europe | |
|---|---|---|---|---|
|  | 1973–79 | 1979–85 | 1973–79 | 1979–85 |
| GDP | 2.7 | 0.7 | 2.4 | 1.4 |
| Private consumption | 4.0 | −0.3 | 2.8 | 1.2 |
| Investment | −0.1 | −1.0 | 0.3 | 0.2 |
| Government consumption | 3.4 | 0.8 | 3.1 | 1.7 |
| Exports | 2.9 | 3.0 | 4.8 | 4.0 |

Source: OECD, 1987

made available for new projects to create employment, for industrial policies for enterprises in need, to increase minimum wages and social security benefits, and so on. In the summer of 1975 new predictions made by the CPB on the basis of its recent vintage model which showed clearly that this course of action was making things worse. Instead, the CPB concluded that the government had to reduce its deficit and lower taxes and social security premiums. This led to a U-turn in economic policy: the cabinet of Den Uyl introduced a policy to restrain the growth of the public sector (it was allowed to increase by no more than 1 percent of national income per year, which was much less than in the previous years) (Toirkens 1988: 32 ff). The strong upturn of 1976 postponed more drastic measures, but in 1977 new projections of the CPB created the basis for a new round of budget cuts, this time introduced by a Conservative-Christian Democratic cabinet led by Van Agt (1977–81). Little came of their plans as they were obstructed by cabinet ministers who represented other interest groups (for example, the Minister for Social Affairs) and by active opposition in parliament (for backgrounds see Chapter 4, pp. 68–9). Moreover, almost every attempt to reorganize government finances was accompanied by 'supplementary' plans to mitigate its effects on employment, which caused additional expenditure, and many of the proposed cuts were never put into practice (Toirkens 1988). The end result was that the budget deficit increased sharply despite the enormous income from the gas reserves. The government deficit went up from less than 2 percent of GDP in the early 1970s to almost 9 percent in 1982–3. This was to become the dominating political problem of the 1980s.

## DEPRESSION AND REORIENTATION 1979–1985

Consumers, firms, and government responded in roughly the same way to the economic problems of the mid-1970s: they had all tried to borrow a way out of the recession. This had been a rational solution for the adverse economic tide in times of negative (or very low) real interest rates. The sharp upturn in international interest rates that began in 1979 – caused by a switch towards restrictive monetary policies in the USA and UK – blocked this way out and exposed the vulnerability of the Dutch economy to changes in the real interest rate. The downturn of the international economy that followed the second oil crisis of 1979 was therefore accompanied by a decrease in the rate of inflation and a surge in (real) interest rates, so that the economy was actually hit twice: by the contraction of demand and by the strong rise in real interest rates.

During the 1970s expansionary policies had mitigated many of the adverse effects of the exogenous shocks: generous industrial policies bolstered important parts of declining industries and energy policies resulted in only modest increases in domestic energy prices for many producers.

But in the early 1980s the financial problems of the state became so dramatic that serious budget cuts had to be introduced. Some measures had already been taken by the successive cabinets of Van Agt (1977–82), but the first radical package was introduced by the (first) Lubbers cabinet (1982–6) as part of the *regeerakkoord* (the coalition agreement). It implied serious cuts in the real wage of public servants and in social security benefits; the real income of the aged, the disabled, and the sick was to fall by more than 10 percent in the first half of the 1980s. Other measures were less 'successful' – for example, the number of government employees continued to grow – but the increase in government consumption slowed down markedly after 1980 (Table 9.6). The Lubbers I *regeerakkoord* was followed by a long (and still unfinished) row of measures to reduce public spending in order to lower the budget deficit, but also and increasingly to decrease the level of taxation in the economy and reduce the role of the state.

The private sector reacted in a similar way to the pressures of the early 1980s. Consumption declined sharply (Table 9.6) after the collapse of the market for houses in 1980–81; the market for consumer credit also contracted. The profitability of Dutch industry, which had been declining almost without interruption during the 1970s, continued to fall steeply until 1982–3. A wave of bankruptcies swept through the economy: an estimated 27,000 entreprises went bankrupt at the cost of about 150,000 jobs (Lakeman and Van de Ven 1985: 158). Many firms that had been kept alive by government subsidies during the 1970s now went into liquidation.

Table 9.6 shows some of the reasons why growth between 1979 and 1985 was much slower in the Netherlands than elsewhere: the stagnation in private and public consumption is the big difference with the preceding period, but the decline in investments was also relatively strong. Only exports continued to grow rather rapidly, which was probably caused by the gradual improvement in international competitiveness (see below). Compared with the OECD average (and with the exports of the main trading partners) export growth was, however, modest and Dutch industry continued to lose market share.

However, at the depth of the depression there began a process of reorientation that was to bear fruit in the decade to come. An important agreement was concluded by trade unions, employers' organizations and the government in 1982 to aim at restraining the increase in wage costs. The unions were actually prepared to renegotiate the indexation of wages. In return, the government promised that it would no longer intervene in wage negotiations (as it had done unsuccessfully six times between 1971 and 1982 (Van Hulst 1984: 224–5)) and the employers' organizations promised seriously to consider the demands for the redistribution of labour through shortening the work week (Van Bottenburg 1995: 195–6). The agreement of Wassenaar (named after the village where it was

171

reached) inaugurated a new phase of wage moderation: the increase in nominal wage costs declined from 6.5 percent in 1982 to an average of 1.7 percent in 1983 to 1989, and remained at a relative low level in the 1990s (CPB 1995: 158–9).

The retreat from wage policy by the government in 1982 was part of a wider reorientation of its policies. In 1983 it became known that the RSV, the huge combination of ship building and metalworking firms which had received a large part of the subsidies for industrial policy, was virtually bankrupt. This led to a public scandal and an official inquiry by the Dutch parliament into the allocation of subsidies (totalling 2,700 million guilders) and the management of the RSV (the first official parliamentary inquiry after 1946). The inquiry was broadcast on television in 1984–5 and became a media event. MPs exposed the follies of captains of industry, high-ranking public servants and (former) ministers of economic affairs. In general the inquiry showed the lack of planning of government and RSV management and the absence of control over the expenditure of large government funds. It accelerated the ending of all kinds of subsidies to ailing industries and the move towards a more 'offensive' industrial policy, aimed at promoting technological change and stimulating growth industries (Van Zanden, at press).

Privatization was another part of the ideological offensive of the 1980s. In 1982 the first programme to privatize a number of state-owned firms was launched. Its purposes were dual: to strengthen the supply side of the economy by increasing the efficiency of these companies, and to bring in money for the government to reduce its deficit. But it was not a radical departure from previous policies; already in the 1960s the government had sold part of its shares in well-run companies (Hoogovens, KLM) and the conversion of the state mines into the chemical company DSM had also involved loosening the ties with the government. In the 1980s the process was accelerated: state enterprises such as the postal services and the postal bank were first converted into state-owned firms, in order to increase their competitiveness. After a while the government began to sell its shares in a number of tranches, thereby concluding the process of privatization. The relatively small share of the government owned sector of the economy naturally implied that the impact of this policy was relatively small (Andeweg 1994).

Other parts of the switch towards the supply-side policies of the 1980s were the attempts to reduce public spending in order to lower the deficit and, after that had been accomplished, to reduce taxes and social security premiums. These measures resulted in a reduction of the share of taxes and premiums in GDP with more than 12 percent between 1982 and 1995; this success has been sketched in Chapter 4, pp. 69–70. Various measures were taken to try to solve some of the structural problems in the labour market: benefit levels were reduced, and access to social security schemes was

172

made more difficult to obtain, minimum wages were frozen and marginal taxes and premiums on minimum wages were lowered in order to encourage entrepreneurs to hire these workers.

A remarkable aspect of the rather radical change in government policy is that it was shared by all major parties involved. The policies of the Conservative/Christian-Democrat cabinets Lubbers I and II were not much different from those of their successors in which the (left-wing) Labour Party participated. And the basic aims and goals of the policy were supported by trade unions and employers' organizations alike. In the early 1980s a new consensus emerged in Dutch politics. The similarities with the post-1945 consensus are quite striking (see Chapter 7, p. 133). In 1945 the consensus was based on a historical compromise between labour and capital – concluded in the Stichting van de Arbeid – and it was stimulated by the common experience of the war. In the 1980s the CPB seems to have played a leading role in creating a climate for renewed concensus. Its diagnosis of the causes of the economic problems – high wage costs, the large public deficit, and the big public sector – became generally accepted. Moreover, almost all proposals for a change in economic policy were subject to extensive assessments by the CPB; when its models predicted negative results for employment or the government deficit, the measure was usually called off. In a similar way, every *regeerakkoord* was screened by the CPB and adapted when the predictions of its consequences on growth and employment were not sufficiently positive. The influence of the CPB reached even further. Before every election the CPB simulated the effects on the economy of the mix of proposals put forward in the platforms of the major parties; they 'predicted' how these measures would affect employment and growth. The results of these simulations were widely published and played a role in the campaigns (Passenier 1994: 291 ff). Within the wider contest for the favour of the electorate the parties also had to bid for the 'favours' of the CPB models (some politicians became experienced in proposing the right mix of measures that would give the best projections by the CPB). In the 1993 elections even the radical left-wing party (Groen Links) cooperated with the CPB on how to translate their ideas into the instruments of the CPB models. In brief, the overriding influence of the CPB resulted in a political discourse that was largely dominated by its neo-liberal models, projections, and ideas. On this basis the new consensus was reached quite easily.

## NEW DYNAMISM 1985–1995

The combination of these measures and the results of the 'new' policy of wage restraint of the unions brought about a sharp improvement in international competitiveness, a strong recovery of the profitability of industry and a gradual reorganization of public finance. As a result the (relative) performance of the Dutch economy improved markedly after about 1985 (see introductory section). The best proof of the renewed dynamism was probably the way in which the economy was able to cope with the recession of 1992–3 that was largely caused by the negative side-effects of German unification. Whereas the previous period of high interest rates had wrought havoc among Dutch industry and had led to the worst depression since the 1930s, the economy was now able to withstand the adverse economic tide. GDP in Germany, France, and Belgium fell by 1 percent or more, but in the Netherlands growth continued, albeit at a slower pace.

The outlines of the new growth phase have already been sketched in previous chapters. It was accompanied with the relative decline of the large multinationals (the big six) and the growth of the number of small and medium-sized firms. Following the new neo-liberal orthodoxy, the government tried to reduce its role in the economy and successfully cut its expenditure. Attempts to increase flexibility in the labour market met with some resistance by the unions, but their position was weak as union density had fallen sharply since the 1970s. The expansion of the female labour force and of part-time labour was another particular feature. The demand for labour grew fairly rapidly since about 1985, especially in the service sector. The Dutch 'job machine' was linked to the slow growth of wage costs, which in turn was the result of wage moderation by the unions and government policies to cut (marginal) tax rates in the lower segments of the labour market.

Compared with the situation in the 1970s and early 1980s the economy seemed revitalized and was much more dynamic. Yet, the 'new growth' of the 1980s and 1990s surely had its limitations. First, as in the 1950s, it was based on keeping down wages, which was not a very promising growth strategy in the long run. For example, low wage costs mean that firms do not have strong incentives to increase productivity and will therefore not invest in labour-saving technology. As a result, the growth of labour productivity has been rather low (in contrast to the preceding period, see introductory section), and the growth of GDP per capita was not rapid either (for example, compared with growth in the pre-1973 period). This was also caused by expenditure constraints: the 'low wage' strategy combined with the continuous budget cuts of the government resulted in a slow growth of domestic consumption expenditure (Table 9.7). As in the early 1980s exports were the main outlet for the growth of production (Table 9.7); investment, however, continued to grow rather sluggishly (see below).

In the 1950s the low-wage strategy resulted in an undervalued currency which boosted the exports of Dutch manufacturers. In a system of floating exchange rates this was no longer possible. The effects of the new low-wage strategy were therefore somewhat more complex. The primary consequence was that the price of labour relative to that of capital goods, energy, and other inputs declined which would probably result in increased

174

*Table 9.7* Growth of GDP, 1985–1994 (average annual growth rates)

|  | Netherlands | OECD Europe |
|---|---|---|
| GDP | 2.53 | 2.20 |
| Private final consumption | 2.50 | 2.51 |
| Government final cons. | 1.66 | 1.83 |
| Gross investment | 2.12 | 2.60 |
| Exports | 4.62 | 4.11 |
| Imports | 4.27 | 4.87 |

*Source*: OECD 1995

employment in the long run (for example, through a slow-down in the scrapping of old technologies or through changes in the capital–labour ratio of new vintage technology). The effects on the development of international competitiveness are not as obvious: in theory, in a perfect system of floating exchange rates the relative decline in wages (and prices) would result in a compensating rise in the effective exchange rate, leaving international competitiveness largely unaffected. However, the European attempts to create a zone of stable exchange rates and the various crises in the EMS regime in the 1980s and 1990s – resulting in large-scale capital movements and sudden fluctuations in the exchange rates with pound sterling, other less stable European currencies, and the dollar – made the effects of the policy of wage moderation far more complicated.

The fundamental premise of Dutch monetary policy was the stability of the exchange rate with the Deutsche Mark. This created opportunities (to improve competitiveness vis-à-vis the German economy where wage moderation was almost non-existent) as well as problems (the guilder shared the strong upward trend in the effective exchange rate of the Deutsche Mark). The opportunities were used effectively. Whereas unit labour costs in industry increased by only 5 percent in the Netherlands between 1983 and 1993, they went up by 37 percent in Germany in the same period (Table 9.8). The difference in the rate of inflation was much smaller. The result was that in the Netherlands the share of wage costs in the value added of industry declined almost 12 percent, while it increased by 14 percent in Germany (Table 9.8). All other indicators of the development of international competitiveness show the same picture: Dutch industry was able to improve its position, particularly with regard to Germany. The strong improvement of the competitive strength of Dutch industry was therefore not only the result of wage moderation but also of the fact that on its main export market it competed with a German industry which was unable to adjust to the increases in the effective exchange rate of the Deutsche Mark. To some extent the Dutch economy could profit from the increased economic problems of Germany.

However, the reliance on Germany as a major export market also had

*Table 9.8* Comparison of competitiveness of the Netherlands and Germany, 1983–1993 (indices, 1983 = 100)

|  | Netherlands 1993 | Germany 1993 |
|---|---|---|
| Unit wage costs in industry | 105.2 | 137.0 |
| Prices of private consumption | 118.6 | 125.8 |
| Wage costs as a share of value added | 88.3 | 114.1 |
| Market share of export goods | 108.5 | 80.6 |
| Relative export prices (common currency) | 92.5 | 108.7 |
| Relative unit wage costs (common currency) | 96.4 | 129.9 |

*Sources*: OECD 1995; CPB 1996: 176–7

side-effects: economic growth in Germany was relatively slow despite the impetus of unification. Moreover, on the German market Dutch exports had to compete with those of other countries that were not handicapped by a strong currency. Especially during and after the various EMS crises this resulted in increased competition, for example, by Italian producers and in stagnation of the Dutch share in German imports.

Relations with the rest of the world economy were characterized by an ongoing appreciation of the guilder during the various crises on international capital markets. Relative unit labour costs shot up in 1986–7, when the dollar collapsed, and again in the early 1990s (during the crisis in the EMS), which had negative consequences for the growth of exports and the profitability of industry (export shares fell in 1987, 1989–90 and again in 1992). For the parts of industry that were dependent on exports to the dollar or pound sterling areas the periodic declines in the value of these currencies led to strong increases in competitive pressure and a decline in profitability. Part of the relative decline of the multinationals in manufacturing (Philips, Fokker) should be attributed to these recurring problems.

On average the economy did rather well with the combination of wage moderation and a strong currency. In the long run the relatively slow growth of labour productivity can become problematic, as it is clear that in all kinds of labour intensive processes Dutch workers will never be able to compete with 'low-wage countries'. According to one 'dissident', Kleinknecht, the continuous improvement of production processes and products that is needed to keep ahead of international competition is not sufficiently stimulated by the low-wage strategy (Kleinknecht 1996). The fall in R&D expenditure during the late 1980s and early 1990s is seen as proof of this growing weakness. It is well known that the reasons for this fall are the budget cuts of the government, which also affected expenditure on research and, more importantly, the decline in R&D expenditure by the large multinationals. The share of the five largest firms (Shell, Unilever, DSM, AKZO, Philips) in private spending on R&D has declined from two-thirds in 1987 to 55 percent in 1993 (OECD 1996: 83). The relative decline of the multinationals – also in the field of R&D – is not (yet) sufficiently compensated for by the rise of R&D expenditure of small and medium-sized companies.

Another weakness of economic development after 1985 was the sluggish growth of investments. Although international competitiveness was strong and profits were high – according to the OECD estimates the rates of return on capital in the business sector were continually among the highest in Europe (OECD 1995) – investments grew at a lower rate than GDP, which was in stark contrast with the strong increase in investments in the period before 1973 (Table 9.7). This is particularly striking because the decline in investments had been rather pronounced between 1979 and 1985 (Table 9.6). The decline in public investments – the result of the ongoing attempts to cut spending – was substantial. Its share in GDP fell almost continuously from 4.9 percent in 1971 to 2.4 percent in 1988, after which there began a modest recovery. Gross private investments showed some recovery after the strong decline in the early 1980s, but its modest growth since 1985 cannot easily be explained.

One of the explanations for the sluggish growth of investments is that there has occurred a structural shift in business strategies in the 1980s. As has been explained in Chapter 3, before the 'globalization' of capital markets in the 1980s Dutch firms were relatively free from these pressures. Managers were in complete control of business strategy and focused on the long-term growth of the firm. This 'continental' model of the firm was reinforced by all kinds of legal constructions to reduce the influence of shareholders. The 'revolution' of the shareholder in the 1980s has, however, led to a number of changes. As in the USA, managers have come under stronger pressure to increase profitability in the short turn in order to pay out higher dividends and push up share prices. The slow growth of investments must perhaps also be seen in this light: long-term growth objectives became less important, which reduced investments and expenditure on R&D, and were replaced by all kinds of short-term measures to increase efficiency (such as 'downsizing' and the sale of unprofitable activities).

Domestic savings do not seem to have been a bottleneck for the expansion of investments. In fact, savings were generally sufficient to cover the large deficits of the government during the 1980s and, apart from a few years in the late 1970s (1978–80), to allow for a healthy surplus on the balance of payments. When the public deficit began to decline, this surplus increased to 3 or 4 percent of GDP in the late 1980s and early 1990s (OECD 1996). This is another indication that domestic expenditure became (too) slow as a consequence of the government's budget cuts, wage moderation, and the slow growth of investments in the private sector.

At the same time foreign direct investment increased rapidly – it boomed to about 5 percent of GDP in the years after 1988 – which was part of the strategy of the multinationals to spread their activities more evenly across the globe. Large insurance companies and banks followed the example of industry, and sometimes took the lead in the internationalization of their activities (Gales and Sluyterman 1993). Moreover, as part of the general policy of deregulation, restrictions for the large pension funds were liberalized, which made it possible to export large amounts of Dutch savings to the USA and other EC countries.

## FOREIGN ECONOMIC POLICIES AND THE DEVELOPMENT OF THE EU

During the 1970s the development of the EC was dominated by two issues: the admission of the UK, Ireland and Denmark and the resulting conflicts about the British contribution to the EC budget, and the monetary problems of the decade.

The entrance of the UK had a big impact on the role of the Netherlands in the EC. Before 1973 it had positioned itself as the closest ally of the British and Americans and had defended this 'Atlantic' cooperation against 'continental' (i.e. French) desires for a separate political and military union. As part of this policy the Netherlands had argued strongly in favour of the enlargement of the EC with the UK. When this goal was attained in 1973 the British began to act as the 'dissidents' or the 'natural' opponents of the French (and the Germans), while the role of the Netherlands became more modest.

The economy appeared to have profited from the enlargement: international trade with the UK, which had relatively declined during the preceding decades, shot up. Helped by the increased importance of North Sea oil, the British share of imports increased by almost 80 percent (from 5.3 percent in 1972 to 9.4 percent in 1982); exports to the UK went up more gradually (from 7.4 percent of total exports in 1972 to 9.3 percent in 1982 and 10.3 percent in 1987) (CBS 1994). Trade with the other new member states also expanded relatively rapidly, but its importance was much smaller.

The heavy reliance on exports to the old and new members of the EC proved to be a mixed blessing during the 1970s and 1980s. After the decades of stormy growth before 1973, the European economy stagnated during the 1970s and 1980s, which must have depressed Dutch exports in the long run. Other, more favourably developing markets – in the Middle East, North America, and Asia – had been relatively neglected and had declined in importance since the 1950s. In 1973 about 75 percent of Dutch exports went to the enlarged EC, and this percentage remained almost constant in the following decades (it was 74 percent in 1993 when Spain, Portugal, and Greece were included) (CBS 1994).

In the field of monetary policy the Netherlands became the natural ally of Germany. In their view the failure of the 'snake' agreement showed that a better coordination of domestic economic policies was needed before a system of more or less constant exchange rates could successfully be implemented (according to the German–Dutch point of view this implied that anti-inflationary policies along the German model had to be introduced before other currencies could be linked to the Deutsche Mark). As a result, until 1978 no new attempts were made to introduce a more robust system of exchange rate management. In 1978 the German Chancellor Schmidt changed his position and together with France he launched the plan for the EMS. The fear that the ongoing devaluation of the dollar would cause an even stronger appreciation of the Deutsche Mark was probably behind the plan; Schmidt hoped to create a kind of buffer around the Deutsche Mark which would relieve the upward pressure on its value. The Dutch monetary authorities – especially the Central Bank – were rather concerned about these plans (as was the Bundesbank), but they were unable to exert much influence (Szász 1988: 155 ff). The old fear that the new system would not force the countries with a (too) high level of inflation into more orthodox monetary policies was behind the feeble resistance.

The EMS proved to be much more successful than the Central Bank had expected. Although realignments of the different currencies had to take place periodically (until 1987), it eventually forced the French into restrictive monetary policies (after the failure of the Mitterand experiment between 1981 and 1983) (Temperton 1993: 16–17). In general, the period witnessed a continuous decline in international disparities in the rate of inflation, and the differences between Germany, Belgium, the Netherlands and France became very small indeed (see Table 9.5). This was, of course, to a large extent a side-effect of the end of the inflationary boom of the 1960s and 1970s that came about as a result of the diminishing of tension on the labour market (to use an understatement) and the restrictive monetary policies after 1979.

The other problem that dominated the debate about the future of the EC in the late 1970s and early 1980s was the reform of the Common Agricultural Policy (CAP). In Chapter 4 it has already been explained that the change from being a net importer of agricultural products to sizeable exporter lay behind the strong rise of EC expenditure on the CAP until it absorbed more than 70 percent of the EC budget in the early 1980s. Moreover, it led to the accumulation of enormous stocks of butter, meat and grain, and in general seemed a classic example of the inefficiency of government intervention in the 1980s. The continuing problems about the British contribution to the EC budget can largely be attributed to the fact that they hardly profited from the CAP subsidies, while they paid a large part of its costs, being a net importer of agricultural products (Swann 1988: 215 ff).

A reform of the CAP was therefore one of the priorities of EC policy during the early 1980s. The Council of Ministers – in this case the ministers responsible for agriculture – was, however, only slowly moving towards plans for reform, because these would undoubtedly create problems with their supporters, the farmers and their organizations. Basically there were two options: to increase the level of intervention by introducing production quotas which would 'solve' the problem of overproduction; or to introduce market-oriented reforms by bringing prices more in line with those on the world market (supplemented with other measures to sustain the incomes of the farmers). In 1984 a first series of measures was taken to reduce the overproduction of milk by fixing quotas; these quotas were subsequently lowered. Dutch farmers fervently supported these measures because they would more or less fix the strong position they had gained in the EC market for milk products (Strijker 1990: 105). Later reforms to reduce the over-production of grain followed a more market-oriented course and aimed at lowering prices. Pressures from the USA, which had made liberalization of trade in agricultural products one of the priorities of the Uruguay Round of the GATT, also contributed to the switch towards market-oriented reform.

The Dutch position towards these reforms has been ambivalent. Since the days of Mansholt, Dutch members of the European Commission had been highly influential in the formulation of agricultural policy. The Commissioner (for agriculture) and, until 1994, the Minister of Agriculture were seen as representatives of the agricultural interest group, which did not generally favour the lowering of subsidies from which Dutch agriculture had benefited so much. There was, however, a growing awareness that the sector had become so efficient that it should be able to meet the challenge of international competition, and together with the general rise of neo-liberal economic ideas this helped to redirect policies. As a result the resistance against radical changes in the CAP, which had been character-istic for the 1970s and early 1980s, slowly dissipated (Strijker 1990).

In other fields the Netherlands supported the liberalization of the EC far more ardently. With the 1984 bilateral agreement completely to liberalize air traffic between the Netherlands and the UK the two countries took the European lead in the process of deregulation in this sector (Bouwens and Dierickx 1996). Notwithstanding strong resistance from a number of other EC countries, which wanted to protect their heavily subsidized national airlines, the liberalization of air traffic was pushed through in the following decade. At the same time, once again inspired by the American example, steps were taken completely to liberalize capital markets. In the Nether-lands this process was completed in 1986 and became part of the pro-gramme for the realization of a unified market in 1992.

The plan for the creation of a unified market gave new impetus to the process of European integration after 1984. The Maastricht Treaty of 1991, in which the European Union was formed, was in many ways the conclusion of this period. The ambitious plans for a European Monetary Union, to be formed at the end of the 1990s, were undermined in the following years by a number of developments. The one-sided restrictive monetary policies of the Bundesbank, to stem the economic problems of German unification, led to increased tension within the EMS. Since 1987 no new realignment of currencies has taken place, probably in order to force countries with a substantial rate of inflation into more deflationary policies. However, the choice of keeping exchange rates as stable as possible proved to be a mistake. In 1992 and 1993 the 'weak' currencies were forced to leave the EMS and the system crumbled under the pressure of large-scale speculative capital movements. The EU thus reaped the sour fruits of the liberalization of international capital markets which it had made possible.

Since 1991 the conditions for joining the EMU which were formulated in the Maastricht Treaty have contributed much to the general deflationary climate in the European economy. All countries, from the richest (Germany which has great difficulty with the costs of unification) to the poorest (even Greece now seems to think of implementing some of the decisions it agreed upon), are now united in their attempts to cut expenditure and lower budget deficits in order to live up to the strict rules set by the Bundesbank. This may be regarded as an unexpected outcome of the long twentieth century, which was, among other things, a complex and prolonged experiment in national economic policy.

# BIBLIOGRAPHY

Abma, R. (1977) 'Het Plan van de Arbeid en de SDAP', *Bijdragen en mededelingen betreffende de geschiedenis der Nederlanden*, 37–68.

Addison, J.T. and Siebert, W.S. (1993) 'The U.K.: labour market institutions, law and performance', in J. Hartog and J. Theeuwes (eds) *Labour Market Contracts and Institutions*, Amsterdam, 351–384.

Albeda, W. and Dercksen, W.J. (1985) *Arbeidsverhoudingen in Nederland*, Alphen aan den Rijn.

Alber, J. (1981) 'Government responses to the challenge of unemployment: the development of unemployment insurance in Western Europe', in P. Flora and A.J. Heidenheimer (eds) *The Emergence of Welfare States in Europe and America*, London, 151–186.

Alberts, W.H.M.E., Boomen, P.H.J. van den, Fischer, E.J. and Gerwen, J.L.J.M. van (1982) *Marges van de vakbeweging*, 's-Gravenhage.

Andeweg, R.B. (1994) 'Privatization in the Netherlands: the result of a decade', in V. Wright (ed.) *Privatization in Western Europe*, London, 198–214.

Andriessen, J.E. (1987) 'Het economisch eldorado', in A. Knoester (ed.) *Lessen uit het verleden*, Leiden/Antwerpen.

*Annual Report of the Commissioner of Patents* (1880–1993) Washington DC.

Ark, B. van and Jong, H.J. de (1996) 'Accounting for economic growth in the Netherlands since 1913', *Economic and Social History in the Netherlands* 7, 199–242.

Armstrong, P., Glyn, A. and Harrison, A. (1984) *Capitalism since World War II*, London.

Arrighi, G. (1996) *The Long Twentieth Century*, London.

Arts, W. and Wijck, P. van (1994) 'De lange-termijndynamiek van de Nederlandse inkomensverdeling', in H. Flap and M.H.D. van Leeuwen (eds) *Op lange termijn*, Hilversum, 37–60.

Bain, G.S. and Price, R. (1980) *Profiles of Union Growth*, Oxford.

Bakker, A. and Lent, M.M.P. van (1989) *Pieter Lieftinck 1902–1989*, Utrecht/Antwerpen.

Bakker, G.P. den, Bochove C.A. van and Huitker, Th.A. (1987) *Macro-economische ontwikkelingen, 1921–1939 en 1969–1985*, 's-Gravenhage.

Bakker, G.P. den and Sorge, W. van (1996) 'Interwar unemployment in the Netherlands', in J.L. van Zanden (ed.) *The Economic Development of the Netherlands since 1870*, Cheltenham, 137–159.

Barendregt, J. (1993) *The Dutch Money Purge*, Amsterdam.

Barendregt, J. and Visser, H. (1997) 'Towards a new maturity', in M. 't Hart, J.

Jonker and J.L. van Zanden (eds) *A Financial History of the Netherlands*, Cambridge, 152–194.

Barnouw, D. and Stellinga, R.S. (1978) 'Ondernemers en ordening in bezet Nederland: de organisatie-Woltersom', *Cahiers voor de politieke en sociale wetenschappen* I, 4.

Baudet, H. and Fennema, M. (1983) *Het Nederlands belang bij Indië*, Utrecht/Antwerpen.

Baudet, M.J. and Wijers, G.H. (1976) 'De economische betekenis van Nederlandsch – Indië voor Nederland', *ESB* 61, 885–888.

Beaton, K. (1957) *Enterprise in Oil*, New York.

Beld, C.A. van den (1963) *Conjunctuurpolitiek in en om de jaren vijftig*, 's-Gravenhage.

Bie, R.J. van der (1995) '*Een doorlopende groote roes*'. *De Economische ontwikkeling van Nederland, 1913–1921*, Amsterdam.

Blaisse, P.A. (1952) 'De Nederlandse handelspolitiek', in P.B. Kreukniet (eds) *De Nederlandse volkshuishouding tussen twee wereldoorlogen*, Utrecht/Antwerpen.

Blanco Fernandez, J.M. (1993) *De Raad van Commissarissen bij NV en BV*, Maastricht.

Blanken, I.J. (1992) *Geschiedenis van Philips Electronics N.V.* III (1922–1934), Leiden.

*Blatt für Patent-, Muster-, und Zeicherwesen* (1894–1990), Berlin.

Bloembergen, E. (1943) *De Naamlooze Vennootschap in een tijd van ordening*, Utrecht.

Bloemen, E.S.A. (1981) 'Bezieling en "esprit d'equipe". Industriële research in Nederland in het interbellum', in P. Boomgaard *et al.* (eds) *Exercities in ons verleden*, Assen, 153–167.

—— (1988) *Scientific Management in Nederland 1900–1930*, Amsterdam.

Bloemen, E.S.A. (ed.) (1992) *Het Benelux-effect*, Amsterdam.

Bloemen, E.S.A., Kok, J. and Zanden, J.L. van (1993a) *De top 100 van industriële bedrijven in Nederland 1913–1990*, Den Haag.

Bloemen, E.S.A., Fransen, A.W., Kok, J., and Zanden, J.L. van (1993b) 'De vermogensontwikkeling van Nederlands grootste industriële bedrijven, 1913–1950', *Jaarboek voor de geschiedenis van bedrijf en techniek* 10, 133–160.

Blom, J.C.H. (1985) 'Onderzoek naar verzuiling in Nederland', in J.C.H. Blom and C.J. Misset (eds) '*Broeders sluit U aan*', Amsterdam, 10–29.

—— (1989) *Crisis, bezetting en herstel*, Den Haag.

Bochove, C.A. van and Huitker, Th.A. (1987) 'Main National Accounting Series 1900–1986', Occasional Paper nr. NA-017, CBS, Voorburg.

Boekestijn, A.J. (1992) 'Een nagel aan Adam Smiths doodskist: de Benelux-onderhandelingen in de jaren veertig en vijftig', in E.S.A. Bloemen (ed.) *Het Benelux-effect*, Amsterdam, 143–168.

Bottenburg, M. van (1995) *Aan den arbeid!*, Amsterdam.

Bouwens, A.M.C.M. and Dierickx, M.L.J. (1996) *Op de drempel van de lucht*, Den Haag.

Brandes de Roos, R. (1927) *Die Industrie, der Kapitalmarkt und die industriellen Effekten in Holland*, Den Haag.

Broeke, W. van den (1989) 'Het spoor terug gevolgd', in J.A. Faber (ed.) *Het Spoor. 150 jaar spoorwegen in Nederland*, Utrecht, 11–51.

Broekema, C. (1920) 'Landbouw', in H. Brugmans (ed.) *Nederland in den Oorlogstijd*, Amsterdam, 279–316.

Brugmans, I.J. (1969) *Paardenkracht en mensenmacht*, 's-Gravenhage.

Burger, A. (1993) *Voor Boerenvolk en Vaderland*, Amsterdam.

Burger, D.H. (1975) *Sociologisch-economische geschiedenis van Indonesia*, Wageningen/Amsterdam.

CBS (1898–1996) *Jaarcijfers voor Nederland* (from 1968 onwards *Statistical Yearbook of the Netherlands*), 's-Gravenhage.

—— (1935) *Overzicht van den omvang der vakbeweging*, 's-Gravenhage.

—— (1947) *Economische en sociale kroniek der oorlogsjaren 1940–1945*, Utrecht.

—— (1949–1966) *Statistiek der naamloze vennootschappen* (from 1964 onwards *Winststatistiek der grotere naamloze vennootschappen*), Utrecht/Hilversum.

—— (1951–1975) *Statistiek van de investeringen in de nijverheid*.

—— (1955) 'De Nederlandse volkshuishouding in de periode 1945–1955', *Maandschrift van het CBS*, 50, 4, 288–335.

—— (1958–1995) *Nationale Rekeningen*, Zeist/'s-Gravenhage.

—— (1959) *Zestig jaren statistiek in tijdreeksen*, Zeist.

—— (1984) *Vijfentachtig jaren statistiek in tijdreeksen*, 's-Gravenhage.

—— (1989) *Negentig jaren statistiek in tijdreeksen*, 's-Gravenhage.

—— (1994) *Vijfennegentig jaren statistiek in tijdreeksen*, 's-Gravenhage.

—— (1994b) *Milieustatistieken voor Nederland*, 's-Gravenhage.

Chandler, A.V. (1990) *Scale and Scope. The Dynamics of Industrial Capitalism*, Cambridge/London.

Cleef, B.D.M. van and Kuijpers, R.A.C. (1991) 'Leden van de vakbeweging', *Supplement bij de sociaal-economicsche maandstatistiek 5*.

Clemens, A., Groote, P. and Albers, R. (1996) 'The contribution of physical and human capital to economic growth in the Netherlands', *Economic and Social History in the Netherlands* 7, 181–198.

Clerx, J.M.M.J. (1986) *Nederland en de liberalisatie van het handels- en betalingsverkeer (1945–1958)*, Groningen.

Compaijen, B. and Butter, F.A.G. den (1991) *De Nederlandse economie, 3: Het jaarverslag van de Nederlandsche Bank*, Groningen.

CPB (1965–1996) *Centraal Economisch Plan*, 's-Gravenhage.

—— (1976) *De Nederlandse economie in 1980*, 's-Gravenhage.

Crouch, C. (1993) *Industrial Relations and European State Traditions*, Oxford.

Dankers, J.J. and Verheul, J. (1993) *Hoogovens 1945–1993*, Den Haag.

Darmstadter, J., Dunkerley J. and Alterman, J. (1977) *How Industrial Societies Use Energy*, Baltimore.

Davenport, M. (1982) 'The economic impact of the EEC', in A. Boltho (ed.) *The European Economy*, Oxford, 225–258.

Davids, C.A. (1995) 'Diffusie en creativiteit. De technische ontwikkeling van Nederland in de negentiende eeuw in vergelijkend perspectief', *NEHA-jaarboek* 58, 72–88.

*De Kroniek van dr. mr. A. Sternheim* (1928/29–1938/39).

DeMonchy, E.P. (1928) 'Commerce and navigation', in *The Netherlands and the World War* II, New Haven.

Dendermonde, M. (1961) *Nieuwe tijden. Nieuwe schakels*, Arnhem.

Dercksen, W.J. (1986) *Industrialisatiepolitiek rondom de jaren vijftig*, Maastricht.

Dercksen, W.J., Fortuyn P. and Jaspers, T. (1982) *Vijfendertig jaar SER-adviezen* I, Deventer.

Deterding, H. (1934) *An International Oilman*, London.

Douw, L. (1990) 'Meer door minder; ontwikkelingen in de structuur van de landbouw na 1950', in A.L.G.M. Bauwens *et al.* (eds) *Agrarisch bestaan*, Assen-Maastricht, 35–53.

Downs, A. (1972) *An Economic Theory of Democracy*, New York.

Driehuis, W. (1975) 'Inflation, wage bargaining, wage policy and production structure: theory and empirical results for the Netherlands', *De Economist* 123, 638–679.

—— (1978) 'Labour market imbalances and structural employment', *Kyklos* 31, 638–661.

Driehuis, W. and Zwan, A. van der (eds) (1978) *De voorbereiding van het economisch beleid kritisch bezien*, Leiden/Antwerpen.

Drukker, J.W. (1990) *Waarom de crisis hier langer duurde*, Amsterdam.

Eichengreen, B. (1996) 'Institutions and economic growth: Europe after World War II', in N. Crafts and G. Toniolo (eds) *Economic Growth in Europe since 1945*, Cambridge, 38–72.

Eng, P. van der (1987) *De Marshall-hulp*, Houten.

Esping-Andersen, G. (1985) *Politics Against Markets*, Princeton.

Fischer, E.J. (1983) *Fabriqueurs en fabrikanten*, Utrecht.

Flanagan, R.J., Hartog, J. and Theeuwes, J. (1993) 'Institutions and the labour market: many questions, some answers', in J. Hartog and J. Theeuwes (eds) *Labour Market Contracts and Institutions*, Amsterdam, 415–447.

Flierman, A.H. (n.d.) '*Het centrale punt in de reederswereld*', Weesp.

Flora, P. (1981) 'Solution or source of crisis? The welfare state in historical perspective', in W.J. Mommsen (ed.) *The Emergence of the Welfare State in Britain and Germany*, London, 343–390.

Flora, P. and Alber, J. (1982) 'Modernization, democratization and the development of welfare states in Western Europe', in P. Flora and A.J. Heidenheimer (eds) *The Development of Welfare States in Europe and America*, London, 37–81.

Fortuyn, P. (1980) *Sociaal-economische politiek in Nederland 1945–1949*, Groningen.

Fritschy, W. (1994) 'Financieel beleid onder – of ondanks? – Colijn', in J. de Bruijn and H.J. Langeveld (eds) *Colijn. Bouwstenen voor een biografie*, Kampen, 199–234.

Gales, B.P.A. and Sluyterman, K.E. (1993) 'Outward bound: the rise of Dutch multinationals', in G. Jones and H.G. Schröter (eds) *The Rise of Multinationals in Continental Europe*, Aldershot, 65–98.

Gerretson, C. (1939/1942) *Geschiedenis der 'Koninklijke'* I–III, Utrecht.

Gerwen, J.L.J.M. van (1993) *De Centrale centraal*, Amsterdam.

Goey, F. de (1990) *Ruimte voor industrie*, Rotterdam.

Griffiths, R.T. (1986) 'Enkele kanttekeningen bij de eerste industrialisatienota's van J.R.M. van den Brink', *Bijdragen en mededelingen betreffende de geschiedenis der Nederlanden* 101, 110–117.

—— (ed.) (1987) *The Netherlands and the Gold Standard, 1931–1936*, Amsterdam.

—— (1990) 'The Schuman Plan', in R.T. Griffiths (ed.) *The Netherlands and the Integration of Europe 1945–1957*, Amsterdam, 113–136.

—— (1996a) 'Backward, late or different?', in J.L. van Zanden (ed.) *The Economic Development of the Netherlands since 1870*, Cheltenham, 1–22.

—— (1996b) 'The Dutch economic miracle', in J.L. van Zanden (ed.) *The Economic Development of the Netherlands since 1870*, Cheltenham, 173–186.

Griffiths, R.T. and Schoorl, E. (1987) 'The single issue pressure groups', in R.T. Griffiths (ed.) *The Netherlands and the Gold Standard, 1931–1936*, Amsterdam, 139–164.

Groot, M.N. de and Bauwens, A.L.G.M. (1990) 'Vijftig jaar landbouwbeleid in Nederland; consensus en conflict', in A.L.G.M. Bauwens *et al.* (eds) *Agrarisch bestaan*, Assen/Maastricht, 146–169.

Grubb, D., Jackman, R. and Layard, R. (1983) 'Wage rigidity and unemployment in OESO countries', *European Economic Review* 21, 11–35.

Haavisto, T. and Jonung, L. (1995) 'Off gold and back again: Finnish and Swedish monetary policies 1914–1925', in C.H. Feinstein (ed.) *Banking, Currency, and Finance in Europe between the Wars*, Oxford, 237–268.

Harmsen, G. and Reinalda, B. (1975) *Voor de bevrijding van de arbeid*, Nijmegen.

Hartog, H. den, and Tjan, H.S. (1974) *Investeringen, lonen, prijzen en arbeidsplaatsen* CPB Occasional Paper, nr. 2, 's-Gravenhage.

——— (1976) 'Investment, wages, prices and demand for labour', *De Economist* 132, 326–349.

Hartog, J. and Theeuwes, J. (1993) 'Postwar unemployment in the Netherlands', Leiden University, Research Memorandum 93.01.

Heerding, E. (1986) *Een onderneming van vele markten thuis*, Leiden.

Heide, F.J. ter (1986) *Ordening en verdeling*, Kampen.

Hen, P.E. de (1980) *Actieve en re-actieve industriepolitiek in Nederland*, Amsterdam.

Hobsbawm, E.J. (1994) *The Age of Extremes. The Short Twentieth Century 1914–1991*, London.

Hofstee, E.W. (1981) *Korte demografische geschiedenis van Nederland van 1800 tot heden*, Bussum.

Holtfrerich, C.-L. (1980) *Die deutsche Inflation 1914–1923*, Berlin/New York.

Horlings, E.H. (1995) *The Economic Development of the Dutch Service Sector 1800–1850*, Amsterdam.

Houwink ten Cate, J. (1995) ' *De Mannen van de Daad' en Duitsland, 1919–1939*, Den Haag.

Hulst, N. van (1984) *De effectiviteit van de geleide loonpolitiek in theorie en praktijk*, Amsterdam.

ILO (1952) *Yearbook of Labor Statistics*, Geneva.

Immink, J.W.A. (1892) *Reservefondsen bij Naamlooze Vennootschappen*, Utrecht.

Jong, L. de (1970–1988) *Het Koninkrijk der Nederlanden in de Tweede Wereldoorlog* III, Amsterdam (1970), IV (1972), VII (1976), Xb (1981/82), XII (1988).

Jonge, J.A. de (1968) *De industrialisatie in Nederland tussen 1850 en 1914*, Amsterdam.

——— (1996) 'The role of the outer provinces in the process of Dutch economic growth in the nineteenth century', in J.L. van Zanden (ed.) *The Economic Development of the Netherlands since 1870*, Cheltenham, 23–40.

Jongh, J.G. de (1919) *De reservevorming der Nederlandsche Naamlooze Vennootschap*, Rotterdam.

Jonker, J.P.B. (1989) 'Waterdragers van het kapitalisme; nevenfuncties van Nederlandse bankiers en de verhouding tussen bankwezen en bedrijfsleven (1910–1940)', *Jaarboek voor de geschiedenis van bedrijf en techniek 6*, 158–190.

Jonker, J. (1996) *Merchants, Bankers, and Middlemen*, Amsterdam.

Kaa, D.J. van de (1980) 'Bevolking: a-symetrische tolerantie of accomodatiepolitiek', in *Nederland na 1945*, Deventer, 82–101.

Kaelble, H. (1990) *A Social History of Western Europe 1880–1980*, Dublin.

Keesing, F.A.G. (1947) *De conjuncturele ontwikkeling van Nederland en de evolutie van de economische overheidspolitiek 1918–1939*, Utrecht/Antwerpen.

Kersten, A.E. (1982) *Maken drie Kleinen een grote?*, Leiden.

Klarenbeek, D.L.M. (1995) 'Reconstructie van de Top-100 van industriële bedrijven in Nederland gerangschikt naar het totale aantal werknemers, 1930–1990', Utrecht, Scriptie Universiteit.

Klaverstijn, B. (1986) *Samentwijnen. Via fusie naar integratie*, Arnhem.

# BIBLIOGRAPHY

Klein, P.W. (1973) 'Depressie en beleid tijdens de jaren dertig', in J. van Herwaarden (ed.) *Lof der Historie*, Rotterdam, 289–336.

Kleinknecht, A. (1996) 'Potverteren met loonmatiging en flexibilisering', *ESB* 81, 622–625.

Klemann, H.A.M. (1990) *Tussen Reich en Empire*, Amsterdam.

—— (1997) 'De Nederlandse economie tijdens de Tweede Wereldoorlog', *Tijdschrift voor geschiedenis* 110.

Kloosterman, R.C. (1994) 'Amsterdamned: the rise of unemployment in Amsterdam in the 1980s', *Urban Studies* 31, 1325–1344.

Kloosterman, R.C. and Elfring, T. (1991) *Werken in Nederland*, Schoonhoven.

Knibbe, M. (1993) *Agriculture in the Netherlands 1851–1950*, Amsterdam.

Knoester, A. (1989) *Economische politiek in Nederland*, Leiden/Antwerpen.

Knotter, A. (1980) 'Sociaaldemokratische opvattingen van loon en loonstrijd in Nederland (1918–1940)', *Tijdschrift voor sociale geschiedenis* 6, 3–44.

Kohl, J. (1981) 'Trends and problems in postwar public expenditure development in Western Europe and North America', in P. Flora and A.J. Heidenheimer (eds) *The Emergence of Welfare States in Europe and America*, London, 307–344.

Kok, J. (1990) 'The moral nation', *Economic and Social History in the Netherlands* II, 7–36.

Korver, T. (1993) 'The Netherlands', in J. Hartog and J. Theeuwes (eds) *Labour Market Contracts and Institutions*, Amsterdam, 385–414.

Kreukels, L.H.M. (1986) *Mijnarbeid: volgzaamheid en strijdbaarheid*, Assen/Maastricht.

Krips-van der Laan, H.M.F. (1985) *Praktijk als antwoord*, Groningen.

Kuijpers, I. (1996) *Een stille revolutie: de Nederlandse arbeidersbeweging en de overheid 1914–1920*, Utrecht.

Kuijpers, I. and Schrage, P. (1992) ' "Als uw machtige arm het wil . . ." ', in B. de Vries *et al.* (eds) *De kracht der zwakken*, Amsterdam, 247–272.

Lakeman, P. (1984) *Het gaat uitstekend*, Weesp.

—— (1991) *100 jaar Philips*, Amsterdam.

Lakeman, P. and Ven, P. van de (1985) *Failliet op krediet*, Weesp.

Leeuwen, M. van (1996) 'Trade unions and the provision of welfare in the Netherlands 1910–1960', paper presented at seminar on economic history, Utrecht.

Lewis, H.G. (1963) *Unionism and Relative Wages in the United States*, Chicago.

Liagre Böhl, H. de, Nekkers, J. and Slot, L. (eds) (1981) *Nederland industrialiseert!*, Nijmegen.

Lieftinck, P. (1973) *The Post War Financial Rehabilitation of the Netherlands*, Den Haag.

Lijphart, A. (1968) *Verzuiling, pacificatie en kentering in de Nederlandse politiek*, Amsterdam.

Lindblad, J.Th. (1988) 'De handel tussen Nederland en Nederlands-Indië, 1874–1939', *Economisch- en sociaal-historisch jaarboek* 51, 240–298.

—— (1996) 'The economic relationship between the Netherlands and colonial Indonesia, 1870–1940', in J.L. van Zanden (ed.) *The Economic Development of the Netherlands since 1870*, Cheltenham, 109–119.

Lindert, P.H. (1994) 'The rise of social spending, 1880–1930', *Explorations in Economic History* 31, 1–37.

—— (1996) 'What limits social spending?', *Explorations in Economic History* 33, 1–34.

Louwes, S.L. (1980) 'Het gouden tijdperk van het groene front; het landbouwbeleid in de na-oorlogse periode', in *Nederland na 1945*, Deventer, 223–249.

Lubbers, R.F.M. and Lemckert, C. (1980) 'The influence of natural gas on the

Dutch economy', in R.T. Griffiths (ed.) *The Economy and Politics of the Nether-lands since 1945*. Den Haag, 87–114.

Maddison, A. (1991) *Dynamic Forces in Capitalist Development*, Oxford.

—— (1993) *Standardised Estimates of Fixed Capital Stock: A Six Country Comparison*, Milan.

—— (1995) *Monitoring the World Economy 1820–1992*, Paris.

Marris, R. (1967) *The Economic Theory of 'Managerial' Capitalism*, London.

Meade, J.E., Liesner, H.H. and Wells, S.J. (1964²) *Case Studies in European Economic Integration*, London.

Meere, J.M.M. de (1983) 'Long-term trends in income and wealth inequality in the Netherlands 1808–1940', *Historical Social Research* 27, 8–37.

Meester, G. and Strijker, D. (1985) *Het Europese landbouwbeleid voorbij de scheidslijn van de zelfvoorziening*, 's-Gravenhage, WRR-voorstudies V46.

Messing, F.A.M. (1988) *Geschiedenis van de mijnsluiting in Limburg*, Leiden.

Mierlo, J.G.A. van (1988) *Pressiegroepen in de Nederlandse politiek*, Den Haag.

Milward, A.S. (1984) *The Reconstruction of Western Europe, 1945–1951*, London.

—— (1987²) *War, Economy and Society 1939–1945*, Harmondsworth.

—— (1992) *The Rescue of the Nation-State*, London.

Ministerie van Landbouw en Visserij (1977) *Landbouwverkenning*, 's-Gravenhage.

Minne, B. (1995) 'Onderzoek, ontwikkeling en andere immateriële investeringen in Nederland', *Onderzoeksmemorandum no. 116*, Centraal Plan Bureau, 's-Gravenhage.

Mommens, T.E. (1992) 'Belgische en Nederlandse visies op het landbouwprobleem en de vorming van de Benelux in de jaren vijftig', in E.S.A. Bloemen (ed.) *Het Benelux-effect*, Amsterdam, 109–128.

Noort, P.C. van den (1965) *Omvang en verdeling van het agrarisch inkomen in Nederland, 1923–1963*, Wageningen.

Nordvik, H.W. (1995) 'Norwegian banking in the inter-war period: a Scandinavian perspective', in C.H. Feinstein (ed.) *Banking, Currency and Finance in Europe between the Wars*, Oxford, 434–457.

OECD (1972) *The Research System*, II, Paris.

—— (1978) *Policies for the Stimulation of Industrial Innovation*, II–2, Paris.

—— (1987) *Historical Statistics 1960–1985*, Paris.

—— (1995) *Employment Outlook*, Paris.

—— (1996) *OECD Economic Surveys 1995. The Netherlands*, Paris.

Oomens, C.A. and Bakker, G.P. den (1994) 'De beroepsbevolking in Nederland 1849–1990', *Supplement bij de sociaal-economische maandstatistiek* 2, 's-Gravenhage.

Passenier, J. (1994) *Van planning naar scanning*, Groningen.

Peacock, A.T. and Wiseman, J. (1967) *The Growth of Public Expenditure in the United Kingdom*, London.

Pelkmans, J. (1986) 'De voltooiing van de interne markt: economische voordelen en beleidsimplicaties', in W.G.C.M. Haack (eds) *Europese economische integratie*, Utrecht, 83–121.

Popta, K.B. van (1995) 'Bezuinigen in de jaren 1982–1994', in W. Fritschy, J.K.T. Postma and J. Roelevink (eds) *Doel en Middel*, Amsterdam, 213–228.

Post, J.G. (1972) *Besparingen in Nederland 1923–1970*, Deventer.

—— (1973) 'Timing in de Nederlandse conjunctuurpolitiek', *ESB* 58, 990–995.

Post, J.H. (1990) 'Nederland als specialist in agrarische produktie', in A.L.G.M. Bauwens *et al.* (eds) *Agrarisch bestaan*, Assen/Maastricht, 110–124.

Posthuma, J.F. (1955) 'Tien jaar Herstelbank', in *Tien jaar economisch leven in Nederland*, 's-Gravenhage, 1–45.

Pott-Buter, H.A. (1993) *Facts and Fairy Tales about Female Labor, Family and Fertility*, Amsterdam.

Regt, A. de (1984) *Arbeidersgezinnen en beschavingsarbeid*, Meppel.

Rietkerk, G. (1991) *Onderneming en vermogensmarkt*, Leiden/Antwerpen.

Rijksverzekeringsbank (1935) *Ongevallenstatistiek*.

Roland Holst-van der Schalk, H. (1902) *Kapitaal en arbeid in Nederland*, Amsterdam.

Rooy, P. de (1979) *Werklozenzorg en werkloosheidsbestrijding 1917–1940*, Amsterdam.

Ru, H.J. de (1981) *Staatsbedrijven en staatsdeelnemingen*, Nijmegen, Stichting Ars Aequi.

Schaar, J. van der (1987) *Groei en bloei van het Nederlandse volkshuisvestingsbeleid*, Delft.

Schaïk, A. van (1986) *Crisis en protectie onder Colijn*, Amsterdam.

Schiff, E. (1971) *Industrialization Without National Patents*, Princeton.

Schrover, M., Nijhof, E. and Kruizinga, P. (1992) 'Marx, markt, macht', in B. de Vries *et al.* (eds) *De kracht der zwakken*, Amsterdam, 193–246.

Seegers, J.J. (1987) 'Produktie en concurrentievermogen van de Nederlandse industrie in het Interbellum', *Economisch- en sociaal-historisch jaarboek* L, 186–211.

Sijes, B.A. (1966) *De arbeidsinzer: de gedwongen arbeid van Nederlanders in Duitsland. 1940–1945*, 's-Gravenhage.

Sluyterman, K.E. and Winkelman, H.J.M. (1993) 'The Dutch family firm confronted with Chandler's dynamics of industrial capitalism, 1890–1940', *Business History* 35, 152–183.

Smidt, M. de and Wever, E. (1990) *De Nederlandse industrie*, Assen/Maastricht.

Smits, J.P.H. (1990) 'The size and structure of the Dutch service sector in international perspective', *Economic and Social History in the Netherlands* II, 81–98.

—— (1997) *Economic Growth and Structural Change in the Dutch Service Sector 1850–1913*, Amsterdam.

Smits, W.F. (1979) 'De Nederlandse concurrentiepositie binnen de EG', *ESB* 64, 457–461.

Sterks, C.G.M. (1982) *Begrotingsnormen*, Groningen.

—— (1984) 'De conjuncturele invloed van de Rijksbegroting 1961–1983', *Maandschrift Economie* 48, 56–71.

Stevers, Th.A. (1967) 'Welke factoren bepalen de verandering in het niveau en de structuur van de belastingen in de 19e en 20e eeuw', in *Smeetsbundel. Opstellen aangeboden aan prof.dr.M.J.H.Smeets*, Deventer, 327–354.

—— (1976) 'Begrotingsnormering 1814–1939', *Economisch- en sociaal-historisch jaarboek* 39, 101–147.

Strijker, D. (1990) 'De relatie met het buitenland in handel en beleid', in A.L.G.M. Bauwens *et al.* (eds) *Agrarisch bestaan*, Assen/Maastricht, 97–109.

Stuurman, S. (1983) *Verzuiling, kapitalisme en patriarchaat*, Nijmegen.

Swann, D. (1988[6]) *The Economics of the Common Market*, Harmondsworth.

Szász, A. (1981) 'Het wisselkoersdebat', in E. den Dunnen (ed.) *Zoeklicht op beleid*, Leiden/Antwerpen, 303–323.

—— (1988) *Monetaire diplomatie*, Leiden/Antwerpen.

Temperton, P. (1993) 'Introduction', in P. Temperton (ed.) *The European Currency Crisis*, Cambridge, 3–49.

Thiede, G. (1984) '10 Jahre Versorgungsberechnungen für die EG', *Agrarwirtschaft* 33, 136–142.

Tijn, Th. van (1974) 'Bijdrage tot de wetenschappelijke studie van de vakbonds-geschiedenis', *Mededelingenblad* 45, 98–108.
—— (1976) 'A contribution to the scientific study of the history of trade unions', *International Review of Social History* 21, 212–239.
Toirkens, J. (1988) *Schijn en werkelijkheid van het bezuinigingsbeleid 1975–1986*, Deventer.
Trienekens, G.M.T. (1985) *Tussen ons volk en de honger*, Utrecht.
US Department of Commerce (1975) *Technology Assessment and Forecast*, IV, Washington DC.
—— (1979) *Technology Assessment and Forecast*, IX, Washington DC.
*Van Oss' effectenboek* (1915/16) Groningen.
Veen, D.J. van der and Zanden, J.L. van (1989) 'Real wage trends and consumption patterns in the Netherlands (*c*.1870–1940)', in P. Scholliers (ed.) *Real Wages in 19th and 20th Century Europe*, New York, 205–228.
Vissering, G. and Westerman Holstijn, J. (1928) 'The effect of the war upon banking and currency', in *The Netherlands and the World War* IV, New Haven.
Vlak, G.J.M. (1967) *Het Nederlandse valutaegalisatiefonds 1936–1940*, Assen.
Voogd, R.P. (1989) *Statutaire beschermingsmiddelen bij beursvennootschappen*, Deventer.
Voogd, C. de (1993) *De neergang van de scheepsbouw en andere industriële bedrijfstakken*, Vlissingen.
Vries, Joh. de (1968) *Hoogovens IJmuiden, 1918–1968*, IJmuiden.
—— (1976) *Een eeuw vol effecten*, Amsterdam.
—— (1983[4]) *De Nederlandse economie tijdens de 20e eeuw*, Bussum.
—— (1989) *Geschiedenis van de Nederlandsche Bank* V, part 1, 1914–1931, Amsterdam.
—— (1994) *Geschiedenis van de Nederlandsche Bank* V, part 2, 1931–1948, Amsterdam.
Vries, J. de and Woude, A.M. van der (1995) *Nederland 1500–1815. De eerste ronde van moderne economische groei*, Amsterdam.
Vries, W. de (1970) *De invloed van werkgevers en werknemers op de totstandko-ming van de eerste sociale verzekeringswet in Nederland (De ongevallenwet van 1901)*, Deventer.
Vrolijk, H. (1982) 'Opkomst en neergang van de Nederlandse herstructurerings-maatschappij', in H. Vrolijk and R. Hengeveld (eds) *Interventie en vrije markt*, Amsterdam, 49–92.
Wassenberg, A. (1983) *Dossier RSV*, Leiden.
Wee, H. van der (1983[2]) *De gebroken welvaartscirkel*, Leiden.
Weststrate, C. (1959) *Economic Policy in Practice: The Netherlands 1950/1957*, Leiden.
Wieringa, W.J. and Zijp, R.P. (1979) 'Het werkfonds 1934', in P.W. Klein and G.J. Borger (eds) *De Jaren Dertig*, Amsterdam, 130–141
Wijngaarden, C.N. van and Griend, W.F. van der (1971) *De Rijksbegroting, verleden en toekomst*, Alphen aan den Rijn.
Wilensky, H.L. (1975) *The Welfare State and Equality*, Berkeley.
Wilson, C. (1954) *The History of Unilever*, London.
Windmuller, J.P. (1969) *Labor Relations in the Netherlands*, New York.
Windmuller, J.P. and Galan, C. de (1979[3]) *Arbeidsverhoudingen in Nederland*, 2 vols, Utrecht/Antwerpen.
Winsemius, J. (1945) *Vestigingstendenzen van de Nederlandse nijverheid*, 's-Gravenhage.
Woltjer, J.J. (1994) *Recent verleden*, Amsterdam.

Zanden, J.L. van (1986) 'Inkomensverdeling en overheidspolitiek, 1938–1950', *ESB* 71, 768–771.

—— (1987) *De industrialisatie in Amsterdam 1825–1914*, Bergen.

—— (1988a) 'Nederland in hct Interbellum', *ESB* 73, 172–178.

—— (1988b) 'Geleide loonpolitiek en de internationale concurrentiepositie van Nederland, 1948–1962', *Maandschrift economie* 52, 464–477.

—— (1991) *The Transformation of European Agriculture. The Case of the Netherlands*, Amsterdam.

—— (1996a) 'The dance around the gold standard: economic policy in the Depression of the 1930s', in J.L. van Zanden (ed.) *The Economic Development of the Netherlands since 1870*, Cheltenham, 120–136.

—— (1996b) 'The economic development of the Netherlands and Belgium and the "Success" of the Benelux', in J.L. van Zanden (ed.) *The Economic Development of the Netherlands since 1870*, Cheltenham, 187–203.

—— (1997) 'Old rules, new conditions, 1914–1940', in M. 't Hart, J. Jonker and J.L. van Zanden (eds) *A Financial History of the Netherlands*, Cambridge, 124–151.

—— (at press) 'The history of an empty box? Industrial policies in the Netherlands', in J. Foreman-Peck (ed.) *A Century of European Industrial Policy*, Oxford.

Zanden, J.L. van and Griffiths, R.T. (1989) *Economische geschiedenis van Nederland in de 20e eeuw*, Utrecht.

Zanden, J.L. van and Verstegen, S.W. (1993) *Groene geschiedenis van Nederland*, Utrecht.

# INDEX

330.9492 Zanden, J. L. van.
Zan
    The economic history
   of the Netherlands,
   1914-1995.

| DATE | | | |
|---|---|---|---|
| | | | |
| | | | |
| | | | |
| | | | |
| | | | |
| | | | |
| | | | |
| | | | |
| | | | |
| | | | |
| | | | |
| | | | |